With our compliments....

CENTERED LEADERSHIP

CENTERED LEADERSHIP

Leading with
Purpose, Clarity,
and Impact

JOANNA BARSH

AND JOHANNE LAVOIE

CROWN
BUSINESS
NEW YORK

Published in the United States by Crown Business, an imprint of the Crown Publishing Group, a division of Random House LLC, a Penguin Random House Company, New York.

www.crownpublishing.com

CROWN BUSINESS is a trademark and CROWN and the Rising Sun colophon are registered trademarks of Random House LLC.

Crown Business books are available at special discounts for bulk purchases for sales promotions or corporate use. Special editions, including personalized covers, excerpts of existing books, or books with corporate logos, can be created in large quantities for special needs. For more information, contact Premium Sales at (212) 572–2232 or e-mail specialmarkets@randomhouse.com.

Library of Congress Cataloging-in-Publication Data

Barsh, Joanna.
Centered Leadership : Leading with purpose,
clarity, and impact / by Joanna Barsh and Johanne Lavoie.
pages cm
1. Leadership. I. Lavoie, Johanne. II. Title.

HD57.7.B3676 2014
658.4'092—dc23

2013031300

ISBN 978-0-8041-3887-1
eBook ISBN 978-0-8041-3888-8

Printed in the United States of America

Book design by Chris Welch
Jacket design by M80 Design

10 9 8

First Edition

To our loving husbands and daughters:
You fill our hearts to the brim and then some.

Centered Leadership map of capabilities

PRECONDITIONS

Desire to lead | Talent and knowledge | Capacity for change

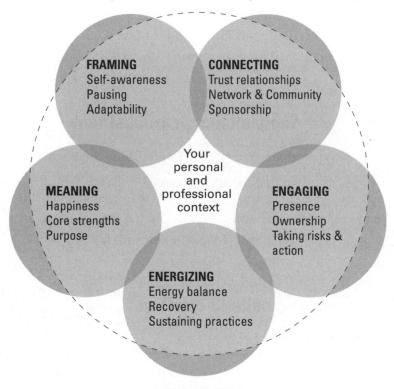

FRAMING
Self-awareness
Pausing
Adaptability

CONNECTING
Trust relationships
Network & Community
Sponsorship

Your
personal
and
professional
context

MEANING
Happiness
Core strengths
Purpose

ENGAGING
Presence
Ownership
Taking risks &
action

ENERGIZING
Energy balance
Recovery
Sustaining practices

OUTCOMES

Leadership impact | Fulfillment | Resilience

SOURCE: The Centered Leadership Project

CONTENTS

PART TWO: MEANING

PART THREE: FRAMING

PART FOUR: CONNECTING

PART FIVE: ENGAGING

PART SIX: ENERGIZING

PART SEVEN: THE JOURNEY CONTINUES

INTRODUCTION

I'm sitting in my gently aging apartment on a weekday afternoon in cold, rainy April and no longer wondering what it will feel like to be sixty years old and retired. Because I *am* sixty years old, with a successful career just completed. "But you don't look sixty!" you graciously say; I don't feel sixty, either. Thanks to my parents, I have the same brown hair and girlish look. I'm still short ("vertically challenged," notes my husband, David; "fun-sized," chirps my daughter Jetta). But something *in* me has changed. I'm having more positive impact than I ever imagined. I'm more productive. I dream bolder. And I laugh more. I'm filled to the brim with a wondrous potion that I started drinking a short while ago.

Of course, my personal milestones are of no concern to you except for one: It's been about ten years since I've begun my personal leadership journey and about six since writing *How Remarkable Women Lead* and launching The Centered Leadership Project at McKinsey & Company. My learning arc continues to soar as I pursue my vision to awaken more centered leaders in this world before I leave it. Centered Leadership is no magic potion, but something even better—a way of leading and living. What do I mean, exactly?

In essence, this book is about learning how to manage your own thoughts, feelings, and actions to unleash your full potential. It's not just about *wanting* to make your mark, but about *how* to lead with purpose, clarity, and positive impact. It's about how to become the kind of leader who is well grounded, faces the future with hope, adapts to find opportunity, achieves results, and embraces learning. It's about mastery of the skills needed to unleash the performance of your team and organization, too. That does sound like magic, doesn't it?

It's not. Centered Leadership is very real.

Those of you who read *How Remarkable Women Lead* may recall my epiphany at age fifty, when I woke up into a life that should have seemed perfect. I had been a senior partner at McKinsey for a decade by then and loved my job. I had two wonderful daughters and a great marriage, a New York apartment with a view and a farm with endless views plus cows, chickens, sheep, a few donkeys (though, sadly, no more pig). So why did I feel empty? At the time, David chalked it up to midlife crisis and sensibly counseled me to buy a pair of shoes—as any loving husband would do. And I did. Those Cinderella pumps twinkled for a moment. Two weeks later, I was back to feeling empty—and invisible. Glass slippers—or even a closetful of them—could not shoo away these blues. They were there when I woke up; I went to work in a dark mood. I was amazed that people said "Good morning," since I was convinced that they did not see me.

Don't get me wrong. I had good days—even great days—when my heart raced and my brain lit up with ideas, and client discussions were exhilarating; or when my children and I danced ourselves silly; or when I won a new client; or when on a family adventure. Most of the time, though, I went through the motions. I wondered if this was all there was. Have you ever been there?

People tell me I'm courageous, creative, bold, visionary, powerful, and fearless. After a lot of hard work, I'm ready to accept that I am those things. I'm also cautious, closed-minded, tentative, pragmatic, vulnerable, and fearful. I've known this side of me for a longer time. It's taken me the last five years to accept that where there is dark, there is also light. Both reside in me, as they do in you. What I could not see at first was my role in creating my invisibility and emptiness. I was the problem and I am the solution.

Fortunately, I had an idea to interview successful women leaders around the world and across all fields, to sit at their feet and absorb what they knew. It was not a rational plan, but I knew this journey would help me to find what I was missing. David urged me to build a video archive of women leader interviews. My colleagues were supportive; they assumed this would be a short-lived renewal project.

But since that first step in 2004, I never stopped, taping more and more interviews. This process of gathering and gestating brought me closer to a breakthrough. Fast-forward to 2008. A new approach to leadership emerged when we combined: the interviews; our team's review of academic research across leadership, organizational behavior, neuroscience, evolutionary psychology, and positive psychology; global research; and internal training. One year later, this new approach had grown into a best-selling business book, a grassroots movement taking root across the world, and a leadership development pilot program. We called it Centered Leadership, and I became its founder, one of its facilitators, and its number-one student, participating in sessions to continue my journey.

As the title implies, *How Remarkable Women Lead* spotlighted the strengths of women, strengths that men share but that the West traditionally labels as feminine. As we continued our research, however, we found these strengths increasingly at play in the workplace among successful men. For example, we found more men seeking other aspects of meaning at work over pay or status. And though some male environments look down on any emotional display, we noticed that others are waking up to how positive emotions—those women often bring to the table—can forge connections, counter fear, and encourage creativity.

More than a few good men read *How Remarkable Women Lead*, sheepishly, and saw themselves in the stories of the women leaders. In the following three years, hundreds of men came to our sessions because they wanted what we offered. We learned that while men and women respond differently, the approach has an equally powerful effect for both. Centered Leadership is as much for men as it is for women.

That's because Centered Leadership teaches leaders to embrace the "and" that lies within them: how we can access our masculine *and* feminine sides. We can be powerful *and* vulnerable. We can be in the movie *and* watch ourselves in it at the same time. We can be practical *and* visionary. Accepting ourselves and holding our polarities is an important step in becoming centered, men and women leaders alike.

All companies need more leaders with the skills to lead significant change in an uncertain, volatile, and fast-paced environment. Centered Leadership fits that requirement. Our approach helps leaders gain greater self-awareness and self-reflection. With those, comes greater choice of thought and action. In effect, these men and women learn to create their own purpose, with greater clarity, to embrace broader perspectives and flexibility in action. Boldly, they step up and into their full leadership potential to make a profound difference in their organization, community, even the world.

Remarkably, this stuff works! In the end, who wouldn't want the keys to unlocking her or his own potential?

So, over the next five years, we taught Centered Leadership in half-day, one-day, three-day, five-day, and ten-day programs for men and women. I continued to interview women and men leaders. I met more than 30,000 people from twenty countries. I laughed and (OK, wept, too), sang and danced with some of the most remarkable leaders I've ever encountered, sharing in their transformations and learning from them. In the process, I morphed, in front of their eyes, from an invisible woman grappling with emptiness into a three-dimensional being bursting with energy. I thank McKinsey for every day I've been given to study Centered Leadership, teach it, live it, inspire it, and write about it.

I've been lucky—make that *really* lucky—to have spent most of my last five years at McKinsey leading the The Centered Leadership Project's transition from a concept into learning programs, in partnership with remarkable human beings, including Johanne Lavoie (whom you'll meet soon). The clients who embrace Centered Leadership use it to ignite and develop everyone from their leadership team, to change leaders, to rising senior executives, to young talent—wherever their need is greatest.

Consider this book a companion piece to *How Remarkable Women Lead*. If you're like me, it's not enough to know what Centered Leadership is about. You're hungry for real learning—the *"how"*—to take your own leadership journey. That's our intention here. So if the first book was my invitation to you to understand Centered Leadership, this book is our practical field guide.

Building on five years of research, we draw on five more years of hands-on learning in Centered Leadership seminars, workshops, and programs to help you master these capabilities. You'll find a valuable tool kit in here—filled not just with concepts and tools but with exercises and work sheets, actionable tips and practices—to help you make the difference you most want to create through your leadership. We still call our work The Centered Leadership Project because it is a living and dynamic thing, enriched by all the facilitators and participants who have joined us.

Johanne and I share a dream to turn on scores of leaders who aspire to make a significant difference. You're part of our dream. If you desire to lead—to envision what should be but does not yet exist and then turn that into reality—we'll help you build the capabilities to do it. Putting our tools into practice, you can reach previously unimagined places. This is a big promise, but we're ready to deliver. What I want more than anything is to awaken that desire in you, to help you use your unique strengths at work and in life, and to channel your energy to light up the world.

You are a positive force. I'm sure of it.

PART ONE

INTRODUCTION TO CENTERED LEADERSHIP

1

YOUR CENTERED LEADERSHIP JOURNEY

In which we introduce the program that Fortune 100 companies have been using with success to increase their leadership capacity

I
n 2009 a combative colleague cornered me to ask, "What makes the leaders you interviewed remarkable? What makes Centered Leadership distinctive? What's your elevator speech?" The tiny voice in my head piled on, *Do you even have one, Joanna?* I froze. "It's the Force!" I responded. His eyes rolled, and he walked away, as my inner voice chided, *Think you're Obi-Wan Kenobi? Really? What were you thinking?* Oh, dear; I wasn't.

The route to Centered Leadership

That conversation prompted me to think hard about the video interviews and what had drawn me to each remarkable leader. Not everyone had magic, but most did and they weren't born with it. These were people who saw opportunity everywhere. They exuded positive energy. They understood themselves—their thoughts, feelings, and actions—and they were open to others, welcoming opposition. They were eager to connect; they touched others deeply. They faced big challenges and took personal risks with the confidence that if things didn't work out, they would move on. They bounced back from failures with unstoppable energy. They were driven by purpose; they were a force.

It took years to articulate what my intuition understood—how to explain Centered Leadership in an elevator ride. I was not looking to describe every possible leadership capability or to fully explain leaders. I just wanted to know, in a nutshell, what distinguishes leaders who have a profound and positive impact on us versus other leaders who do a fine but unremarkable job. *I was looking for the smallest combination of capabilities that matter.*

So we—a team of colleagues and experts—set out to explore. After poring over reams of research in relevant academic fields, we were ready. And when we settled on meaning, framing, connecting, engaging, and energizing as the smallest combination, I felt complete without knowing why on a conscious level.

We tested these dimensions in two worldwide quantitative surveys of executives working in a range of industries and companies. And what we found astounded us.

A small segment of men and women—about one hundred people— regularly practiced four or all five of Centered Leadership's dimensions and reported a high level of leadership effectiveness, a high level of satisfaction at work and at home, and a high level of preparedness for the current challenging environment. My mathematician husband, David, tactfully asked if possibly we had uncovered a random coincidence, but here's the clincher: In contrast, hardly any of the 1,300 men and women who didn't practice any dimension regularly felt that way. My resident skeptic then asked for cause and effect: Did these practices really lead to greater leadership success and personal fulfillment, or was it the other way around? Hundreds of workshops convinced us that the practices made the difference. We observed how individuals practiced Centered Leadership to be their best at work more of the time, to feel more in control of their destiny, and to have a positive effect on those around them.

But it doesn't happen overnight. It's a journey.

Five parts make a whole

What's intriguing is that the five dimensions of Centered Leadership work better *together* than alone. Use just one and you'll be able

Centered Leadership map of capabilities

PRECONDITIONS

Desire to lead | Talent and knowledge | Capacity for change

FRAMING
Self-awareness
Pausing
Adaptability

CONNECTING
Trust relationships
Network & Community
Sponsorship

Your personal and professional context

MEANING
Happiness
Core strengths
Purpose

ENGAGING
Presence
Ownership
Taking risks & action

ENERGIZING
Energy balance
Recovery
Sustaining practices

#1

OUTCOMES

Leadership impact | Fulfillment | Resilience

SOURCE: The Centered Leadership Project

to make incremental improvements in your leadership. Use them all in concert, and you'll have lasting impact. Centered Leadership practices build on and reinforce one another, bringing you the inspiration, motivation, and energy to continue. It is, like life itself, a gestalt. Here is the unifying map, refined since *How Remarkable Women Lead*.

Since 2008, we have honed the dimensions of Centered Leadership, and Johanne recognized how all of Centered Leadership resides within each dimension:

- **Meaning:** Still the most powerful factor, meaning is the anchor of Centered Leadership. It begins with happiness: Meaningful engagement offers longest lasting fulfillment; and it taps our core strengths (and gives us energy). By knowing what really matters to us we can discover our purpose, which in turn inspires us to gain conviction, courage, and confidence we may not realize we have. We lead through vision, which helps us reframe challenges as opportunities, connect deeply with the hearts and spirits of others, take on risk, and exude positive energy.

- **Framing:** We see the world through invisible frames of our own making. You may think you know yourself, but how self-aware and self-reflective are you in the throes of panic? With practice, we can learn to see ourselves "in the movie" of our own lives—noticing what triggers our emotions and reactive patterns of thoughts and actions. Once we pause, we become aware of our fears—how they serve but also how they limit us. With acceptance we can adapt, choosing to reframe our mindset or belief, which enables a different behavior to emerge. Choosing our experience in any situation releases a rush of positive energy. Reframing opens a window for us to build on strengths, help others move forward, and see more possibilities, too.

- **Connecting:** For some, forging true connection does not feel like real work. Not so! Reciprocity is the currency of work relationships, but genuine trust building turns that transaction into much more. Those who cultivate meaningful community from their networks are able to scale their leadership visions. In particular, sponsors—powerful people who take a risk on us—accelerate our growth. Belonging is a powerful driver of meaning; strong relationships increase our openness to reframing; and, with that support, we take risks and act. This is how Connecting creates energy.

- **Engaging:** Presence happens when you align your intention (what you really want to have happen) with your attention (what you choose to focus on) and your emotions (how you experience the moment). That alignment helps you balance fear with hope. Hope shows you the upside of opportunities and challenges, helps you accept the personal risk of acting, and as you do, you take ownership of your future. As I leaned into Engaging, I felt enormous power—a scary feeling. That power enables our pursuit of purpose, helps us see more opportunity, draws others to us, and, once again, releases positive energy.

- **Energizing:** It is disappointing to learn that work-life balance is a myth, but there is a solution: learning to manage our sources and uses of energy so we can work *and* live more fully. With attention to our bodies, minds, emotional well-being, and spiritual health, we can sustain high performance more of the time, bounce back quicker, and practice recovery when we need it. Energy is the fuel for each dimension, and, at the same time, more energy is released as you unlock each one. Energized leaders and teams build on strengths, pause and reframe in challenging moments, attract and mobilize others, accept risks, and take action!

In practical terms, mastery of these five dimensions enables us to extend our range of choices and actions. Centered Leadership is as much about *doing* as it is about *knowing* and *being*. That helps us become better leaders of teams and organizations: We see more possibilities, handle adversity instead of avoiding it, and transform ourselves to meet complex challenges without easy solutions. Equally powerful for men and women, Centered Leadership works across cultures, across industries, across pretty much everything.

David sees humanity at its best in Centered Leadership's five-dimension design. Johanne sees mindset and behavioral change infused throughout. I feel a force just waiting to awaken—what I thought I had been missing but actually had inside me all the while.

Now *that's* what I call an elevator pitch.

The road ahead

You picked up this book for a reason. Something about your professional hopes or aspirations wants your attention. Something about your untapped leadership potential is longing to be heard. Ask yourself what that might be. As you read, notice whether you're experiencing the high positive energy of hope, excitement, and joy or the high negative energy of fear, anxiety, and stress. Every now and then, step back to integrate what you are experiencing and learning, discussing your insights with others. How are you changing, and what is changing in you? You are the scientist, but you are also the subject.

Each section on your Centered Leadership journey begins with a chapter explaining the key concepts and their effect on me—your guinea pig. Mind you, I put myself out there, showing you the "before" and "after" and how I transformed. That's a pretty vulnerable place to be (just sayin')! Then, we teach you the specific tools, skills, and practices using Johanne's exercises that enable you to interact with them, using your real life challenges. We've relegated further resources to footnotes so that you can remain in the learning experience. After each "tool kit" chapter, you'll find stories of remarkable men and women leaders who demonstrate that practice in action. Here is a quick summary (tools, skills, and practices are in italics):

■ **What you'll find in Meaning:** We'll help you discover your core strengths and show you how to tap into them in pursuit of your leadership vision. Specifically:
  - Recognize and use your *unique strengths* by reflecting on what energizes you and what you value most about yourself.
  - Dig into what really matters to you through *visualizing your far future* and using *appreciative questions* that help you unblock the path to it.
  - Reflect on your past, your future, and your essence, integrating them to inform discovery of your *purpose*.
  - Begin to give voice to your *vision* for your leadership today.

- **What you'll find in Framing:** We'll help you recognize the frames through which you are currently experiencing difficult or draining situations. Then we'll teach you how to use choice to shift your mindset and broaden your range of behaviors and actions in line with your growth aspirations. Specifically:
  - Become *aware of the fears or unmet needs* that get triggered in you, knowing that, through acceptance, you regain your power to choose your actions.
  - Access your natural ability to *pause in the moment* of an upset to see yourself and the pattern of how you tend to react.
  - *Make the choice* to shift your belief in order to experience new behaviors.
  - Create your own *sustaining practice* to help you integrate your desired mindset and behaviors.
- **What you'll find in Connecting:** We'll help you learn how to build trust, develop your network strategically, forge a close-knit community, cultivate sponsor relationships, and become an effective sponsor yourself. Specifically:
  - Build *greater trust,* creating greater belonging and meaningful relationships.
  - Develop your *desired relationship network* and forge *communities* in service of your leadership vision.
  - Coach your (potential) *sponsors* to be more effective in helping you make your vision a reality; pay that forward by learning to be a better sponsor.
- **What you'll find in Engaging:** We'll help you build or expand your presence to live into your intention, and offer you ways to assess risks and take action to lead positive change in your team or organization. You will:
  - Align your *attention* with your *intention* and *emotion*, allowing others to see you and hear you more clearly through compelling *storytelling.*
  - Enlist hope to balance fear, *learning to say no by saying yes* first to your priorities and listening to the *internal voices* that tap into hope.

- Build courage to take risks and bolder actions through *tools that help you assess risk.*
- Solicit counsel through a *"mini-board"* process that increases support and coaching.

■ **What you'll find in Energizing:** We'll help you actively manage your own energy sources and uses to refuel in the short and longer term. Specifically:

- Heighten your *emotional literacy,* recognizing positive and negative emotions and their impact on your energy and your effectiveness in that moment.
- Cultivate *mindfulness* through practices that develop your capacity to reflect and stay present to your experience.
- Build in *daily recovery routines* to refill your physical, mental, emotional, and spiritual energy during the workday.
- Adopt your own *sustaining energy practices* to renew for the longer term.

Our destination? Positive impact. Fulfillment. Resilience.

Can you think of anything better?

We cannot.

2

INTRODUCING YOUR GUIDES

In which we share our professional and personal context and describe the leadership journey that awaits you

Back in 2008, we knew that Centered Leadership was more than a list of leadership qualities; it was a *map of capabilities* that people could master with deliberate practice. Here's how we figured that out: We introduced new training to McKinsey colleagues in North America, and before we could catch our breath, word had spread across the globe. Our goal was to train a few hundred, but we trained thousands. I felt part of a wave, and very few things in life beat that. Still, in quiet moments I was nagged by the feeling that our training was missing the mark. We taught people the concepts, sparked flashes of insight, and offered practical tactics, but we did not help people actively *build* new capabilities. Everyone "got" Centered Leadership but struggled with mastery, including me.

Making Centered Leadership real

I needed help. So I called Scott Keller, a leader in McKinsey's Organization practice, and said, "Centered Leadership is creating a wave, and that's magical." So far so good. Then I decided to be vulnerable. "But I don't know how to design a capability-building program. You know how to do that, Scott, so will you help me?"

Pause.

Pause.

Pause.

Hey! the tiny voice in my head scolded, *Now you've gone and exposed yourself as a complete fraud. "I don't know how to design a capability-building program!" What propelled you to self-destruct? Really!*

"Scott? Are you there?"

"Scott?"

He's doing e-mails while you're dyin' here! I told myself.

Nope. Scott was thinking. He replied, "I'll introduce you to Johanne Lavoie. She'll help you with design. She rocks. Hell, yeah, Joanna!" (Scott really likes heavy metal and he draws on those two phrases with regularity to great effect. I never fail to feel the energy.) Johanne had an electrical engineering degree, an MBA, and ten years' experience in McKinsey Argentina, Brazil, and Canada. She was a coach and facilitator with five years of designing learning programs. Perfect.

This story would end there except for the fact that . . .

Johanne refused on the spot.

Johanne refused a second time, and I became convinced that the story really did end.

Her reason? At the time, Centered Leadership was all about how remarkable *women* lead, and she did not believe in teaching something different to women. Many of you might think the same: If women have the same potential as men, why should they need special training to lead in the same context? The idea of teaching a new leadership approach in a women-only program was against Johanne's principles.

So she said no, in no uncertain terms; and we both walked away.

Not so fast.

I was frustrated that senior, male colleagues who attended briefings on Centered Leadership told me they understood it, practiced it, loved it—and then wished me good luck with the women! I remembered "mucho macho" Dave's advice: "The Centered Leadership Project will only be taken seriously if *men* think it is important." What made me think that teaching women would be different?

Now it was my time to pause.

As luck would have it, Johanne read my book and had an epiphany.

"Joanna," she said, weeks after turning me down. "I love your book! To me, the leaders you interviewed are *positive deviants*—courageous women who delivered results and felt fulfilled. They made it despite all the obstacles, finding ways to influence the system to create positive change. By listening deeply, you uncovered a feminine archetype of leadership that lives in everyone and that we all need to address complex problems, to stand in uncertainty, and to tap our creativity and intuition." And she was just getting started! Johanne saw Centered Leadership as an extension of the path she had been on—with more rigor and completeness. She "got" that Centered Leadership helps leaders be more of who they are, mastering the skills to create significant change. She told me that she loved designing learning journeys for leaders—in effect, leadership *capability-building* programs.

As a small child, I used to watch television with my grandmother and our favorite program was *You Bet Your Life* with Groucho Marx. He would interview contestants and if they said the secret word revealed to the audience earlier, they received $100! Jo had just said the secret word: "Capability-building." Yes!

So I asked again, and she joined me in this journey.

Joining forces

When I met Johanne, I wasn't sure what I had signed up for. Imagine Jo, living with her husband, Rob, and their two girls deep in the Canadian Rockies. She skied, ran, or biked every day—carrying bear spray because grizzlies roamed the same trails. Jo's path to Centered Leadership looked very different from mine. From age twelve on, Johanne saw herself taking care of her family. Tenacity and courage served her well in many ways, as her achievements showed.

But sometimes things happen off plan—way off plan—and that was Jo's trial and the greatest source of her growth. In her late twenties, Johanne and Rob decided to start a family. But she could not conceive. Medicine could provide no logical answer or solution. Jo recalled, "I felt powerless. My tenets in life, what *drove* me—success comes with hard work (and suffering is part of it), all problems can be solved with Cartesian logic, you can control everything your mind decides—literally didn't work. I had to reframe at the deepest level." Johanne's strength is to be in full control. Learning to let go was not easy.

It meant reintegrating what she had locked away: vulnerability. So Johanne reached out for help. "Life found a way to put great teachers on my path. These are people I would not have paid attention to before but, out of despair, I did; and they opened my world to new practices and bodies of science. I started asking new questions. I began to realize that, perhaps, my mindsets were the source of my challenges."

Two daughters and a lot of life later, Johanne's fascination with the human capacity to learn and grow created meaning far greater than what she had given up. She decided to shift her professional program to live into her vision: touching the inner life of leaders, helping them create and sustain change. That was when Jo began to train as a coach and facilitator. Johanne believed wholeheartedly in change—experiencing it firsthand through the birth of her two daughters, relocation to the mountains, and a new path.

What had the Universe brought me? Exactly what I had asked for. Every time Johanne and I talked, sparks flew. She was stubborn. I was stubborn. (Johanne reframes this as a creative process where differences give birth to new and better ideas. I remember this as arguing!) But Jo is an independent thinker who, having seen the beauty of Centered Leadership's bold vision, simple structure, and rigorous clarity, loved it. She helped me turn ideas and intuition into a valuable curriculum, unique exercises, and, over five years, a distinctive and powerfully effective program. We enlisted a community of practitioners who helped complete our program for personal transformation, leading others, the business, and transformational change.

Now, "transformation" is a word bandied about enough that you may have passed it by, but I'll pause on it, with your permission.

Yes, we offered exercises, new tools, and practices from the start. But those are not transformational on their own. Centered Leadership was crying out to be experienced, practiced, used in daily work and life. *The missing piece was a process* to help you dive deep enough to gain consciousness of what drives you, what you stand for and value, what stands in your way. Only then can you open yourself to a journey to transform the outcomes you create at work and in life. And, like a great road trip, this is an adrenaline-fueled adventure that sparks your ability to be in the moment, feeling alive and energized.

That said, only a few leaders attend a program. It will take thousands of leaders to create positive change in your company or community and—call us dreamers—in the world. So we're bringing you that Centered Leadership learning journey in this book as best we can. We want to give you the experience of our Centered Leadership programs, only between two covers. We encourage you to find some way to make the process interactive and energetic. Dog-ear the pages. Write in the margins. Rip the pages out, if you'd like. Or, if marking up a printed book is not your style, write in a notebook by your side.

Although you can approach this as a solitary experience, you'll accelerate learning by sharing experiences. Of course you're not exactly on your own because we're with you, but you may want to discuss your learning with a coach or mentor, too. Or take this journey with a friend; many of our exercises are meant to be shared. You might even form a learning circle or "mini-board" of colleagues to work together. Whatever approach you choose, we hope you go beyond a "read-only" format. This book is meant to be used.

Come back to it over time, and reread passages or chapters that call out to you. Be patient with yourself. Some questions may not spark insight right away, but in time, you'll experience flashes of insight—aha! moments. Then set action experiments—fieldwork—to practice a new skill.

Welcome on board

If you're just starting out, we'll help you head down the path, open to opportunities coming your way. If you are midcareer and worried about how to balance greater responsibility at work with home and family, we'll help you face those questions with courage. If you're working from home, looking for work, or a full-time parent and wondering how to make your mark, you'll find lots of ideas in here. And if you're a senior executive who wants to inspire and mobilize others with more results and less drain—that's in these pages, too.

The Centered Leadership journey beckons to anyone who feels, as I did, invisible at work. It's for anyone who feels stuck—who wants to achieve more. It's for anyone who is frustrated that implementation is not unfolding as envisioned. And it's for anyone who dreams about having positive impact beyond what's in reach today.

But in order to do that, you must start with yourself. If you stay with us on this journey, you'll begin to think, feel, even look different. It happened to me. In the middle of a Centered Leadership workshop, a woman named Sara walked up to me and said: "Joanna, I've been watching you for years. Something has changed. You look great! You are visibly happy and excited about what you're doing. I can feel your energy from the back of the room! Can I buy you lunch and find out what you're having? I want some!" I could not have asked for a better gift. Sara had uttered words I had hoped people would say one day.

Ten years into my journey, I continue to grow. I wake up most days feeling hopeful. I feel more present and genuinely alive more of the time. I get more done and I get more out of what I do. Even better, I have touched so many more people, who, in turn, pass on the spark. For the first time in my life, I feel connected to a broader community.

What's more, today I'm as joyful and playful as I was at four. At the same time, I'm wiser (and calmer). I have found my purpose, counseling men and women at dozens of companies in as many cities on every continent (yes, including Antarctica); providing thousands with the tools to take their places as leaders; and pioneering Centered Leadership at our firm. Meanwhile, Johanne is teaching an army of gifted facilitators as programs unfold in all parts of the world. In other words, the journey continues—especially, now that you're here.

With that, welcome on board.

3

SETTING OUT

*In which we begin our journey by practicing a Check-In, setting
agreements, and familiarizing ourselves with how adults learn*

I don't know about you, but every family trip we take starts long
before we leave. Explorers know that preparation is the most important part of any journey. So think of this chapter as preparation. Luckily, you already have everything you'll need. You may not
yet realize it, but you possess the insights and capacity required to
become a Centered Leader: It's all within. This book is about learning
how to access it.

Checking in

We invite you to do a quick exercise to help you recenter and reflect
on what you want to get out of our time together. This is a great ritual
that Jo introduced to me. I wholeheartedly embrace it and encourage
you to do the same, whether you are by yourself or in a group. Take a
moment and reflect on these three sentences:

[handwritten note in margin: check in with your team]

Check-In

- Right now, I am feeling . . . (or: Right now, I am physically sensing . . .)

  Confused about next chapter of my career. Whether I will be able to make it in M.U.

- What I want to learn, experience, or bring more to the fore in my leadership is . . .

  Ability to lead challenging clients. build long-term relationship w/ partners.

- What may keep me from being present (or get in my way) is . . .

  Day-to-day frustration.

Maybe you're thinking, "How much time do I have to answer these questions? It could take an hour and I've only set aside ten minutes!" So take ten, and listen deeply to yourself. I'll go first, to show you:

1. *Right now, I am feeling* . . . excited and scared writing this chapter. I'm excited because this is the start of a big, messy, creative project. I'm scared because I risk falling short of your expectations and fear that I will fall flat on my face publicly.

2. *What I want to learn, experience* . . . I want to put Centered Leadership into your hands in a way that you will value and use. I want to be at my best on every page—vulnerable, imaginative, wise, inspiring, and funny.

3. *What may keep me from being fully present in this moment is* . . . if I let my fear take over and I worry about your critique, I will get distracted or, worse, use big words to say little.

Now it's your turn to check in. If you're in a group, listen with genuine curiosity as others speak. This is your first tool! Its purpose here is simple: *to help you be more present, open, and aligned with yourself and others.* That's worth a comment.

Most days, we go about our business hardly aware. There is so much to do and not enough time to do it in. Who has time to stop and be present in the moment? If we're honest, we feel a rush—a bit of a thrill—when we're too busy to catch our breath. We love the adrenaline high and we're proud of our ability to fix things, to get stuff done, to be in the vortex of what goes on at work. We love being productive, achieving results. We feel important. We feel valued and needed. We *are* valued and needed. And yet, how often do we take the time to think about what we want to accomplish—what is really important to us?

I remember the Check-In at the start of a Centered Leadership program with a group of high performing managers at a technology company. Most of them were "the fixers" at work, the people who made it happen. Despite feeling productive and valued, they felt stressed and overwhelmed. They wanted more downtime; they wanted to be more strategic and knew it was a requisite for advancement. Engrossed in tasks, they had lost sight of aligning their intention and their work.

All that from a Check-In?

Check-Ins are amazingly brief, yet go deep. They happen without dialogue. You'll be surprised how much you can voice in a minute when everyone is listening intently. Ten people can do this exercise in under ten minutes.

The first time we invite people to check in, they hesitate. They say, "I don't want to go first!" or "He just said what I was going to say!" or simply, "Pass." That's exactly how I felt when Johanne turned to me. I felt silly sitting in a circle and was squirmy. I felt tense; I didn't know what to say. I felt ashamed—I worried I would not sound smart. I felt embarrassed about opening up, sharing too much. It can feel awkward to disclose feelings, voice an intention, even express discomfort. But once you get going, the experience can be profound.

Use the Check-In with your team. If that step feels too big, ask for one word that captures what people are thinking or feeling at that moment. In that version, we hear words such as curious, reflective, confused, energized, excited, inspired, upset. Even one word can communicate a lot. Check in with yourself at times during the day. It will get you in the habit of noticing your emotions and making action a conscious choice. So, *please* give this tool its due. Introduce it in your next meeting. Change the CI questions, if you like, to reduce discomfort until you gain familiarity with the tool. For example:

- Today I wanted to come here because . . .
- What really matters to me in this discussion is . . .
- What will make this a great meeting for me is . . .
- The biggest opportunity I see for myself and others is . . .
- The most important issue I would like us to address is . . .

With practice, you'll realize the value of the ritual, and when you do, others will, too. You'll be more productive; you'll feel more connected. To quote Scott, the team will rock.

What are your leadership challenges?

People learn more easily when they are personally engaged—solving their issue or addressing their question. Accordingly, take a moment to think about what you dream of achieving at work, in your community, in your family. *What is the nature of the leadership challenges you face?* Name your top three in the space below:

My Top Three Challenges

1. _____

   _____

2. _____

   _____

3. _____

   _____

What kind of leadership challenges are they? Drawing on Ron Heifetz's research, Johanne offers a checklist to identify whether your challenges are adaptive or technical:

____ A. Is the problem definition clear with discoverable cause and effect (and correct answers possible)? OR

____ B. Are the issues complex, ambiguous, and unprecedented?

____ A. Can you reach a solution with relevant experts, best practices, or your own experience? OR

____ B. Do you need the collective intelligence of multiple stakeholders to discover a solution?

____ A. Does implementation depend on efficient execution, standardization, and follow-through on a detailed plan? OR

____ B. Are you looking to rapidly prototype ideas and quickly learn from mistakes, adapting as you go?

____ A. Will command-and-control authority get you the best outcome? OR

____ B. Is your role more to ask the right questions and lead through a process of engagement?

For each of the three challenges you named above—and overall—estimate your mix.

My mix of challenges

	Percent A	Percent B
Challenge #1	%	%
Challenge #2	%	%
Challenge #3	%	%

Are you leaning to leadership challenges that look more like B? If so, it would be natural to feel stress from not knowing, living with uncertainty, letting go of control, engaging people outside of your authority, and opening up to change. How will we learn to master all these messy, complex skills on the job—especially when the challenge is important and urgent?

Most of us are not content to sit at a desk and listen up as some authority figure jabbers away at the front of the room. Research suggests that adults don't acquire, develop, or master new skills in classrooms. We want to explore that knowledge *ourselves,* to live it, to contribute to it. As Jo explains, we learn in four stages:

- **Stage 1: Unconsciously unskilled:** One leader demonstrated this phase when she confidently burst out: "I can do anything I set my mind to. If I had to operate on you right now, I could. I might need help but I could do it!" Thank god for my good health that day. Until we have some incident—a curve ball—that upsets and creates self-awareness, we remain unconsciously unskilled, not knowing what we do not know. With self-awareness, we can choose to stay in the comfort zone of our habitual beliefs; or we can *choose* Stage 2 . . .
- **Stage 2: Consciously unskilled:** We've accepted that our old mindset and behavior did not get us the outcomes we wanted, and

we care enough to want to grow. Now that we're open, we're willing to try on new beliefs or practices. It's unsettling, though, and
it takes humility to be a "beginner" when the stakes are high. How
exhausting and energizing is early learning! But with commitment
we move to Stage 3 . . .

- **Stage 3: Consciously skilled**: Our new tools and new approaches
  have helped us adopt new mindsets and create new possibilities.
  We're still learning, though, and we'll fall back without attention.
  Now it's up to us to practice, practice, practice the new behaviors
  until we find that our comfort zone has expanded to include them.
  We're on fire, learning at lightning speed; and with enough practice,
  we move to Stage 4 . . .

- **Stage 4: Unconsciously skilled**: In this stage, we have integrated
  what felt unnatural before. We're not even aware we're using these
  skills and behaviors now, because they naturally emerge out of our
  new mindset. We still need humility as we may find ourselves falling back at times; yet we continue to develop new skills and behaviors with less effort, starting the cycle again with joy and energy.

Remember when you learned something new that seemed incredibly challenging at first? I recall a 1990 company ski retreat for our
newest consultants. As the partner in charge and with my boyfriend
(now husband) looking on, I was too embarrassed to admit that I was
a rank beginner. Put yourselves in my ski boots:

There I am, at the top of the bunny hill, about to be tested. Suddenly
the hill looks huge. I feel a tightening knot in my stomach. Everyone
has zipped down, and it's my turn to win *Advanced* Beginner status.
The tiny voice coaches, *Better make the grade, Joanna, or you'll be off
the team*. I bend down, poles parallel to the ground like a racer. Looking good! As I take off, I hear, *Pittifaldi Barsh!* I'm thrilled with my (increasing) speed. A crowd to my right is yelling, and I race on, heartened.
Flying (literally), I ski over a bump and crash at the bottom. A random
instructor dashes over to pick me up, worry written all over his face.

Uh-oh.

Looking halfway up the hill, I see my colleagues and their words now make sense, "Turn right, Joanna! Stop! Snowplow! Watch out!!!"

Aha!

I've been "unconsciously unskilled"—until now. This was my curve ball. Still embarrassed, I'm now conscious and ready to learn.

I take lessons all weekend, eager to learn new behaviors. David sticks by me with only a little teasing. In time, I no longer fall off the ski lift and can make it down intermediate slopes upright. My belief shifts from "I just need to make it" to "I can ski at my level and enjoy it!" Soon the new me tastes freedom as I gain control to safely navigate new routes. I sense that, with practice, each motion in my body and each movement of my skis will better align. That is the long road to mastery.

But what does skiing have to do with anything in this book?

Everything. Becoming aware, choosing to grow, and practicing to increase mastery are no different with leadership. As you set out with us on this adventure, let's be beginners together. Learning your purpose; gaining clarity through self-reflection; building communities through trust; and being fully in the moment and energized feels hard because it *is* hard work. These skills are challenging to learn; they require us to transform. But, as with most things in life, if they aren't difficult, they probably aren't worth doing.

And you're not alone. Remarkable leaders are regular people like you and me. They get stuck like the rest of us, sometimes hijacked in the action when they should be outside it and cool-headed. We're all human and imperfect by design. That's why we've created a tool kit for you—to help you experiment, make mistakes, gain feedback and learn. As you practice, you'll grow and eventually achieve the mastery not possible in a classroom. This cycle never stops unless you decide to stop it.

Setting agreements

In our programs, we always set agreements at the outset—promises and requests you make to create a safe environment for learning.

Since I have the pen, I'll put some down. If you're using this book in a group, we encourage you to ask for and record agreements together.

First on the list is confidentiality. A program of personal transformation demands it. But what other agreements should we make? Here are a few we care about deeply:

- **Trust:** Accept people for who they are; be honest and let go of judging yourself, too.
- **Be present:** Be here with your body *and* mind so that you can make meaningful connections with learning, with yourself, and with others if you're working together.
- **Step out of your comfort zone:** Be bold and see what happens; it feels exciting and a little bit scary to learn and yes, it is hard to change but possible.
- **Have some fun:** When we play in the childlike stance of wonder, we're most likely to discover new insights and play eases learning.
- **Practice listening:** Be curious, actively listening for what is not said but is felt or thought. Allow uncomfortable silences for reflection, letting the speaker (that could be you) experience discomfort without trying to fix it.
- **Practice speaking:** Share what you're feeling or thinking but hesitant to express, in the spirit of openness and learning.

As a bonus, last comes my favorite: Turn off all machines that go "ping!" If you're sitting by your computer, smartphone, tablet, TV, or plain old telephone, turn them to silent. Give yourself the gift of full attention.

After all, this program is *about you* and *for you*.

4

AT MY BEST

In which you begin your journey as a leader by grounding yourself in the characteristics of leadership that you most admire, which lie within you

Imagine a leader who is truly distinctive in your mind—someone who has had a profound impact on you. This could be a leader from any walk of real or imagined life—work, politics, religion, family, school, books, or movies. Choose someone who stands out in comparison to other leaders, someone who moved you in some way at some point.

Got one memory and the name of that leader?

Jot down or think through the characteristics that distinguish this leader. Please be as specific as you can. In other words, what did they do—or not do, what did they say—or not say, and what impact did that have on you?

A leader I admire

Binny Wim. → she has a purpose of why
she wants to do healthcare & she made it happen

If you're doing this exercise in a group, ask your friends or colleagues what comes to mind for them—and then, why. Make a collective list, remembering that the characteristic must be distinctive or unique for at least one of you. Once you have twenty or more characteristics, you are ready to sort them. Use the three buckets below:

Distinctive leadership

IQ and technical qualities,

e.g., scary smart, quick decision maker, strategic

Smart

Emotion/energy qualities,

e.g., honest, open, touches others, passionate

Passionate

Meaning qualities,

e.g., purposeful, inspiring, values based

Purposeful.
Inspiring
Caring.

I find the three lists fascinating, because participants always place more characteristics on the second two lists versus the first. Why? We *expect* our leaders to be smart and skillful, but that's not what makes them distinctive. The second two lists distinguish remarkable leaders who inspire, align, engage, and mobilize for action.

Take a close look at the qualities you recorded. Are many of them ones to which you aspire? If so, I'm not surprised. We all admire and want to be like leaders who bring out the best in us. Most participants are taken aback when they realize that the traits we admire in others are traits we have ourselves. Same for you? Try Jo's mini-exercise:

Positive projection

(Please finish this sentence.)

"I admire ____Lenders who have a vision /purpose____ for his or her ____Chieer_____, just like me."

Fill in the name of the leader you admire, along with the characteristic you admire. Say the sentence out loud at least once. It's even better if you do this with a discussion partner. You might feel uncomfortable, but try it anyway. Ask people around you—family members, friends, work colleagues—to observe how they see you express this attribute. Johanne says, "If you spot it, you've got it."

Recognizing in yourself those characteristics you admire in a distinctive leader is a step toward becoming one. Reflect on times when you demonstrated these strengths. It doesn't have to be at work. It doesn't even have to be in the last ten years. Once you find the memory, relive it. I'll give you a personal example. In this exercise, I thought of my mother—who rose to leadership when circumstances required. Let's go back fifty years:

Harriet Jane becomes a divorced mother of two with little money, limited education, no skills, and no way to earn. But she prevails. I still remember what she says to calm my fears about money: "We will always find a way. I will become a cashier at the supermarket if I have to." Instead, Harriet Jane remarries, moves us to New York City, teaches herself to design clothing, and, in a matter of years, becomes an avant-garde fashion designer. To my child's eye, she is Rumpelstiltskin spinning gold out of straw: hopeful, creative, bold. Invisibly, Harriet Jane's strength and fortitude fill me with equal resolve. Her belief that almost anything is possible takes root in me. Her visionary sight becomes mine. And her capacity to touch others grows in me, too. Harriet Jane instills in me that wish to appreciate what is inside—our creativity, our individuality, our humanity.

Years after her death, I now recognize and accept that what I admired in my mother exists in me. That didn't happen automatically. So if you struggle with this exercise, let's try a different approach.

Who am I at my best?

Recall a high point over the last few years at work—when you felt passionate, engaged, energized, and in your most resourceful state. Jot down your story (in the present tense) here:

My high point

What am I doing, thinking, and feeling?

_____
_____
_____
_____
_____

(continued)

(continued)

What do I value most about my work and about myself, in this moment?

_____

_____

_____

_____

_____

If you can, share your story with someone. And when you have given voice to that moment, stop and reflect on how you feel. Turning to that colleague, ask: "How did you feel hearing that story? What does it tell you about me?" Take some notes here:

What does that experience say about me?

_____

_____

_____

_____

_____

Others can help us see ourselves in new ways. We reveal more to them about ourselves and, in particular, about our strengths.

So let's take that one step further. We invite you to gather feedback from people who know you from different realms of your life—not just work. Aim for at least four but up to ten people. This request is a bit different from what you may have done elsewhere. Ask others to articulate *what they see in you when you are at your best.* We have a template for you (see Request for feedback, next page). Simply give each person a copy and let them know that their feedback is confidential and not for evaluation purposes.

Request for feedback

I am participating in a Centered Leadership development program. In this context, I am collecting feedback to help me understand my strengths, how I can use them more, and what may limit my personal leadership impact. Please complete this brief questionnaire and return it. Thank you so much.

When I am at my best in your eyes, what do you observe me doing? Please use a few specific examples to help me understand—events or situations. What behaviors do you observe? What is the impact of my behaviors on you and/ or others?

_____

_____

_____

_____

What may be getting in the way of me being at my best more often? Please use examples again—events or situations. What behaviors do you observe? What is the impact of my behaviors on you and/ or others?

_____

_____

_____

_____

What other friendly advice can you offer me to bring my best self forward more of the time? Please suggest the smallest steps you counsel me to take that may make the biggest difference.

_____

_____

_____

_____

PLEASE RETURN THIS FORM TO: _____

I don't know how you'll feel when you read what others have written, but I hope you will receive the feedback with appreciation, curiosity, and openness to learn about what others see in you. Watch out for self-judgment—and self-blame. I remember giving out my forms in 2008 to friendly colleagues, a sponsor, a client, and my husband. As I read their handwritten scribbles, it was clear that they saw me. Let me repeat: They *saw* me. For the first time, I realized that I was not invisible. They admired my courage, my creativity, my vision. They also saw how I undermined myself by expecting the worst from others. And I'd thought I had that well covered up! I cried because I felt ashamed, so exposed. I still aspired to perfection and could not accept these parts of myself. The feedback burned for days.

And there was more. What was the future they envisioned for me? They saw me speaking and writing, traveling the world to seed Centered Leadership. At the time, I thought that was just plain dumb. Six years later, I'm living the future they imagined. Clearly, it takes time for some of us to gain self-awareness, to accept, to appreciate ourselves. That part of my journey was rocky and steep. And I'm still on the path.

These may be your hardest steps, too, in your journey. But, boy, are they worth it. If you do nothing more with this chapter, I hope you think deeply about the leaders you admire. And know that what you admire is in you, too.

Let's unleash it together. We have the map. We have our destination. We're packed. Johanne is in the car. So what am I waiting for?

You. You make it all worthwhile.

And now that you're here, we're ready to go.

Turn up the music, roll down the windows, and hit the gas! It's going to be a great ride.

PART TWO

MEANING

5

BECOMING SOULFUL

In which we introduce Meaning and its three dimensions—happiness, strengths, and purpose—and what you'll find in this section

What do you mean when you talk about meaning? I've come to believe that meaning is what we crave to be sure we are living fully—that we are making our contribution, using our short time on Earth well. So universal is our fear of meaninglessness, it is said that we human beings are "meaning makers." For me, meaning is the difference between having a life with few regrets (with loving husband, loving daughters, great job and community) and a truly remarkable life in which I feel complete and resilient, experiencing joy wholeheartedly. Meaning is what happens in moments when I feel at one with the universe—when I feel love for everyone and everything around me, including myself. And that's a good feeling.

We made Meaning the anchor of Centered Leadership; our research showed that it carried about five times the clout of any other dimension. So if you're looking for a place to start your Centered Leadership journey, this is a great one. With that, let's begin.

The roots of meaning

It all begins with happiness. And yet, the pursuit of happiness does not necessarily lead to meaning. A riddle, you ask? Not exactly. The pursuit of meaning leads to happiness; but, as happiness experts teach us, happiness itself doesn't guarantee a meaningful life.

Long-lasting happiness, what experts call *fulfillment*, is the kind of happiness we seek. Where does it come from? Jonathan Haidt draws on Sonja Lyubomirsky, Kennon M. Sheldon, David Schkade, and Martin Seligman when he coins a formula for lasting happiness: 50 percent from your genetic set point, 10 percent from the conditions of your life, and another 40 percent from voluntary activities you choose. It may seem unfair that unaware parents contribute half our total happiness. Luckily, as Haidt posits, this set point is more of a range; with conscious effort, we can engage in activities that get us to the top of it. That's where we're headed.

But pause for a moment on *conditions*—that 10 percent. Conditions are the little things that, if improved, would make you marginally happier in your day-to-day life—such as quieter neighbors or a shorter commute. Take a moment to list your most important conditions:

Conditions I would improve if I could

_____   _____

_____   _____

_____   _____

_____   _____

_____   _____

_____   _____

_____   _____

The great thing about conditions is that we humans are adaptable; even when our conditions dramatically improve (beyond our wildest dreams), we settle into the new status quo quickly. The same holds true for most conditions that bother us (as anyone can attest who has learned how to tune out noisy neighbors).

Actually, our threshold for acceptable conditions is quite low. Great conditions don't boost your happiness for long. If you had to let them go, you could adapt to worse conditions. I think a lot about this, because my mother-in-law had to leave everything behind—to survive and, ultimately, to make a new life from scratch. Material things are temporary. Even intangibles, like life itself, are temporary. I know I can live with less and still be happy. I bet you can, too.

Back to the equation. What about that remaining 40 percent? Happiness has three levels: pleasure, active engagement, and choosing activities that really matter to us, that allow us to fully use our strengths, that take us to a higher plane where we feel part of something bigger than ourselves.

Aah, pleasure. What gives you pleasure? Tal Ben-Shahar, in *Happier*, suggests we make a list. Did you know that, on average, people are happiest at mealtimes? Food carries strong *sensory* and *emotional* components. What provides you with sensory and emotional pleasure? Mine are: espresso in the early morning as the sun rises on a summer's day. A cheap chocolate bar from Halloween. Stupidly funny movies. Brand-new shoes, especially red leather ones that remind me of the first day of school. Yeah. Write your list here:

My pleasure list (happiness, part 1)

_____   _____
_____   _____
_____   _____
_____   _____
_____   _____
_____   _____
_____   _____

So many things in life give pleasure. Music. Books. Movies. Flowers, boats, cars, shoes—there's a catalogue for everyone. Once we start to think about what gives us pleasure, we notice it everywhere.

But as good as it feels in the moment, pleasure is the most fleeting form of happiness. It evaporates almost as soon as it's consumed, and we want more—more chocolate, more toys, more sex, more everything—we stop only when we feel sick (until the craving starts up again). Pleasure served up regularly but in small amounts is best.

Active engagement is what allows us to *extend* that happiness feeling. Why is it that you always feel energized when engaged in certain activities or events? Think about those experiences—ones that trigger something more than momentary delight. Recall the experience (or look at a photo) of a special vacation or celebration—and notice what you feel in that moment of recall. On their own, Johanne notes, these things don't *make* us happy; they trigger us to *choose* to feel happiness. An important distinction—we make the choice. Please list the activities or experiences that trigger you to choose to feel stronger fulfillment.

What engages me (happiness, part 2)

_____	_____
_____	_____
_____	_____
_____	_____
_____	_____
_____	_____
_____	_____

This list, you may find, goes beyond fleeting sensations and emotions; the good feeling lasts longer. I'll share a few of mine: taking in the views from our apartment (an artist by training, I delight in watching the weather); our daily walk to school and work (I'm with people I love and feeling good about exercising); walking on our farm (beauty in nature brings me joy).

The third level of happiness is the longest lasting, and we can achieve it by choosing to engage in activities that truly matter to us. These activities engage us on a deeper level. Most often we get there by drawing on our strengths. Martin Seligman, a father of positive psychology, defines strengths as those universal characteristics or virtues we had as children. They exist in any culture and era. Johanne defines strengths as what we value most in ourselves—characteristics that give us energy when used. They represent what is deeply true about us. Any definition you like works for me, as long as these strengths are not skills in disguise!

What engages me *and* is really important (happiness, part 3)

_____   _____
_____   _____
_____   _____
_____   _____
_____   _____
_____   _____
_____   _____

For example, I lose track of time working on Centered Leadership programs with Johanne and our colleagues. My creativity is turned on; I feel a part of something bigger. When we dig down to this level, we are on the road to living our true purpose.

I found it striking that most interviewees or participants underscore that relationships—people they've helped, their families, their friends—are the most important things on their list. We share a deep human need for belonging. When we belong, we experience the longest-lasting feeling of fulfillment. And helping others is often the key to purpose.

Purpose, a much harder one to get our arms around, delivers meaning. Simply put, it is what you can do with all that is uniquely you. It becomes your calling. Though some people know their purpose as a child, it could take decades to find. If you have not yet crystallized yours, please don't worry. You are on a journey of discovery. As you seek it, Johanne suggests this question for reflection: What do I stand for regardless of my work, community, or family context? Without your knowing it, your purpose may reveal itself. At least that's how it happened to me.

When I started my journey in 2004, I badly wanted a purpose. Sure, I loved my work. But the universe had certainly not spoken to me (I'm sure I would have noticed if it had)! Then one day, years later, I realized that I was engaged in activities that gave me energy; I was using strengths that I valued in myself; I was part of something bigger. And there it was. I had a purpose.

Looking back now, it seems obvious. As a young child, I spent hours in imaginative play—making up stories and using anything at hand to enact them: myself, friends, dolls, even my thumbs. As a young adult, my first dream was to be an artist or moviemaker. I wanted to touch everyone through funny stories, moving stories; I wanted to paint and fill people's lives with color. In contrast, my own reality was sometimes painful, but mostly quotidian except in daydreams.

Two degrees in English literature later, I knew what my calling was *not*. And three years into a retail career, I was knee-deep in cement. I reached out and my stepfather suggested Harvard Business School. I applied, got lucky, and started the following September. After that, friends interviewed with McKinsey, and so I did, too. Lucky again. But not purpose-driven. I recall working very hard and looking no further than a few months ahead. I tried to remain busy so as not to think.

Exactly when did my calling show up?

Not for a long, long time. Meanwhile, a lot more life happened. Including love at first sight (David), and love at first sight again (Gaby and then Jetta). And countless ups and downs and plateaus in between. More than twenty years passed.

Over the years, I wandered into storytelling. In 2004 I started interviewing remarkable leaders as I kept on being a consultant, daydreaming and seeking patterns without realizing. These remarkable women and men were my characters and teachers. For example, I remember Shikha Sharma in late 2008, so kind and sitting perfectly still as she described purpose: "This whole thing of Hindu philosophy, sometimes I think I do understand and sometimes I think I don't. It talks about how you have to find what you were born to do, do it, and leave the results to destiny. Free will is in finding purpose in your life and choosing to go out and do it. Forget about results. The results will happen one day."

Like Shikha, I wasn't sure I understood, so I kept on listening.

Then one day it clicked, as I sat in a circle with men and women in a Centered Leadership program. The group was practicing mindfulness. As I relaxed, I let go more and more and began to feel the grandness of the circle of strangers who were becoming seen by me. I no longer felt separate because of my physical being; I became a part of each person just as they were a part of me. I floated above the group. In a flash, I saw myself reintegrated with the child I was at four and I felt love and kindness for her. I looked to a colleague next to me and felt his presence, vastly different and yet so much the same. His reserve, his pain, and his separateness seemed to melt away. I understood my purpose: to move people by witnessing their uniqueness and courage to be great.

At your peak

Once we're living our purpose, we find meaning daily in our work. Let's look for meaning in times when you were feeling energized and on fire: when you were operating at peak performance and in your most resourceful state. Scan your last few years to find mountain peaks in your work. (We'll face the bottom-of-the-ocean lows in an-other chapter, so for now please shine a light on these highs.) Scan the past five years and note some of your proudest achievements. What was it about those times that made you feel like you were making his-tory? Are they marked by challenge, growth, and accomplishment?

Spend a moment exploring one work experience (or if none come to mind, use a personal example). Feel free to take the same experience you reflected on in chapter 4 or, better yet, choose another. Were you alone or part of a team? Were you working on daily business or a spe-cial project? Did you have a goal that felt urgent and maybe impossible, yet you achieved it anyway? Go back to that experience and explore why this moment—this accomplishment—moves you. Here is some space to jot down your notes:

My peak experience (the situation, what we accomplished, how I felt)

Situation

_____

_____

_____

Goal/what you achieved/what you created

_____

_____

_____

What about this high point makes it stand out for you?

_____

_____

_____

It's wonderful to see how energized people get as they remember, share, and report on their peak experiences. (Do you see the link to happiness's third level?) Usually the goal or achievement was high in importance and urgency for the company. Often, the person was on a team of high performers with clear roles, close alignment, effective processes, clear metrics of success, and skilled leadership. The team collaborated, resolved conflicts early, trusted and respected each other. The team debated and argued, but people found it creative and energizing versus blaming and draining. Participants reported that it was an honor to be part of this team's experience—highly challenging and memorable for life.

Workshop participants also recall experiencing strong emotions. When we are operating at our best we work in a high-performance mode, and that's emotionally and physically exhausting. Yet we're motivated to push ourselves to new heights. We don't recall the experience as necessarily fun (it's usually damn hard work), but we're fully engaged. As we learn to work together, accomplishing more than we could achieve on our own, we feel great love for fellow team members. Stretching ourselves to the max allows us to feel a closeness we have not experienced before at work.

Participants also recall how the most meaningful work differs from "business as usual." Perhaps the challenge was a new product launch or turnaround; a company merger or divestiture; a dramatic change in strategy—generally, way out of the ordinary. Often, people volunteer, but not for the rewards. Some want to learn and grow personally. Others do it for the team. Still others want to make a significant contribution to the company or serve their customers better. Many do it in service of broader society. People differ in terms of what matters most to them, and though not everyone would sign up again right away, what marks the experience is a feeling of being part of something bigger than oneself.

In other words, what distinguishes most peak experiences is *meaning*. Without meaning, that project or initiative was still an opportunity to contribute and develop. *With* meaning, it's a remarkable achievement. Sadly, meaning all too often gets lost in the hustle and bustle of daily work, trampled in our frantic race to do more and get ahead. As you recall the way you felt during your peak moment, estimate how often you feel that way at work:

What percentage of my time do I spend in a peak experience?

Over the last five years _____%

Over the last year _____%

Over the last six months _____%

Most people choose a startlingly low percentage, yet wish they could live at their high point more of the time. What is your goal? Write it down so you can revisit it:

I aspire to live at my high point _____ **% of the time**

It might be tempting to plug in 100 percent, but caution: It's not possible to be in peak performance all the time.

The pages ahead

We've designed Centered Leadership to help you find meaning in your work and life through the three core elements of Meaning: deepening our *happiness* by choosing to engage in activities that bring us energy; explicitly drawing on our *strengths*; and living into *purpose*. We've already talked about ways to raise your levels of happiness by finding pleasure and fulfillment in the world around you. Next, we guide you to build on your strengths. After that, we help you develop your emerging vision so that you can begin to lead with meaning, personally and professionally.

As you embark on this leg of the journey, please remember to be kind to yourself; appreciate that each of us takes our own route in our own time. Whether it takes years or comes to you in a flash doesn't really matter. All routes can bring learning. We're going to practice dreaming; and, though your first dream may not work out, interim visions are great stepping-stones on your way to purpose.

And then again, your second or third dream just might be the one that works out.

By the way, thinking about Meaning may be uncomfortable. David, the happy pessimist, warns that dreaming could lead to less happiness when the dream falls apart! That's a downside, for sure, but I encourage you to stay with dreaming awhile. Once you set out down the path toward Meaning, you'll find yourself on your way to achieving the most elusive of goals: inspiring yourself and others to achieve greatness.

6

BUILDING ON YOUR STRENGTHS

In which you identify your strengths and how to draw on them
more to release positive energy at work—and at home

Back in 2007, I decided to take Martin Seligman's strengths assessment to get a third-party opinion on my core strengths. So I marched over to the computer and registered on his site, www.authentichappiness.org, to find my rank order of "signature strengths." You see, I was determined to *prove* my leadership. My thought process went something like this: Because of my height—I am five feet tall if I stand up really straight—the (male) leaders in my firm probably never saw me (no one's fault, really). My plan was to print out this assessment as "Exhibit A." When they saw my leadership strength revealed in black and white at the top of the list, I would be set. A layup! Put yourself in my shoes.

I take the assessment and, twenty minutes later, the test results show up on the screen (my personalized list of strengths, ranked from first to twenty-fourth), and my eyes race to the top of the page.

What the . . . ?

I frantically scan my top five strengths, my top ten, panic rising. I finally find leadership—at number 15.

Not what anyone would call a *top* strength.

Deep breath, Joanna. Breathe.

With visibly less excitement, I return to the top and see my number 1 strength staring back at me: industry, diligence, and perseverance.

That nagging little voice can't resist: *How glamorous, Joanna! You're industrious!* My daughters pipe up next. Gaby reasons, "Mom! You love to wash dishes—that's industrious." And Jetta chortles, "You should be a housekeeper, Mom—then you'd be happy!" I deflate with disappointment, realizing that I really do love to wash dishes.

And over the next three weeks, I wonder why industry, diligence, and perseverance are my top strengths. Sure, consulting is a good job for someone who perseveres. But there has got to be more. How am I applying this strength in my work and life?

And then it hits me. I love getting around obstacles in the road. I do that as part of problem solving. But there's more. I see that I've always flourished *because* of obstacles. After all, I went to business school against all odds (I was an English and fine arts major in college). I joined McKinsey at a time when women were barely 20 percent of the class; and one of my professors had informed me that my chance of getting in was about zero. I had two children late in life, when those odds were low. I worked (crawled) my way back from maternity leaves during a recession each time. I advanced to partner and then director with (really) low odds. Mathematician David puts it this way, "If we were to run a Monte Carlo simulation on one thousand Joannas, only one would make it to director. It's just the probabilities, honey." We both know I didn't win some grand cosmic lottery. I worked with diligence in the face of obstacles; and, with a lot of help, I persevered, regardless of how many years it was gonna take.

So what happened when I became a senior partner and there were no more obstacles in the road?

I put a big obstacle in the road.

And with that, I entered what people politely call a "career valley"—actually, I fell off the cliff for a year. That opened up opportunity . . . to work my way back to higher ground through industriousness! I was praised for my diligence and perseverance.

I wasn't ready yet to accept my strengths. I wanted the ones displayed by our "gold standard" partners. So I set my sights on becoming a rock: Think about it. Rocks are large, stable, and strong; these leaders were mature, broad-shouldered, and dependable. By comparison, I felt more like a stone—interesting, fast-moving, yes, but also at first glance, unimpressive. Skipping across the water, I looked cool; but next to a boulder—well, you didn't even notice me.

So I worked on my "rockness." I wore black. I walked slowly in higher heels. I laughed less. I self-regulated, containing my unpredictable ideas and bottling up my emotions to appear constant. I worked hard to suppress creativity, humor, and zest (all high on my strengths list). The result? I was less happy, worked even harder, and had less success. I was tired and down. I didn't feel authentic. I got sick of myself and I'm pretty sure even my mother didn't like me. At least that's what she told me at the time.

This was my moment of truth. I realized I was trying to be someone else and not doing a very good job of it. *What was I thinking?* This was not a path to distinctiveness. This was a path to nothingness. I wondered whether turning away from my strengths had something to do with why I continued to feel empty and invisible.

It got to the point where I had to do something. And I did. I accepted my strengths with gusto, leaning in, stepping up, jumping off, swimming, and spreading my wings to fly. Once I started living into my strengths, I created what I most wanted—leadership. Assessments are not silver bullets, but with one I have recommitted to what I value about myself. I have not been the same since.

Finding your strengths

There are many ways to find your top strengths, including asking others what they observe when you're at your best. To recap: Strengths boost your energy when you use them; they are what you believe has always been true about you. For example, you might think of yourself as a great problem solver, and that's a good start. What's underneath? Curiosity? Love of learning? Tolerance for ambiguity? Courage? If you've taken company assessments, you may think you know your strengths, but as I learned, it's not enough to simply *think* you know. If you want to build on these strengths, you've got to know them, and also value and accept them. Let's explore your strengths more fully through Johanne's next exercise starting with a centering practice. Imagine her guiding us:

Quick Centering Practice

- Please settle comfortably on your chair—legs uncrossed and feet on the floor, hands free and resting gently on your lap, back straight with head sitting comfortably on your spine.
- Close your eyes to reduce outside stimuli and feel your body relaxing; start at the top of your head and slowly work your way down—feeling your facial muscles relaxing, the furrow between your eyebrows opening, your jaw dropping, your tongue receding. Feel your neck and shoulders relaxing, stress falling away.
- Take in a few deep breaths and exhale as fully as you can; forcefully blow out the air in order to bring new oxygen in. After two or three deep exhales and inhales, breathe normally and begin to notice your breath—the rise and fall of your chest or the air flowing in and out.
- Rest for a few moments, focusing on your breathing. As thoughts enter your mind, just observe them and let them go. Each time, come back to your breath.

Aaaah. I love this practice because I feel relaxed and attentive afterward, more curious and open.

Now that we're present, Johanne offers some questions to help us get in touch with our strengths. She encourages us to read each question, then close our eyes to experience it.

When you are finished, use the space below to jot down some notes so you can remember your images, words, feelings, and sensations. Imagine that you are in the movie of your life: What do you see? Writing in the present tense helps to take you there.

Building on strengths exercise

1. I am picturing myself as a young child. What fantasy games do I love play-ing? What do I get to do and who do I get to be? In activities like reading or sports, what characters or players do I imagine myself to be?

    _____

    _____

    _____

    _____

2. As a young adult, what activities do I feel drawn to? When do I feel most passionate and so absorbed in an activity that I lose track of time?

    _____

    _____

    _____

    _____

3. Today, what activities leave me feeling strong, energized, and alive? At work, at home, and in my community?

    _____

    _____

    _____

    _____

4. Looking at my reflections, what do I value most about these activities and about myself in these moments? What do these memories say about me?

    _____

    _____

    _____

    _____

Once you have done this reflection, share your stories with someone. If you're on your own, find a friend to talk to or use a journal to hold a dialogue with yourself. Perhaps you're reading this book alongside colleagues or friends; if so, pair up to share, delving as deeply as you can, opening yourself up to be seen. Don't be afraid of expressing hidden thoughts and feelings; your partner will be inspired by your openness. When it's your turn to listen, try to hear what's beneath the words—unspoken thoughts and feelings. As you practice acceptance, intriguing insights reveal themselves. They always do.

This discussion is where you find gold. You may find curious connections between the stories, but also between the two of you. Allow yourself the dreaming time for the images, words, feelings, and insights to flow. In other words, get curious about who you were as a child and who you are today.

Now let's explore one level deeper. Johanne designed this next exercise as an "appreciative interview," with gratitude to David Cooperrider, who has been a great source of inspiration for Centered Leadership. We're hardwired through school and professional work to value the paradigm of problem solving. In consequence, we focus on what is wrong; we search for mistakes until we find the culprit. In contrast, this interview's goal is to help you reflect on your hopes and what really matters to you. With the mindset of possibility, we naturally ask questions that inspire a different kind of discussion.

The best way to do the interview (or reflection) is while walking. Walking takes awkwardness out of personal conversation. It sets a rhythm conducive to intuition, encouraging the mind to go to deeper places. We invite you to see for yourself. You'll be amazed what happens when you meander along on a beautiful day in a safe place conducive to wandering. Plan on twenty to thirty minutes per person.

As you listen, observe the words and images that carry energy for your partner. How will you know? He or she will light up. Just watch for changing facial expressions or energy. With genuine curiosity, when you spot that energy, ask your partner to tell you more. Also observe your own energy. It's often difficult to recognize our own strengths. It's much easier to see our strengths in others.

Partners' walk interview

1. Thinking back to leaders who have had a profound impact on you—what qualities do you admire most in them? What are the ways you manifest these very same qualities through your own leadership?

    _____

    _____

    _____

    _____

2. What would the people who know you best say are the top strengths they value in you? (If you handed out the Request for feedback form from chapter 4, reflect on their observations.)

    _____

    _____

    _____

    _____

3   Come back to the question: What do you believe to be true about you always—as a leader, as a human being?

    _____

    _____

    _____

By this time, you should be pretty jazzed about what you're learning, and hopefully, you've discovered insights that you want to think more about. Maybe you found patterns between your three stories or rediscovered something true about yourself that you've forgotten since childhood. How did you find the process? What surprises did it reveal? What did you learn about your discussion partner that was different from what you might typically learn? Revealing what is true about ourselves often fosters greater closeness than sharing family information or talking about what we did this past weekend.

Maybe you are having difficulty with this exercise. For some, re-flecting on personal strengths is uncomfortable. If so, please note that this focus is not selfish. Only when we understand, appreciate, and ac-cept ourselves can we do the same for others.

Think about how you use your strengths at work. How might you use them more? What would you do differently or do less of to free up energy and time for your strengths? What about at home? What might you do more of to use your strengths daily? Having strengths is one thing; using them is another. When you live into your strengths fully, you release tremendous energy in yourself that, in turn, sparks posi-tive energy in everyone around you. And that sets off a (good) chain reaction. Miracle stuff!

Many of us believe that we'll be happy only when we perform at our best. We work very hard to enjoy that momentary luxury of basking in achievement. But the converse is actually the case, as Johanne dis-covered: "When I play to my strengths, I do what I love; that makes me happy, and so I become a high performer!" That's the right way around.

Does that mean that we should forget about weaknesses and just do the "strengths thing" all day long? Of course not! Centered Lead-ership is about the "both/and." In this case, we must *both* work to tap into our strengths *and*—at the same time—work on our development needs. While it's true that focusing on our strengths is critical to find-ing meaning, shoring up weaknesses helps us work more efficiently. I don't need to convince you. For most of us, focusing on weaknesses comes naturally. Most of us grew up in an environment of deficit-based learning. Grades were our yardstick. When I brought home a 96, my father would ask—in jest, of course—"What happened to the other four points?" I focused on my mistakes and everyone else's, too. By the time I reached McKinsey, I assumed that everything in life could be—and was—graded. And so I strove for perfection. That's why re-ceiving feedback is so hard to do.

Many organizations struggle with teaching their managers to give and receive feedback well. Too often, something in us is triggered, and we avoid or botch it. We get defensive, leave the discussion demoralized; everyone feels awful. But when we genuinely share the strengths we see in others, we build connection. The receiver generally responds with greater openness and acceptance—making the discussion more caring and genuine. *Everyone* has core strengths to acknowledge and leverage, even those who may do better elsewhere.

Live into your strengths, and in time you'll discover your purpose. That was the case for Wangechi, in our first story. We hope you're as inspired by her as we are.

STORY 1

Wangechi Lives into Her Strengths

In which we meet Wangechi Mutu, a visual artist born in Kenya, who finds meaning and happiness by deepening her many strengths

I met Wangechi Mutu through her husband, Mario Lazzaroni. When I saw Wangechi's explosive work at a gallery opening, that did it—I had to learn about her artist's journey. Indeed, her story underscores the power of building on strengths.

Discovering her strengths

Wangechi was born in Kenya nine years after the country gained independence—a hopeful time. "Kenya," Wangechi told me, "is an incredibly beautiful country without, at that point, too much upheaval. It's a place where you can be easily inspired."

As a little girl Wangechi always drew. She drew on the walls when she didn't have paper. She dressed up and created characters out of things around her. Creativity, in her words, "was an obsession. I never thought that it was something that one could or ought to do. It was like breathing." Then Wangechi went to Catholic school, where her visual art was somewhat stifled, though her creativity flourished. Her turning point happened when she got the lead role in a school production of *The Desert Song*. She recalls, "You couldn't have made me happier. At fifteen, I was a shy teenager. It was incredible that I'd gotten this role that would allow me to do what I wanted to do onstage . . . I thought, *Wow, I could do this sort of thing—creating personas or embodying other things.*" The floodgates had opened.

When a mentor encouraged her to apply to the United World Colleges, she did and attended high school in Wales. The school was perfect for an insulated girl wanting to stretch. She realized, "Oh my god, this is it!" Her teacher put a sketchbook in each student's hands and told them to make that a part of everyday life. The kids were confused about what to do, but the teacher urged them to do anything they wished with it. Wangechi learned: "Art begins when you wake up and continues into your dreams; the teacher was encouraging us to think of ourselves as eternally creative. That just blew my mind." She understood then that drawing was not so much a skill as creativity was her core—inherent—strength.

Still, her family figured this foray into the arts was temporary and Wangechi would settle down after high school.

Not so.

After school, Wangechi went to live and work on a faraway island, Lamu, to help create an environmental museum out of an antique fort. She remembers, "I wanted to go somewhere where I could do something that fed back into this creative impulse and was relevant to society, to the community." It was there that she became conscious: "My heart was in love with knowing I was an artist."

Lamu was too close to home and so Wangechi packed up and moved to New York City. Where else would a budding artist go?

Enabling her strengths

New York had its dark moments: "I was this driven, manic, foreign girl, running around trying to survive." Another of Wangechi's strengths—determination—revealed itself in New York, and it served her well. A dedicated student, she "inhaled everything" she could. I asked her how she became a success. She shared:

> Gosh, Joanna, I don't even know. I'm still reeling from the fact that this happened. I've always been a big daydreamer, a big dreamer. I would think, *The only reason I could possibly have*

come this far is because there's something major I have to do. There is so much talent everywhere. I know it. That I'm able to do this gives me the responsibility to do something amazing with it.

Wangechi headed to graduate school at Yale. When she completed her studies, September 11 happened and with it a time of transition, self-doubt, questioning. Wangechi returned to a tiny New York apartment with just enough space to draw on paper with pen and ink and watercolors. "I painted all of this neurosis and silence into the work." She says, "They were very small watercolors of glamorous women. They're pinups. They're posed. They're sexy. And then, when you look at them again, you realize every single one of them is missing something—a limb or teeth or an eye. Ultimately, they look like they're trying to convince you that everything is OK."

Her collective strengths—her artistic vision and creativity, her compassion for the human condition, her determination—coalesced in these arresting, haunting depictions of "animals and women and people and friends mutating, fighting, arguing, and lovemaking." Wangechi recalls, "It's funny, because these pieces and watercolors on the side, I wasn't planning to show anyone. But that's what everyone wanted to see. Contained in them were all the contradictions and the mixed-up-ness that I was going through in the work. They were full of the mess that we have inside of us, desire and fear, love and anxiety, prejudice, shame, and they were not cleaned up."

Living into her strengths

Wangechi's restlessness pushed her to work larger. Because she was still an emerging artist, her exhibition spaces were not the best. Still, she found ways to create a place people wanted to visit. "Every new space became an opportunity for me to tell the story about being from outside and having to find your place within. It's a story of triumph." Do you see that Wangechi is always hopeful for the future?

It was a move to San Antonio, to Art Pace, that extended Wangechi's range. "We had studios that were also exhibition spaces," she recalls. "People were always walking through. You felt like someone was always watching you. I remember thinking, 'I can't make a drawing in here. I can't focus. I can't sing to myself.' That's when I started working on the wall." Wangechi opened up a deep place that guided her to turn the studio wall into living art and bring the war in Iraq and Afghanistan home:

> The drawings on the wall didn't read the way they do on paper, so I took a hammer and started creating that same mark with a hammer and ink. It looked like a wound. My research at the time had to do with the war. I was touched and moved and disturbed by what was happening and I wanted to create a space where we looked at images of what was going on. There are no pictures of war being shown. It's almost like nothing happens. Anyway, I created these wall wounds taken directly from configurations of bullet holes in the walls of buildings in Afghanistan and Iraq and Iran.
>
> The way buildings react to war is similar to the way bodies react to war—the way they are damaged, the way they're treated, what happens to them. You felt this disturbance and damage and poetic memory of something that had happened or that was happening.

I never saw that wall, but through her clear voice and stark images I felt it. Powerful.

Using strengths to find meaning

Drawing on all her strengths, Wangechi was living fully—regularly experiencing what experts call *flow*. In her words:

> I'm so happy when I'm producing a body of work. It starts like these little tributaries and they're trickling and every single

one has its own rhythm and tune. And then they start to come together. It doesn't happen when I want it to. But slowly they come together and at some point, this massive body—it's like a river—just starts to rush along and take me with it. I know I'm doing the right thing at that point. And I get really, really—like I feel it now—I get goose bumps because it feels like something else has taken over. And it's bigger than me. . . . And those are really happy moments. They give me a reason to feel, OK, I get it. I know why I'm doing this now.

Today, Wangechi finds the inner strength to keep going with what she finds interesting, important, valuable. She ended our interview by sharing her life philosophy: "Humans are incredible. We're survivors. We figure things out, slowly and together, we do. I believe that you can do things. That active and dynamic behavior—creating and making as opposed to destroying—is what got us to who we are. I believe very much in the possibility of things. I do."

7

LEADING WITH PURPOSE

In which you take steps toward finding your own purpose by looking into your future to discover what really matters to you and what you most want to create

D o you remember Meaning's third element—after happiness and strengths? It's purpose; purpose lights up the path. If you did nothing more than use your strengths more each day, as the years passed you would wake up one day to find yourself living into your purpose, as I did. I just want to help you accelerate that fifty-year process if I can. Purpose comes when you can answer these questions: *What really matters to me? What do I most want to create in my life?*

If your immediate reaction is to blurt out, "I don't know," that's normal. Those questions stop a lot of people in their tracks; they have no boundaries and they're challenging. It's natural to feel your mind go blank, as you say "I never really thought about it" or "Thinking about hopes and dreams leaves me cold." So let's sneak up on purpose indirectly. Johanne will guide us into our far futures to visualize the legacy we want to create.

If you like, turn on quiet, lyrical music to help you to allow yourself to imagine. Let's center ourselves to begin. Sit comfortably, feet on the floor and hands gently resting in your lap, eyes closed. Allow yourself to relax, taking in a few deep breaths (exhaling fully) and then focus on your breathing. As your mind wanders, consciously return to your breathing each time. Spend a few minutes focusing on your breath. And when you're ready, hear Johanne:

Imagine you are in nature and walking down a gentle path, bordered with flowers. It takes you into a small wood. You feel light and at peace as you leisurely follow the path. You're safe here and enjoying yourself as the path winds deeper into the forest. You continue walking and, in a little while, you see a lovely cottage. You notice that it is well lit and many people are gathered. You are curious and so you walk up to a window to look. The people who matter most to you are there. You hear them clearly. One by one, they are giving beautiful tributes of how you have touched their lives. You hear the tributes of four people who are important to you from different areas of your life and career—perhaps a sponsor from work, a leader in your community, a member of your family, a good friend. They don't have to be living people or even people you know today—let your imagination run free. What do you hear each one say about you in turn?

After the fourth person finishes, you walk up to the front door and knock. A much older but familiar-looking person—healthy, radiant, and happy—opens the door to greet you. That person is you. You ask for advice, guidance, or wisdom. Knowing you well, what does your older self tell you? You receive this gift with appreciation, and then you enter the cottage to join your celebration.

I always enjoy Jo's guided visualization, because I would never imagine this celebration without help. Somehow, when someone directs me through the exercise, the images appear. Reread the passage above, noticing who comes to mind and what they say:

My celebration tributes

- **Person, role, or context:**

_____

That person's tribute to you:

_____

_____

_____

- **Person, role, or context:**

_____

That person's tribute to you:

_____

_____

_____

- **Person, role, or context:**

_____

That person's tribute to you:

_____

_____

_____

- **Person, role, or context:**

_____

That person's tribute to you:

_____

_____

_____

In the space below, note the insight or advice you received from your much older self:

What my older self tells me:

_____

_____

_____

_____

_____

For each person, imaginary or real, write down what the person says about you, including your older self, without censoring it. This is no time to be modest. Some participants find this exercise very moving emotionally. Others need more time to allow the visualization process to happen. If that's you, take the time. It will happen. I hope my example will help you gain comfort with this exercise:

- **My daughter:** "Mom, you have stood by me always, even when I angrily pushed you away. You helped me accept all parts of me; I stopped punishing myself and others through judging. I'm proud that some of you lives on in me."
- **Head of my firm twenty years from now:** "Joanna, you mobilized a movement, collaborating with others to change our professional DNA. Your boldness and vulnerability made it possible for us to join. Thank you for persevering."
- **A woman leader in the world:** "Mrs. B., you showed me that it's possible. Thank you for encouraging me. I have changed my life, inspired to draw on my strengths, to stand up and be counted. I will pass it on."
- **My husband:** "Jobo, I love you to pieces—for your laughter and silliness, your stability, your intuition, and your spirit. You grounded me when I most needed it. You picked me up when I needed that more. My life is full."

What did my much older self say? "Dear, living into meaning is not something you do when you are very old like me. Then it is too late. Meaning is not about grand gestures and big actions. Small things every day are meaningful. Learn to notice. Use your eyes, your intuition, and also your fears, your imperfections. They all serve. And choose to lead with love. Stop protecting yourself! You are strong enough to bounce back—just look at the evidence."

Now it's your turn. Let the images and words flow.

Reflecting on this exercise, ask yourself what becomes possible when you begin living and leading this way now.

What becomes possible?

What do these tributes say about what I stand for? What becomes possible when I live and lead according to what really matters to me?

_____

_____

_____

_____

_____

_____

Writing is a great start to articulating a vision that will inspire you and those around you. Using this exercise a few times, I began to feel bolder, freer, and more powerful.

As you weave the threads of your best self between both bookends of your life—your imaginative play as a child and your wisdom as an elder—see the vast expanse of possibility ahead. In other words, we invite you to dream about who you can become in the next few years, building on your strengths and insight.

If you're working with a partner, interview each other, taking a few notes to capture the conversation's insights. But note-taking breaks connection, so try to take just enough notes to recall the conversation and, at the same time, support the speaker through curiosity and compassion. Please ask the questions just as Johanne has written them. Some of them may not feel comfortable, but embrace them anyway, letting go of resistance to dreaming. Imagine yourself ten years from today, successful and engaged at work.

Appreciative coaching interview: ten years out

Allowing yourself to think boldly, complete the sentence "I am most proud of the contributions I have made to the lives of others and of who I have become because ... "

_____

_____

_____

_____

If you assume for a moment that everything is possible—and knowing you are worthy and cannot fail—what bolder aspirations or dreams would you allow yourself to have? Now dig deeper: What else? Freeing yourself from all constraints, what else?

_____

_____

_____

_____

Standing in this future and looking back, what actions did you start today that made the biggest difference to achieving deep personal fulfillment and leadership contribution?

_____

_____

_____

_____

Here's my example: *I am most proud of the contributions I have made to the lives of others;* leading with vulnerability and power, I have made it OK for others to bring themselves more fully into their leadership. *Assuming that everything is possible,* I aspire to extend the Centered Leadership community across the world, touching thousands of future leaders—shifting big organizations and even societies. *The actions I started today that made the biggest difference* were to put the program in a structure that is inviting, simple, and clear, working closely with Jo and others emboldened to join us.

Aah!

That's the release you'll have if this exercise opens up a window into your vision. If you don't see it yet, know that it will come. Johanne explains, "This exercise isn't about the answers; it's about living into the questions—letting them guide you down a path you want to explore."

When you're ready, let's go one step further. Any similarity to earlier questions is intentional. Digging a little deeper, you may begin to see your purpose; reflect on what comes up for you—and let the images, words, and feelings flow without judgment or self-critique.

Emerging threads—my purpose

Reflecting on what you stand for, ask: What has always been true about me and that I value about myself? What brings me a sense of purpose? What really matters to me?

_____

_____

_____

_____

Taking elements that feel important, reflect on:

What do I really want?

_____

_____

_____

If I had what I want, what would become possible for me?

_____

_____

_____

If I had that/were that, what would then become possible for me?

_____

_____

_____

If I had that/were that, what would then become possible for me?

_____

_____

_____

No, that was not a typo—we repeat the question on purpose, to help you go further in each iteration until you reach a thought or image or feeling that makes you say, as Wangechi did, "That's it!"

I'll go first: *What has always been true about me* is that I have wanted to create. *It's important to me* to be seen and heard as a unique human being. *What I really want* is to create without limits imposed by fear. *If I had that*, I would be even bolder, trusting my ideas and intuition. *And if I* trusted my ideas and intuition, I would inspire others more. *And if I* inspired others more, I would feel greater connection. *And if I* felt greater connection, I would feel that I have moved people through creative force.

Now it is your turn to explore more, see more, and also accept more about who you are, what matters to you, and what you most want to create. You may find it even more powerful if you use this exercise with a discussion partner. If that is the case, ask the questions of each other, exploring with kindness and honesty.

Now we're ready for Johanne's most important question. I see it differently each time. My vision sharpens as I strip away what is less important. But at first, it felt overwhelming. If this is the case for you, simply reflect and wait; an image may come to mind instead of a statement and, if so, sketch it below:

Emerging threads—My vision

What if my life—*with its unique history, experiences, strengths, values, and passions*—had prepared me ideally to make a unique leadership contribution in my professional context today . . . what might it be?

_____

_____

_____

_____

_____

_____

_____

_____

Please share what comes up with people who know you: family, discussion partner, colleagues, friends. They can help you bring out your vision's boldness; they will reinforce what is distinctive about you. They see your strengths, what is unique about you, and they reflect back like a mirror.

Feedback on my vision

_____

_____

_____

_____

_____

_____

_____

With feedback to inspire you, step out of the movie and see yourself. Refine your statement—make it clearer, sharper, as bold as you dare; no—make it even bolder.

My vision bolder

_____

_____

_____

_____

_____

_____

You know that's it, if you feel a thrill _and_ a twinge of fear and you're excited to see what happens next. You're far enough out of your comfort zone now!

If you're working with a partner, this is a good time to stop and think about what most inspired each of you about the other. If you're alone, take this time to appreciate yourself.

What inspired me:

What inspired me about my partner:

_____

_____

_____

What inspired my partner about me:

_____

_____

_____

What inspires me about Johanne is that she is able to coach someone deftly through a raw moment without fixing it or removing the pain. I admire her sensitivity combined with toughness. What inspires Jo about me is that I am open—and a sponge—unafraid to be a student in front of the room. She admires my courageous leadership.

We are inspired by people who live into their strengths and purpose, showing it with *both* power *and* vulnerability (there's the *both/and* again). We are moved to follow leaders who say: "This is who I am. This is what matters to me. This is the contribution that I want to make."

That brings us to commitments. Writing your vision down is an act of courage, and you should be proud. Truly *living* your vision is an act of leadership. Based on your discussions and ongoing reflection, note your commitment:

My commitment to me

What is the smallest step you can take that will make the biggest difference to living more in line with your vision? What are you ready to commit to now?

_____

_____

_____

_____

_____

_____

What are the implications for you professionally and personally? Think through your promises in terms of what you want to start doing (do more of) and how you will free up time and attention.

Small steps: living into my vision

- *Professionally*, I commit to start doing or intensify:

  _____

  _____

  _____

- *Professionally*, I commit to do differently or reduce time on:

  _____

  _____

  _____

- *Personally*, I commit to start doing or intensify:

  _____

  _____

  _____

- *Personally*, I commit to do differently or reduce time on:

  _____

  _____

  _____

Avoid sweeping statements that, deep down, you know you won't deliver. It's natural to desire giant leaps, but usually we're too busy or it's not feasible. Instead, define specific, purposeful, concrete, and achievable steps that you want to—and can—take.

One final note: The path through Meaning is not linear. Next up is a story about a leader who took zigs and zags, guided always by purpose, until he found the vision that lit up the path.

STORY 2

Geoffrey Pursues His Purpose

In which Geoffrey Canada, president and CEO of the Harlem Children's Zone, discovers his purpose and spends a lifetime pursuing it, drawing others into his bold vision

Geoffrey Canada started dreaming about improving the lives of kids when he was just a child himself. Fifty years later, his dream is reality: The Harlem Children's Zone is breaking down barriers that keep underprivileged kids from becoming middle class.

A first dream

Reading got him into dreaming, as Geoff recalls. "I would read about children growing up in these idyllic neighborhoods where everybody was nice, and everything was clean, and all the parents did all of these great things with their children. It looked nothing like the life that I saw around me. I began to wonder why—in my community—everything looked like it was actually working against children." Geoff decided that if he managed to make it out, he would devote his life to making a difference for them. When I suggested it was one hell of a purpose for a kid, Geoff laughed heartily and replied,

> I had the ability at nine or ten to understand that we are all captured and to some degree captive of the environments that we grow up in. In the South Bronx, if you were a boy you had to be tough. You had to be prepared to fight. We spent inordinate amounts of time preparing for these moments in life when you were going to have to show your bravery. Forty blocks away, kids

thought being smart was what you needed to be and they were spending all of their time doing that. All of those kids who spent hours and hours trying to figure out how to be tough, if they had spent the time trying to figure out how to do algebra and geometry and chemistry, would they have ended up in different places? Absolutely yes. They might not have been Einstein, but they certainly would've been able to graduate college.

Sharpening his focus

It wasn't a straightforward path from vision to action, however. Geoff likes to say that he wandered around in the wilderness but never lost sight of what he wanted to do. After graduate school, he taught at the Robert White School in Boston and then settled in Harlem as the education director at Rheedlen (which became HCZ in time): "For the first third of my career, we were just trying to save a few kids. I always knew that, in the back of my mind, there was this idea that it wasn't just that kids needed a good education. They needed a good community. They needed someplace where, when they woke up in the morning, they felt good, they weren't threatened, they weren't always afraid and intimidated. I didn't know if I would ever get a chance to do that, but I knew that it was the right thing to do."

One of the most difficult things to face is failure of grand ideas. Geoff started with younger kids, and then expanded to help kids through high school. Still, the data showed his vision needed revision; HCZ needed to support the students through college. He shared:

Leadership is not for the faint of heart or the half committed. When you believe in something, you've got to give it your all. The problem is—in giving something your all—if it turns out you were wrong, it's very hard to go back to the drawing board for a novel approach. I was wrong about high school being the answer. I know I said, "Trust me. I got the answer," but I didn't. It's tough. Any of us who have worked hard, and think we're good, and think we're talented—it's hard to look at data that says, *Actually, you're not as good as you thought you were.* You get this feeling: Maybe I'm not the one to solve this problem. Confidence is something that almost everybody struggles with.

Small dreamers can fail quietly, big dreamers take big risks. Geoff told me, "It's one thing to fail and it's just you and your mom who knows. It's another thing when it's in the press, and people are studying it, and everybody is second-guessing what you've done. Once *The New York Times,* or *The Wall Street Journal,* or *The Washington Post* says you failed, as far as the world is concerned, you have failed. That's frightening for a lot of leaders."

But purpose emboldens. Geoff said, "If you believe that you are doing something that is more important than your own personal ego—even when your ego gets stepped on pretty hard—you come back to understanding that this needs to be done." And so Geoff continued to sharpen his vision.

Implementing commitments

The environment was tough; the community had given up. No one put out a welcome mat. Geoff and his team were treated with suspicion and sometimes hostility. "Our job was to convince them that we were going to help that child whether or not that parent ever signed on, ever thanked us." Geoff gathered team members who shared his values—though not necessarily his ideas. They shared his sense of justice—that all Americans had a right to educational opportunity—and were willing to put themselves on the line to accomplish it. Purpose gave them courage.

But what action would change the community's deeply entrenched beliefs? With so much to get done, where to start? His vision to transform a one-hundred-block section of Harlem had to start somewhere. He remembers:

> We saw Harlem twenty-five years ago, and saw the promise—wide streets, low housing, sun—but a third of the community was aban-

doned, trash everywhere. So this idea of getting people to accept that Harlem could come back was a crazy idea. They were giving away housing. It was a joke. How do you get folk who have viewed the world one way to totally change their world view? We did it one building and one block at a time. We said, "Look, let's just fix this one building." It took us a year. Then we said, "Let's fix all the buildings on this block." We got the block straightened out. But people said, "We know what happened on 119th Street because you had Mother Pearl," which was true. She was the image of that block for seventy years. So we fixed 118th Street, and they had another excuse. By the third block, people began to say, "Something's going on." Then an interesting thing began to happen. People started thinking, "Maybe I'm wrong. Maybe you could get Harlem to be different." They began to say, "Will you come to my block?" You can talk to people forever. When people begin to see a reality, and then live a reality, it begins to change some of that cognitive functioning. Trying to convince someone of something that they have not experienced is wasted effort. We need to bring these things alive.

Geoff has always believed that education is the key, but his vision expanded to include safety, health care, shelter, healthy eating, and adult attention. That takes (a lot) more money and the entire community working together to keep the kids on track through college. No wonder that Geoff saw skeptics everywhere, even among his strongest supporters. As he puts it, "My team took a big plunge with me. I said, 'Guys, we're heading down this road, and we're going for victory. This is not just trying to play not to lose. This is, why not change the whole thing and solve this problem?' It was just a dream, right? This crazy person had this dream, and now it's a reality."

Geoff and I talked about the next ten years. He had been worried about finding the right next leader, "whether that leader would love these kids and this community enough so they would do whatever they had to do to be successful." Geoff's vision had grown. He imagined HCZ as a small city with 10,000 poor kids. "Every single day, every single hour, there's a kid in crisis." That takes stamina, a long-term view, and crisis management skill, but Geoff stressed spiritual skill. He told me, "I wasn't worried about the technical side. I was worried about finding someone who could do this with that much love and concern over time." By dreaming ten years out, and then taking small steps with the greatest impact, the board and Geoff found their leader.

Sustaining a thirty-year journey is tough. Geoff shared, "Constantly dealing with people's problems would drain you, and possibly make you yourself depressed. For me, this is about a healthy balance. You have to be physically healthy. You have to feel good. You have to get enough sleep. But you also have to be spiritually healthy. We all have a reservoir of compassion that we draw on. You need to know when that reservoir is empty and how to replenish it." Geoff grounds himself in success, remembering young people who have thanked him.

> I tell folk, "If you get four or five kids who come back and thank you, you've gotten more than most parents get in their lifetime." I've got kids by the hundreds. It is one of the most satisfying things that you can experience—that people who had no chance without your help actually make it. It keeps that glass overflowing. The success factor is allowing yourself to be part of it, to feel like you're part of something that is really important. I had a young man who really struggled here—one of our first Promise Academy high school graduates—who came to see me. He's in college now. He said, "Mr. Canada, I saw you were in tears up on the stage. It was so emotional," and I said, "Yeah, it was." He said, "You know what? When I saw my mentor, I put my sunglasses on because I was crying. It was so emotional for me." I said, "I know." We were just there, the two of us. Young man and an older guy saying we both understood. He should've never made it out of that thing and he did. He knew it and he knew why.

Kids like that young man help Geoff sustain the purpose he shaped a long time ago—to use education to help poor kids have a better life. And so Geoff moves forward to fulfill his purpose, one small step at a time.

PART THREE

FRAMING

8

BECOMING PERCEPTIVE

In which we introduce a powerful approach to working with fear and experiencing challenges as learning opportunities—and what you'll find in this section

Have you ever had an experience where you knew things might go wrong and then, your worst fears realized, everything actually did? Have you been in a situation where you could *see* yourself moving toward disaster but you kept on going? It's like being in a B movie: Ominous music begins to play in your head as you walk into the meeting. You hear a hissing voice, "Don't go down that street. Noooo!" But you do—and the bad guys attack or the meteors hit or the world explodes. Whatever your nightmare situation at work, it probably involves embarrassment, shame, rage, despair, and self-loathing that roll in to stay for days or weeks like the fog in Maine.

It doesn't have to be that way. Even pessimists like me can learn to shift deeply entrenched mindsets and behaviors by reframing. It's the best tool in the kit.

Framing begins with what you see and how you experience a given situation—and how that influences your behavior. We all face challenging situations, sometimes genuinely difficult ones. Other times, the demons are in our heads. These demons are no less fearful because we give them power. By recognizing and accepting that we have the freedom to choose our attitude and create a different experience, we take it back and only then can break free of the pattern. This is the heart of learning to reframe. It might change the results or it might not, but it will change how we experience every situation.

When something in me gets triggered

Before we go to your moments of upset—your "triggers"—Jo will take you on a brief side trip into the brain. Think of your brain as having three parts. The most primitive part (and earliest to develop) is your *reptilian brain*, which regulates automatic body functions such as temperature and breathing. Second, there is the *limbic system*—your emotional brain—that develops through childhood. And third is your *neocortex*—your "executive brain"—with its well-developed frontal lobes, which apply logic but take longest to mature. The *amygdala*—two little almond-shaped glands—sits at the base of your limbic system, right beside your memory center. It has protected humans from physical danger for thousands of years (and still does). Because it exists to protect us from danger, the amygdala is the first to respond when we sense a threat.

Here is what happens: You receive a sensory stimulus that feels like, sounds like, looks like it may be a threat to your physical survival. Your amygdala activates and triggers a memory associated with the stimulus, and even before the neocortex can process, habitual neural pathways get tripped. As a result, you associate the sensation with the memory of something dangerous. Your body goes into high-alert survival mode. Your metabolic rate speeds up, blood flows from your brain to your muscles, your nervous system releases stress hormones, and you shut down "nonessential" body systems such as creativity and intuition. Your range of awareness narrows (down to 30 percent when you are severely triggered) and you react. Boom! The "amygdala hijack" in action.

"The problem is," Jo explains, "the amygdala doesn't distinguish between danger to our physical survival and danger to our emotional survival. So we can be hijacked when we feel threatened at home or at work." And we are. Try these situations on for size:

■ You're in a meeting to resolve a company crisis. Every senior executive is tense. The CEO is aggressive. You work up courage to voice your idea, but when you speak no one notices. Someone says the same thing twenty minutes later and everyone agrees!

- A team member bursts into your office, crying. She recounts a difficult conversation and the more agitated she gets, the more uncomfortable you feel. Soon, you interrupt and offer your (correct) solution to her issue and she begins to argue!

- Your team is presenting to a prospective client. He actively challenges everything they say. Without realizing, you take over the discussion, sweeping aside your colleagues, raising your voice, and speeding up!

- You're at your boss's weekly meeting, presenting your analysis. On page 2, she makes the time-out sign and proceeds to grill you. Impatient, she tells you to pick up a pen and take notes as she dictates explicitly what to do!

- You receive a very good end-of-year performance review and go home to celebrate. Returning from the holidays, you learn that your peer, who doesn't work as hard, was promoted. Really?

I felt a little nauseous writing these scenarios, since I took them from my own reality. Too much emotion, David tells me. And though he firmly believes (thanks to military training) that experience and rehearsal reduce anxiety, that's not been my case. After all, I've been rehearsing for thirty years, but when I walk into a crowded meeting room without a "right" to be there, I still have to force myself to sit at the table. It still upsets me when a discussion turns aggressive, as it always does in performance cultures. When someone looks to me for comfort, I still try to end their suffering—and I get upset at their ingratitude! At times, I find myself crowding out my team; I still get angry when I feel let down. When it feels like someone is micromanaging me, I still go nuts! When the "system" doesn't feel fair, I still get drained; I want to pick up my ball and go home. Anger, rage, frustration, feeling drained are all clues to an amygdala hijack.

What triggers these emotions in me might be of little consequence to you—and vice versa. We all have our stories. Wouldn't it be great not to live out that old drama yet again?

Heading down the spiral to rumination

For years, I was undone by bullying. The first hint of an aggressive tone or a combative debate style caused me to clam up. Fierce challenge, hostility, and condescension triggered the same response on cue: I froze. The longer I remained frozen, the more my internal voice scolded. I blamed myself for being stupid and weak. But there's more. I'm not proud of my resulting behavior. I became a bully myself. The thing was, the person I bullied most was me. Let me show you how this vicious cycle works in a true story.

There I am with my nine-person team, sitting at an enormous round table in a vendor room situated below ground, waiting to present our supply-chain proposal. One powerful light shines down on the table; the rest of the room is veiled in gloom. After a time, thirty executives file in. The most senior sit together at the table, the rest settle in behind. We face a giant, brightly lit screen displaying our PowerPoint presentation. Everything seems to go smoothly until it doesn't.

With a minute to go, a senior executive (let's call him Robert) speaks up aggressively: "I have a question for Joanna and one for Jeff." Robert turns to me, his voice menacing: "Joanna, you said that supply chain could become a strategic advantage—you said it right at the beginning." His eyes narrow as he delivers the punch, "What specifically did you mean?"

Like at a tennis match, thirty heads and sixty eyes turn to me. I find myself in a tightening circle of fear. I feel the glaring light shining on me as the rest of the room darkens. Every face accuses. I freeze. Time slows down. And the little voice in my head hisses, *Why aren't you saying anything? The man asked you a question. You don't know anything about supply chain, do you? Why did you blurt out that stupid statement, anyway? SAY something! How long do you think they'll wait? Can't you think of anything to say? Now they know you're **stupid**! What is wrong with you?* Out the window go my rational thoughts, my emotions, even my body. I dissolve into nothingness.

Once the downward spiral starts, it picks up velocity, and I spin out of control. Somewhere in that psychedelic trip to doom, I wonder if the

CEO will ask me to leave the room, if I will get kicked off the team, if my team will ever speak to me again, if I will get fired from McKinsey, and then, as the trip accelerates, if I will ever find another job, and whether I will become homeless, and—as if my life is appearing in warp speed before my eyes—I wonder if my husband loves me anymore; and then I remember I yelled at my kids and realize that I'm a terrible mother! I spiral so far that I cannot see a way to get back up.

In fact, I never get back up (figuratively). A raw survival instinct takes over, and in a squeaky voice, I say one of the dumbest things I have ever been known to say: "I said supply chain could become a strategic advantage because if you don't have the products on the shelf, customers won't be able to buy them." Robert stares (in disbelief?). Everyone looks away. *Duh, Joanna, could you be more irrelevant?*

I'm a zombie through the question that Jeff fields with ease. It takes about a year for the meeting to end (actually, five minutes). I plaster on a smile (more of a grimace), quickly thank my team (I cannot bear to look at their faces marked by worry and concern), and dash into the car just as projectile tears begin to shoot horizontally from my eyes.

Crying hysterically, I call David, whose manly instinct is to say he will punch the entire executive team in their respective faces. His second tack is to tell me I'm worth a billion dollars. When that doesn't stop the tears, his third is to think up what I might have said, and he rattles off a string of snarky, funny retorts. I laugh and continue bawling. His fourth is to command me to call the CEO and his fifth is to dismiss the entire incident. Nothing works. On the car ride back to the office, rumination sets in: In a continuous loop, that incident brings me increased shame with each instant replay.

Over the next week, dreams wake me up in a state of increased anxiety. Daily, I relay them, feeling fresh humiliation from the retelling. No wonder color drains from the bland days that pass by. I have trouble focusing on work. Even winning the assignment brings little relief. I force myself to call the CEO. And do what? Talk through the experience calmly? Nope. I remove myself from the team but threaten that if there is any new bullying behavior we will stop the work. The CEO assures me that he had already warned Robert about his behavior. That just makes me feel worse.

Once I gained the distance to see myself in this movie (years later), I saw that in framing myself as a victim, I had created my most feared outcome. I also saw that Robert had triggered and created his worst outcome, too. We both needed reframing—badly.

Learning to reframe

That was indeed a god-awful experience. Not actually life-threatening—but, thanks to my amygdala hijack, it felt that way. I spiraled down into a pool of shame; I ruminated and lost the will to act. Do you see it? In a high-stakes, challenging competitive proposal process, my amygdala was on high alert. Robert said something that looked like, sounded like, and felt like the bullying I had experienced as a child. In that old story, I was not grown up enough to protect myself from an angry father. In consequence, as I later understood, every adult run-in with intimidating authority figures fed a reaction pattern that slowly solidified.

Of course, it takes time to undo patterns that took so long to create. For years, I was aware of my triggers but stopped short of accepting them. I punished myself every time I screwed up. I could see it happening but felt powerless to stop it. Accepting this vulnerable part of me—my deepest needs and fears—was my turning point. With practice, I became more adaptive, more reflective and appreciative, more creative in the way I handled each situation. The return on effort—your payoff, to put it in hard-nosed business terms—is enormous.

I lost the opportunity to reframe in that supply-chain assignment, but it created the upset I needed to begin learning the reframing skill. I replaced my mindset of inadequacy and shame with curiosity and compassion for others. With this new belief, new behaviors naturally emerged; I generally came to welcome the support of those "formerly known as bullies." I asked questions and rewarded their tough questions with a smile. Said another way, I finally learned how to stand up to my worst bully—me.

What you'll find in these pages

Johanne has carefully worked out a robust reframing process with three simple steps:

- **Becoming self-aware of what in us is getting triggered.** With self-awareness, we can accept that we created patterns of reactivity but don't have to sustain them.
- **Learning to pause and access choice during an upset.** Pausing offers distance to reflect and choose what we most want to create through shifting our response.
- **Choosing to adopt a new mindset and create a new habit or behavior.** These new behaviors expand the range of actions available to us when we need them most.

Throughout this part, you'll have a chance to delve into your beliefs and how they distort the reality you experience. You'll explore your triggers and fears, your unmet needs, and how your own brain hijacks you. You'll learn to pause in order to slow down and stop your fear-based reaction in its tracks. Our "iceberg" tool will help you understand what is being triggered in you during situations that upset or pose difficulty for you. And you'll practice shifting your frame of mind and integrating a new range of behaviors that *you* choose—to lead from your center in a state of greater resourcefulness, in line with your intention. Finally, you'll get the chance to make this a part of your daily work and life.

We are awed by leaders who not only overcome their triggers, but turn them into opportunities to learn. We seek them out because they *see and hear* us as individuals, sparking our momentum, helping us grow. They inspire us to be at our best.

We can all become that leader. We can all reframe our reality in the moment and learn to inspire others to do likewise.

9

IDENTIFYING YOUR TRIGGERS AND FEARS

In which you become aware of your own amygdala hijacks, what fears and needs lie beneath, and how they both serve and limit you

So, now that you've seen me in my horrible "brain freeze" moment, let's turn to you. How much of the time are you leading in your most resourceful state? If you're thinking, close to 90 percent, then you should be teaching Framing and Reframing! If you're closer to 50 percent, join the crowd. *Most* of us get hijacked in conversations and situations we experience as difficult. Some days, everything just feels difficult. Worse, hijacks can lead to a huge drain in energy, decline in performance, and even chronic stress and illness.

I know what you're thinking: That's why leaders get paid what they do! Well, what would you think if I told you it doesn't have to be that difficult? What if I told you that we create *our own* difficult situations? *Dream on, Joanna!*

Who wouldn't want to have less stress and less angst during the workweek or at home? Who wouldn't want to be agile and resourceful in the most critical situations, without getting tripped up by self-doubt and acting out in ways that make things worse?

If you don't want any of that, skip this chapter.

I hope you'll read on to learn more about your triggers and the fears they tap so that you can, in Jo's words, "Use the energy of your fear to get more out of the situation at hand." Once you realize that you create your own experience of any situation at work or in life, you have freedom to choose your attitude regardless. Yes, there is a cost: your vulnerability. That's a high cost, but in return you'll gain energy and creativity.

What triggers you?

Step 1, self-awareness, happens on a trip into the deepest, darkest waters to face the situations that trigger your worst upset and dredge up fears you keep well hidden. In order to do so, you must relive certain experiences as if they're happening now. Don't worry; you need to do this only in imagination. We won't leave your side and you'll become even stronger and more resourceful in those moments where it most matters.

So what really triggers you?

If you have trouble recalling interactions or behaviors at work that upset you, think about the most recent one at home. Johanne says, "We tend to experience family upsets more vividly as we deeply care about those we love—we take it personally as a reflection of ourselves (good parent, partner, child, friend); it actually matters." So think about recent arguments or knockdown "screamfests" with loved ones. They know your buttons and they're not afraid to push them when triggered themselves. Describe the interactions or behaviors that typically trigger you:

Interactions or behaviors that tend to trigger me

_____
_____
_____
_____

For example, I tend to be triggered by aggressive senior executives who are dismissive, cold, or downright hostile. I'm also triggered when others brush away or ignore my comments.

Now think about your typical physical response; body sensations are great cues to catch ourselves early. We *feel* before we think and act. The best way to do this is to close your eyes, recall the difficult moment as if you are right there, stepping into your own movie. Scan your body for cues. Where do you feel the upset? What is changing from your normal physical state? This list may help you complete your scan. I tend to feel tension in my chest, my heartbeat speeds up, and sometimes, most of these symptoms apply to me!

Checklist for physical symptoms

_____ My heart rate speeds up.

_____ I breathe with shallow breaths.

_____ I sense tension. (Scan your face, throat, shoulders, back, and stomach.)

_____ I begin to feel flushed or sweaty. (Our faces and hands may feel it first.)

_____ I turn red or ghostly white against my wishes.

_____ I feel a sudden onset of nausea or a painful knot in my stomach.

_____ I feel dizzy or the opposite, a sudden laser-like focus.

_____ I feel a surge of energy or the opposite, a feeling that I am draining into the ground.

Check how you are feeling emotionally. My first emotions were shock and shame. Sometimes it's hard to recognize our emotions. This list may help you name yours:

Checklist of my emotional responses

_____ I feel defensive.

_____ I'm angry or upset or enraged.

_____ I'm embarrassed or ashamed.

_____ I feel hurt.

_____ I feel misunderstood.

_____ I'm confused or lost.

_____ I'm disconnected, in shock, or frozen.

In the moment of this upset, how do you tend to react? In other words, what do you do (or *not* do), what do you say (or *not* say)—in the moment? Perhaps you tend to fight back. Notice yourself arguing, talking faster in a more commanding tone, refusing to listen, or sending raging e-mails. Perhaps you have a sudden desire to run away. Because it's not always appropriate to physically leave, you might notice that you disengage figuratively—while your body remains in place. Or you may find yourself rooted to the spot, paralyzed, with nothing to say. (That's me in a nutshell.) Those are physical and emotional cues to your typical amygdala hijack response. Note your patterns in the space below:

In the moment of my hijack

How do I feel?

_____

_____

_____

How do I behave?

_____

_____

_____

(continued)

(continued)

What outcome do I create for me?   *What outcome do I create for others?*

_____   _____

_____   _____

_____   _____

In my case, I dread the situation well ahead of time. My anxiety grows as I enter the meeting. Right away I talk too much or say something ditzy. Someone's tone fans the fear fire in me. My worst expectations (I am about to be humiliated) are met, I create my own spiral, and, when I head down, I feel vaporized—I no longer exist. My performance suffers; it takes more energy and more work to repair the damage.

If we are able to get a bit of distance, we usually realize that the amygdala hijack creates a classic catch-22; the very act drives us to create the experience we most fear. Please don't blame yourself if this is the case. Self-blame destroys any possibility of learning.

Getting friendly with your fears

My giant Gordian knot of fears held all the power. The more I fought them, the more they tightened. I predicted the worst outcomes and took a straight path there. But when we get to know our fears, starting with naming them, we take the power back.

If you're having trouble naming what you fear, here's a list Jo collected: being wrong; being left alone or abandoned; not being accepted; being found out—a fraud; being unworthy; having no value; being rejected, becoming irrelevant; being invisible; losing control; being subjugated; letting others down; being let down by others; hurting others; being hurt; being treated unfairly; not being good enough. And this is just a thought starter! Ask the following question, considering each line below as one layer of the onion. Keep peeling until you get to the real fear driving you:

Peeling back the onion of my fears

What, in me, is triggered in the moment of my upset? My fear of ... my need for ...

Top _____

Second _____

Third _____

Fourth _____

I'll peel back the layers of my own fears to get you started. When I faced Robert in the supply-chain proposal situation, I immediately felt caught in the spotlight. (1). When I feel this way, I'm afraid that I will be hurt (2). Below hurt lies my fear that I will be subjugated (3). And when I peel that layer, I really fear being destroyed (4).

Some people believe they are fearless. Yet even the most fearless people have needs; and when those needs are threatened, they react out of fear. They just don't realize it. If that's the case for you, we suggest exploring what need of yours is threatened in the moment of upset. Here is a starter list of needs: being recognized, being seen; being able to influence the situation or control one's emotions; being right; being independent, self-reliant; being accepted; belonging; providing for others; being respected; and we could go on!

Now ask: *What do I hold true about me that appears threatened in this situation?* If we were to ask your friends to tell us three important qualities that they value in you, what would they say? Or if you're clear on what you value about yourself, go right there.

What is true about me:

What is true (that I value) about me that is threatened: I am . . .

_____

_____

_____

_____

For example, I value my creativity, individuality, perseverance, and integrity. Then, look deep into your triggered moment and ask:

What I'm worried about:

What do I want to have happen but worry something else is happening in-stead? If that outcome did happen, what would it say about me in comparison to what I hold true about myself?

_____

_____

_____

_____

For example, I want clients to see that I'm an outstanding consultant and I believe that I am. But when my fear of not being seen takes over, I behave in ways that trigger clients to be dismissive or hostile. I shut down and they withdraw. Am I seen then? No way!

Scan for a few experiences with similar behaviors, because that will reveal the pattern. Once you find your pattern, you'll pinpoint the fear or need that is important to you. Talk to your friends about their fears or needs; talk to your boss and the people who observe you in high-stress situations. Even better, get a group together and ask each person to write down their biggest fear and find their "fear buddies." Feeling unworthy? Join me to discuss our shame! Hate to let people down? So do I; and do you also tend to micromanage others in consequence? Afraid of losing control? Me, too, so let's make a plan. Afraid of being left all alone? Be alone with me!

How crazy is it that we're having fun while talking about our darkest places? Talking about our fears helps us realize they're not all bad; they're part of the human experience. You'll recognize that as unique as we are—we may feel like islands—we're not alone. *Everyone* struggles with this. Our fears are not a function of circumstance, either. New boss, next promotion, or next job will not erase this fact of humankind. Even if you become president or CEO, you won't be immune. But you *will* be a better leader in that next role if you recognize and address these patterns. Your team members and family will thank you, too.

We can blame the organization, colleagues, our bad luck at work, the economy. Or we can learn to face our fears and use their energy to take action. Sounds irrational? Let's try it together—honoring how our fears have served us, accept that they're going to stay with us and then understand how our fears also limit our growth as leaders. Jo explains, "When we fight our fears we give power to them. What we accept we can transform." So face your fears without fear, using this question to reflect or discuss:

Facing my fears:

How my fears served me to get where I am and continue to serve me in many ways:

_____

_____

_____

_____

For example, my fear of not being seen has caused me to work very hard to prove my credibility. This isn't silly stuff. Even the bravest warriors, daredevils, astronauts, and leaders feel afraid. Their fear urges them to prepare more carefully, focus more, stay alert, build closer relationships. At some point, fears cross the line from being fuel for our action to fire that frightens. When is that? Your body knows and warns you. It's telling you that your choices are narrowing and your resources decreasing; you are no longer at your best. Reflect on how fear limits you and, if you can, discuss that with others.

How my fears limit me:

_____

_____

_____

_____

My fears caused me to pull away. They kept me alone and lonely for a lot of my life. And they kept me from appreciating myself.

Once you recognize how your fears limit you, you're taking back your power. Want to go further? Write a letter to your fear. Go ahead, use the space below. I did it. Only then did my fear of bullies loosen its hold. Now this is the crux: I am accountable for creating my own experience of life in that moment. That scary thought is hugely empowering.

Letter to my fears

Dear _____

_____

_____

_____

_____

_____

_____

_____

Yours truly,

Final thoughts on the darkest place

At this point, you may find it a good idea to take a break. Self-reflection uses up a great deal of energy! The next chapters offer relief—learning to pause and reframe your mindset in order to have access to new behaviors that open a window on personal and professional growth. Before you move on, though, a note of appreciation for you. You have made your needs and fears known, and you've thought about how they serve you and how they don't. Johanne says, "This is the courage to be conscious. Courage comes from the French word for heart. When you respond with love, you learn to receive and accept what life brings."

You've already begun to lead in a new way. You are becoming a more resourceful, Centered Leader. And that's worth celebrating.

STORY 3

Mellody Faces Her Fears
Head-on

*In which Mellody Hobson, president of Ariel Investments,
shares her experience with fears, keeping her power, and
gaining comfort with discomfort*

A friend first told me about Mellody Hobson years ago. She was a regular on *Good Morning America*, president of Ariel Investments, on many boards and even the chairman of one. She was smart and driven and, to top it all off, under forty. So I asked Mellody if she would be willing to interview. She said yes, and we lost touch. Then, five years later, I am invited to speak at a *Fortune* event and . . .

. . . so is Mellody. It's 5:30 p.m. and I know I should network. I am poorly dressed and I've put on five pounds. My mind goes blank. I'm freezing. The downward spiral starts and it's . . . show time!

I channel David, who advises me to turn off my left brain. Here goes. I open my mouth, and this comes out: "When I woke up this morning, I thought about meeting all of you—remarkable, successful senior executives with gorgeous shoes. I was so intimidated that I immediately put on all the jewelry I own." Thank god they laugh (does anyone, possibly, feel the same way?). I end on a high. Then Mellody appears onstage in a bright yellow suit, jewels flashing, and acting fearless.

Fast-forward five months to our interview. Mellody talked, and I listened. Her accomplishments, her strengths, her pure energy, and her openness are remarkable. But somehow, our conversation always came back to fear.

Patterns start young

"No question about it—I was influenced by my situation growing up," Mellody said. "At the time it seemed extraordinarily hard, but I know that it made for my resilience today. My single mom was an entrepreneur in the real estate business in Chicago. She would convert old buildings into condominiums. I call it a boom-and-bust life. We spent a lot of time worrying about money. We used to get evicted, our phone disconnected, our lights turned off. Sometimes we lived in the abandoned buildings. Sometimes my mom heated water on the stove to fill a bathtub. So I was obsessed with security. I wanted to know that I was going to be OK. It's no accident that I'm in the financial services business!" I thought, *Here is a woman who experienced what has plagued me forever. Someone brought Mellody to my door to teach me.*

Her counter to fear was financial independence, and school was the ticket: "I came out of the womb focused in a crazy way. I would not miss school. When there was a snow day, my mother had to turn on the television and show me school was canceled. Once, my school bus got into an accident, and I thought I was going to be late. So I slipped off the bus and walked. They had an alert out and were scouring the neighborhood when they found me at school in my seat. I was aware that school was going to be important to me in gaining security but have no idea how I figured that out."

We are all the same person we were at six years old, just more experienced. Mellody recognized that: "This den of anxiety lives in me that I wish I could dial down. I know I'm going to be fine. A good friend tells me, 'Mellody, the die is cast. You're successful.' It's, like, news flash! But I don't ever feel that way. I always feel like I could do better. It's about the quality of my work, the reputation of Ariel, people feeling that we are substantive and smart and dazzling them—I don't know why."

Fear served Mellody well. It motivated her and energized her, propelling her all the way to Princeton. She mused, "They gave us a thousand pages a week to read and they told us at the beginning, 'You won't be able to get the reading done.' Every minute of every day, I knew I should be reading. That's how I feel at work. Every minute of every day, I could be doing something that would move the needle, but I can't get it all done. And it doesn't matter how many people help me. The opportunity just grows in my mind."

Mellody's darkest place

I wanted to explore the topic of living in the uncomfortable space where, no matter how things seem on the outside, fear can take control if you let it. Mellody was no stranger to that place and told a story about working her way through it:

> I've been at Ariel for three years. I say to John Rogers, the founder, "We need to leave our major joint venture partner" and explain why. It had never been done. John replies, "Why don't you present this to our board?" The board agrees. Then we fly to our partner's headquarters to tell them. John is eleven years older than me but I can tell he's anxious. So we present to the mutual fund board and get sent out of the room. They leave us out in the hall for *an hour*. John's doing the "This was probably a bad idea." I totally understand; this is his life's work. Well, they bring us back and say, "You have four weeks to work out a deal. If you don't work out a deal, all bets are off and you both lose—we assign the funds to someone completely different." It's make or break. It's one of these things where it could have been a disaster, it really could have.

How did Mellody feel at that moment when she knew there was no going back? She replied, "I was thrilled and I was terrified. I was thrillified! On the one hand, this is the most amazing thing. On the other hand, I'm thinking, *Oh my god, they've given me what I want. This is horrible.* I expected them to say no. I didn't think I was going to make it past John's office with the initial, 'We should leave.' Then the board said yes and I think, *That's a fluke.* As it worked its way up the food chain, I'm increasingly in disbelief. And when it happened, stress manifested itself." Propelled by fear, Mellody worked without stopping all summer, living on muffins until the deal was done.

I thought there must be something darker than "thrillifying" and I was right. Mellody shared a story of almost being overwhelmed by fear:

> 2008 was really hard; we lost 48 percent that year. I felt like I'd spent all these years pushing this giant rock up a hill, and then it just rolled down. It was brutal. I spent an enormous amount of time feeling like it was my fault. It was the first time I realized that all of my self-validation was coming from Ariel. Every time we won, I was winning. And now that we were losing, I was losing big. I didn't know what to do.
>
> I remember being at the Starbucks board meeting. Bill Bradley and I were going back to the hotel. I'm all worn out but he asks me to sit with him. He says, "Mellody, I am just checking in. How are you doing? Are you scared?" He's been like a dad to me. It was then that I fell apart, I mean, an ugly cry, buckets all over the table in the middle of the lobby. Bill says quietly, "You have a right to feel fear. You have not given yourself permission to have that moment." After that, I pulled myself together and thought, I'm going to get through it. I needed that experience to be clearer about what mattered.

Quietly I asked Mellody, "What is being triggered in you?" She put it bluntly: "Failure. Eviction, lights turned off. I went back to that place. I was having these dreams. I told Bill, 'I'm dreaming about being homeless but I'm walking around holding Gucci shopping bags with my stuff!' My dreams were telling. They all attach back to Easter dresses instead of light bills. I was powering through. I was the person who thought you should always be doing something. Sometimes there is nothing more you can do." A tough economic year had trig-

gered Mellody's earliest memories of losing everything; fear works
that way.

Eventually, Mellody learned that we need not be captive to our fears;
we can accept and appreciate them and work past them. She said, "The
one interesting thing about humans is we hold the keys to the prison.
The bars are right in front of our eyes. All we have to do is open the door
and let our own selves out, but we won't do it. Once you can recognize
it, you have to decide, 'Am I gonna get out today or not?' "

Moving past fear

Swimming taught Mellody about living with fear. She explained:

> We do this exercise where you swim freestyle the length of the
> pool without breathing. My teacher starts off by saying, "Breathe
> every three strokes, every five strokes, seven, nine, eleven, thir-
> teen, until you get to the other side." You're trying to see how far
> you can go. Every time you fail, you start over. It's a nightmare.
> The more frustrated and anxious you get, the more likely you are
> to need the breath. The first time, it took me an hour to get to the
> other end of the pool. My teacher said, "Mellody, I'm not trying
> to teach you to swim without breathing. I'm teaching you to be
> comfortable being uncomfortable mindfully. Then you can be
> comfortable with discomfort in life."

As we drew to a close, Mellody shared her philosophy on fear: "You
know the guy who jumped from space and broke the sound barrier skydiving? He is in the capsule and they're communicating to him from
Earth. They say, 'It's time to jump.' There's a camera on him—his legs
are dangling out, he's in a space suit. And he's sitting, sitting, sitting.
It's just two minutes but it seems like twenty, and they're saying, 'Are
you going to j—' They're saying it over and over. Later, he recounts, 'I
was terrified.' You don't think the guy who wants to break the sound
barrier in a parachute is terrified!"

Mellody, too, looks fearless but isn't. She continued, "For me to go to the next level to be a better leader, a better teacher, a better friend, I have to wrestle fear down. There's that saying, 'What got you here won't get you where you need to go.' Fear and anxiety got me here, there's no question; but it doesn't take me where I need to go."

Well said, Mellody. We all experience fear, and it serves us well. But for some of us, fear holds us back from growing at work and in life.

Then it's time to take back the power.

10

LEARNING TO PAUSE

In which you learn to step out of the movie and see yourself in it, understand what in you is triggered, and choose what you most want to create

Our fears serve us well, moving us to action. That said, our fears also limit us at some point in our careers. For many, fears can be constant companions—more like demons we would love to leave behind. I'll never forget one tall and imposing woman who approached me after a session to ask, "Is there a book that will help me get rid of fear? I live in fear and I can't take it anymore." I don't want you to think that you can make your fears disappear. They have an essential purpose: to protect and fuel you. But there *is* a way to loosen their hold on you. The first step, as you learned, is to recognize and accept them and their effect on you.

Step two is learning to pause. Pausing gives your executive brain the time to reengage after an amygdala hijack. If you're thinking, *Joanna, this is impossible. My life is crazy busy and I cannot get it all done. You're asking me to* pause? *I'm just tryin' to get through—so cut me a break here!* If you're thinking that taking the time to pause is difficult, you are right. But with practice, you'll get there. And, trust me, you want to learn this.

Pausing in the heat of the moment can shift the discussion productively. It allows you to step out of your "movie" to observe, to pose a question instead of reasserting your point, to break the logjam of two strong characters with competing views, or to observe that no one is stepping up. Pausing is like mindfulness. Johanne explains, "When we pause, we activate the parasympathetic system that slows down our heartbeat, lowers our blood pressure, releases mood-elevating hormones such as oxytocin, and returns our body to its relaxed state. Pausing isn't good just for our mood, but also for our brain functions. When we pause, our neocortex can reengage, and our range of awareness expands. We see more perspectives. We regain our capacity to think and question."

Think about how valuable this can be when you're in a difficult or triggered situation. Maybe it's during a tense meeting where everyone is arguing with you. Or in the middle of a presentation when you suddenly go blank. Or when you walk into a meeting and feel sure that others are sizing you up. In situations that feel tough, pausing is like a professional (self-imposed) "time-out"—a moment when you regroup to gain perspective. Pausing helps you look those demons in the eye and make a deliberate choice to shift your belief.

It sounds incredible, doesn't it? An out-of-body experience in the middle of a deadly meeting? Leaving your "movie" to watch it? The ability to actually *decide* and then be able to be at your best? At this point you may be thinking, Huh? *This sounds fabulous, but how? How do I watch my own movie, and at the same time, continue to be in it?*

With awareness of your signs, you can learn to respond in the midst of the hijack. With the knowledge that you are not in physical danger, you can stop your survival, fight-or-flight response. At first it will take conscious effort to pause—to consciously recognize the warning signs and then use your predetermined "pause strategy." With practice, you can lower your stress simply by breathing deeply. In time, it will become second nature, effortless. For masters, shifting from an oncoming amygdala hijack to the centered state of a pause takes mere seconds.

Putting "pause" in your tool kit

Have you ever been in a difficult situation and done something that helped you shift from taking things personally to seeing them differently? Early on in my first year at McKinsey, I had to present to a roomful of senior clients. Feeling sick (read: hijack coming on), I ran to the ladies' room and gave myself a talking-to. I reminded myself that there was nothing to be afraid of. Everyone else was excited about the meeting; I was the only one seeing the situation as threatening, as if on hallucinogens. I told myself that all I had to do was act normal. It was a pause, all right, and it calmed me down. But that's an extreme way to "get out of the movie"—literally. There are as many ways to pause without leaving the room as there are people who practice it. Check the practices you'd like to test. I've used many of them myself and can vouch for them.

Practices to help you pause

_____ Breathe deeply, exhaling fully (when hijacked, we may hold our breath without realizing it).

_____ Ground yourself by feeling your feet on the floor or the chair holding you.

_____ Uncross your arms, drop your shoulders, relax your face (moving your body into a more open state can calm you down).

_____ Smile and make eye contact with others.

_____ Take notes (slows you down and stops you from speaking).

_____ Ask yourself a question, such as "What's going on in me right now? What is my intention here?"

_____ Say something that stops the reactivity and gives you a breather:

    _____ Exclaiming a mantra, such as "What a great challenge!" or "How fascinating!"

    _____ Saying, "Tell me more" when you cannot think of a question (happens to me all the time).

_____ Turn on your compassion by imagining others to be loved ones.

_____ Remind yourself that others are just like you—human beings doing the best they can.

Replay a recent situation and practice with each option. Some will feel more natural than others; for example, I cannot fake a smile but I'm comfortable making an exclamation and have rehearsed so that it's become second nature. When I exclaim, "What a great challenge!" the aggressive questioner relaxes, satisfied that he is heard. In extreme cases, I put my hand over my mouth, which works brilliantly to stop me from defending when I need to listen. Here is a bit of space to devise your own action experiment.

Action experiment: pausing

Objective

_____

_____

Chosen action

_____

_____

Results

_____

_____

_____

Pausing is what puts you in the position of managing your thoughts, feelings, and actions. Next time you feel an amygdala hijack coming on, consider it a lucky break—time to experiment!

To demonstrate, let's take a look at someone who pauses brilliantly and with grace.

STORY 4

Zoe Pauses Naturally

In which Zoe Yujnovich, president and CEO of Iron Ore Company of Canada, demonstrates how to pause with powerful effect

It's easy for some. Zoe Yujnovich, a leader for the Canadian Iron Ore division of Rio Tinto, is exceptional at pausing in the moment. Johanne introduced me to Zoe because she has this very talent. I wanted to learn how a natural "pauser" does it, whether the trait is somehow innate or even genetic, and if not, the conditions that favor it.

Born in Hong Kong to British parents, Zoe remembers moving around a lot as a child. Constant change in environment likely had something to do with building that pausing skill early on. Indeed, one of Zoe's top strengths is the capacity to adapt to new places and situations. She thrives on it: "I've come to appreciate my ability to get somewhere new and assess the lay of the land and feel at home very quickly. I've learned adaptability by coming to new places, but also sensing the untouchable, unspoken things that happen when you arrive in a new location or a new job."

Embracing constant change

Tracing Zoe's ability to pause while in the "movie" (in order to see herself and reflect on what is happening) takes us pretty far back in her career. "I wanted to be a doctor and then decided to be an engineer at the last minute. No real rhyme or reason but I enjoyed maths. And then, my first job was away from home—in Tasmania on the other side of the continent!" Settling into the mining company, Zoe moved within Australia and then to emerging countries, developed countries, and back again. She shared: "I found confidence in being able to move. Each time I made the move, and the degree of complexity increased in some respects, I would just push a little further, without consciously knowing how far I was pushing it. I never felt uncomfortable in any of the move decisions." Instead, Zoe figuratively took flight: "Sometimes, I wonder if I have enough roots and does that matter to me or my children. I prefer wings; I have a lot of great security through my family."

Her ability to tolerate a tremendous amount of change—to embrace even chaotic change—helps Zoe pause effectively. She has fears and trepidations like all of us, but she gains strength when she steps out of her routine: "I can feel my senses. Everything is at a heightened state of awareness. I find it's in that state that I can exist and so I relax there. I'm not stressed, I just feel present. Perhaps it's when I'm in that most present state that I get the greatest clarity of thought on what I can do to help. It gives me the sense of where my value is in the business."

To illustrate, Zoe recounted a story: accepting a role in Brazil just as she learned that she was pregnant with her third child. She said, "I saw this as an opportunity. It didn't scare me. I've got a great, supporting husband. By the time we arrived, I was seven months pregnant. I was feeling reasonably calm. I look back now and wonder how I did it, but then it didn't feel too out of the ordinary! It was one of those stretch moments."

The business had just received approval for significant expansion. But then, the unexpected happened. Zoe recalled, "I was in a heightened state of awareness, thinking, 'We've just moved here and I'm having a baby.' About one month after I start, they decide to divest. I realize that I'm going to need to be present. I also want to be a mother and take time with the family." That is what most of us would call the "perfect storm," but not for Zoe. She said, "When there is a lot of change happening, I feel almost calmer knowing that it's a process. The time will pass, and we'll get to another space."

One reason why Zoe was able to handle such change is her positive framing. She said, "I'm a nine out of ten in the optimism camp. I have a strong view that if you don't believe it, it doesn't happen. Focusing on the things that don't work doesn't actually help, and it doesn't ever make me feel any better. Being able to look for the good in a bad situation is something I do regularly." So Zoe had the baby in Brazil, and after a four-month leave, came back to work part-time. She led the divestment, skillfully taking the organization through the final closing. Naturally, Zoe then packed up the family and moved—to Canada and her next opportunity on the horizon.

Pausing step by step

I asked Zoe to walk me through what happens to her as she achieves that present, yet detached, pause state. Fittingly, she paused to consider her answer:

> I find myself taking a moment to take stock. It might not be a long time, maybe a minute or two. I used to do points of reflection every quarter or so. I would pull out my little book and do a bit of thinking. I find myself doing that much more regularly, often during discussion. I just came from a meeting. I caught myself—as we were talking—thinking, "Hang on! How am I feeling about that? I'm feeling a little apprehensive about what that might mean. There's another way I could look at this." And recharging in some respects and getting back on the page, using that as another opportunity to drive us forward.

Scribbling her thoughts on the page allows Zoe to figuratively leave the issue and whatever is building up inside. She said, "I find myself almost subconsciously doing that as I go. I can sense that I'm not at ease. You know that feeling in your gut or that sensation that something's not quite right? I'll either jot it down or park it in my mind. It gives me a way of decluttering and focusing again on what I'm here for. And then I get back into the conversation that's unfolding before me. I don't harbor it."

11

LEARNING TO SHIFT MINDSETS

In which you learn to use the "iceberg" to uncover your underlying mindsets and choose a different one to create the experience you really want

Pausing helps us reframe in the middle of a challenging moment, but what about facing (and clearing up) difficult *interactions*? Ones that are complex, upsetting, ongoing, and still resonate months—if not years—later? Pausing is only Step Two on the way to Step Three: making the choice to creatively reframe the situation. This chapter is all about how.

To start, recall a "high-stakes" situation from the past year. You'll recognize it because the outcome matters to you (you care about the relationship, or the outcome affects your ability to achieve your goals, or simply because your energy is draining). Choose one that ended with you not getting the results or the connection you wanted. Somehow, you got way off center. It may even make you cringe to remember. Using your example, we'll guide you through the process from start to finish. Ready to go?

Good. Describe your situation in a few sentences by putting yourself back *in the moment*: re-see, re-feel, and re-experience it. It's not fun to relive your hijack, but actually it's great to have a difficult situation that still packs a punch—its resolution will release more energy. In a short while, physical relief will come from reflection, choosing, and shifting your mindset in order to create the experience you want. Remember to use the present tense:

My difficult situation

Who is involved?

_____

_____

What is your trigger?

_____

_____

What is making this difficult for you?

_____

_____

_____

I'll work through a different example (we all have so many). Sometime in early December, at 6:00 p.m. on a Friday, I'm conducting a long-awaited meeting with the head of our firm to present a proposal for global investment in Centered Leadership. What makes this difficult is that he is leafing through my memo without reading it. We talk aimlessly. I sense that I'm being dismissed. And at 7:00 p.m., I am. I leave the room with nothing. A colleague is outside the conference room, waiting to go to dinner. I'm jealous and upset. Actually, it's worse: I am drained. No way forward. Heading home, I wonder, *What just happened?*

Beneath the "iceberg" of you

How much of an iceberg is visible from the surface? About 12.5 percent on average. For this exercise, Johanne asks us to imagine that we are icebergs. Other people can see what we do (or don't do) and hear what we say (or don't say) *on the surface*; in other words, people observe our behavior and judge us without knowing the seven-eighths of us that lurks hidden in the water:

- Right below the surface lie *your feelings and thoughts*: sensations or emotions; what you fear or imagine; your worries about negative outcomes.
- Farther down lie your *values and priorities*: what is most important to you; beliefs you hold about situations, about yourself, about others.
- And, at the bottom, down in the darkest deep, lie your *underlying needs and your identity*: what you really want for and from yourself; your deeper desires, intentions, or motivations; what you believe to be true about yourself.

Most people don't know us below the waterline, and some of us don't know ourselves at that level. It takes more than time to dive that deep—it takes a willingness to live with discomfort. By the way, this exercise is even more effective with a discussion partner. If you're on your own, allow yourself time to reflect on these questions and explore your own iceberg. Putting yourself back in the moment when you are experiencing the high-stakes situation, use these questions as guides:

Uncovering my iceberg

- Behaviors: What are you doing or not doing? What are you saying or not saying? How are you acting?

_____

_____

_____

_____

- Feelings and thoughts: What sensations or emotions are you feeling? What are you thinking or imagining about the situation, about yourself, about others? What negative outcomes are you worried about?

_____

_____

_____

_____

(continued)

(continued)

- Values and priorities: What is important and at stake for you? What belief do you hold about the situation?

_____

_____

_____

_____

- Underlying needs: What do you really want for and from yourself in this moment?

_____

_____

_____

_____

In my example, I make bold statements and sparkle a bit too much to mask anxiety. I'm thinking that the head of the firm doesn't like my idea. My internal voice hisses, *He really wants you to go, so leave, scram!* What's at stake is that I want to make sure Centered Leadership has a home and that I have a platform for my work. What I really want is to be valued; I want assurance that my work is valued, too.

Over to you. As you think about your difficult situation and your four levels of responses (along with your underlying stress or fear in the moment), are you aware of a pattern? Are there other times when you've acted and felt this same way and had the same "iceberg" responses? These questions may help you find the patterns:

Seeing my pattern

When I am feeling this stress/anxiety/fear, what do I do or not do? How do I act?

_____

_____

_____

When I behave this way, what is the likely outcome for me, others, the situation?

_____

_____

_____

My pattern is clear: When I feel ignored I tense up and make awkward statements I later regret. I talk too much; I press too hard. But when I behave this way, other people challenge me or withdraw. I feel ashamed and leave, frustrated. I *am* dismissed—and even if my idea (baby) is amazing, it will not be loved.

Go now to the very bottom of your iceberg. If you're feeling pretty awful, as I am, cheer up; we're about to hit gold. I love to role-model this exercise with Johanne, who says, "Thank you for going to the bottom, and I promise that I won't leave you there, but let's take a short break before we work our way back up." Please stand up and shake the feelings out.

Move to a different chair. I find that works wonders to let go of the hijack.

Choosing to shift

In this difficult situation, you were operating with a frame of mind that led you to behaviors, which consciously or not (usually not), created the outcome you most feared. The good news—no, the great news—is that you can choose your mindset. Clearly, it's going to take practice, but the mindset that got you to the upset is neither genetic nor destiny. You can create a new experience or way of being by reframing. It does not guarantee other people will change or that you will get the results you would like; but, for sure, you *will* experience that situation differently, and in turn, you will behave differently. The situation will not feel so stressful or fearful—it may even be exciting! In consequence, you will be better able to tap into your full reserves of confidence, strength, and resourcefulness. You will feel more centered. Ready for the climb back to the surface? We are.

Choosing a creative way

First, adopt your desired mindset, imagining your deeper need being fulfilled.

Imagine or recall a time when this need is/was already fulfilled, without the limitation of fear. What emotions are you feeling? What physical sensations are you feeling? What are you thinking? What really matters to you or what do you care about most? Please finish this sentence:

I am _____

_____

In my example, I imagine a time when I was leading a client brainstorming session without pressure to gain approval—a time when I was upbeat and curious. Feeling great, I used humor to energize our discussion. What mattered to me was getting to the best answer. So doing this exercise with you (and I am!), I write: *I am in the room to draw out the best in people because I am valued as a peer who builds confidence in bold ideas.*

It's your turn. With that deeper need fulfilled, you're ready for Johanne's next step:

Go back to your difficult situation but with this desired mindset.

With this new mindset, what behaviors would naturally emerge? In turn, what behaviors would reinforce this new mindset? What would you choose to do or say that would be different? Please finish this sentence:

I . . . _____

_____

In my example, I would reinforce my new mindset of creative leadership by beginning with a Check-In, connecting through questions and compassion to create a dialogue. I write: *I am open, connected, and ask questions with genuine curiosity, drawing on my strengths—as a peer.*

Imagine what becomes possible for you if you live into this new mindset and associated behaviors.

If you lived this new mindset and behaviors, what experience would you create more of? What new way of being becomes possible for you? Please finish this sentence:

What becomes possible for me, my team, my performance is . . .

_____

_____

_____

I write: *What becomes possible for me is to gain broad support for Centered Leadership, enlisting everyone in my vision long term.* If you've followed along with your own situation, you are above water once more.

Whoosh.

You may feel a great relief when you work your way through recognizing your current mental frame, experiencing the shift to other behaviors, identifying that other frame, choosing to shift, and then imagining your difficult situation with that new mindset and behavior.

What does that feel like to you? Most people visibly relax, they feel a burden lifted. They see that they are managing themselves in a more powerful way.

Sustaining your reframing practice

A great thing about reframing is that every new challenge or difficult situation is a marvelous opportunity to practice. And there's no shortage of challenges; they happen most days, in fact. But what if there were a way to sustain the new frame of mind you reached in the last exercise? What if you had it at your disposal to take the sting out of that trigger, any time? And what if you could use that new frame to defang other triggers, too?

Remember the four steps to adult learning? In Step Three, we *consciously* embody our new skills through practice. It may feel awkward at first, because the skill is new. Through practice, you will gain the physical, mental, and emotional capacity to shift when you feel the warning signs. New behaviors will emerge naturally. What used to trigger the old behaviors will no longer have much power. For me, I chose to see my discussion as a lost opportunity but not the only one. Feeling compassion, I realized my colleague was exhausted and not in a position to shortcut an institutional process, but would find ways to support us. I no longer felt brushed off. When senior leaders appear dismissive, I now ask myself what else might be going on. I also learned to hold tough discussions in the morning when I am fresh!

Through practice, you create a reinforcing cycle. Work at it to hardwire both mindset and behavior. That's what Johanne defines as a sustaining practice: observable behaviors that you can repeat over time and that support your desired experience or motivating beliefs. It represents a stretch outside your comfort zone, moving you toward your vision with concrete action. Write it in the present tense to make it real.

Creating your sustaining practice to reframe

Reflecting on your story (from the exercise above), articulate the experience you want to create. Finish this sentence:

I create the experience of _____

_____

Using the guidelines above, write a few observable behaviors that you choose to commit to. Finish this sentence:

As I _____

_____

Define ahead of time how you will know that this mindset and behavior are working. Finish this sentence:

I know I am on the right path (what becomes possible for me) when . . .

_____

_____

Here is my example: "I create the experience of connecting people to get the best outcome." As the discussion begins, I pay attention to asking questions, listening and paraphrasing to noticeably value other views. I'll know that I am succeeding when I feel deeper connection and others become animated, open, and engaged. Conflict is normal, but it won't have the personal rancor that happens when people do not feel seen or heard.

A sustaining practice is the key to shifting our mindsets and behaviors for good. As you get more comfortable using this approach, you can help other people explore their icebergs, too! Get curious and ask your team questions to learn more about their thoughts and feelings, beliefs and values, and what really matters to them. As you learn, you and the team will experience more—accomplish more. We've put it in your tool kit, and it's ready to go.

And next up is a remarkable senior executive who did just that.

Ed Reframes to Learn

In which Edward P. Gilligan, president of American Express, makes his way to the C-suite by learning to see the opportunity in business and in life

Ed Gilligan grew up in Brooklyn with his grandmother, aunt, uncle, parents, and brother. His story is the American dream: modest upbringing in a close-knit Irish immigrant community. He says, "Everybody knew me. I could never go too far without someone hanging out a window yelling, 'Watch yourself, Eddie, I know your mother!' That was the first form of matrix management I ever experienced!" His family aspired to a better future at Brooklyn Union Gas or the priesthood. Ed jokes that he is at American Express only because he could not become a fireman. Reframing opened up unimagined opportunity.

A growth mindset

Ed built his capacity to reframe on a firm foundation—a growth mindset:

> I work for a great company that has reinvented itself. And in the company's last few chapters I've had a role to play in that. You think about different ingredients of success for people, for companies—and a lot of it is a growth mindset. I try to live by some of the underlying principles—a constant quest for learning and choice. Every challenge offers two roads—perhaps feeling victimized or unlucky versus "maybe we failed here but I've learned something that's going to help me succeed."

Ed illustrated this idea just a week after he became one of the company's youngest senior vice presidents ever: "There was a change in leadership and a crisis. I was sitting in my *first* top team meeting with every senior executive and the new CEO said, 'We're going to cut costs and a lot of you won't be here in six months!' I thought, *Oh no! I just got here. Is this the beginning of something or the end?* A more senior executive next to me leaned over and said, 'Ed, there's going to be something in this for us. Just watch closely.'" Within thirty days, two levels above Ed were eliminated and he took on more responsibility.

The biggest test of reframing

When September 11 happened, the corporate card and travel business lost eleven employees, part of a group working in the north tower. Ed recalled the horror. He was not prepared for facing the terrible challenge of trying to help the families as he looked for ways to restore the decimated business. Thousands upon thousands of employees depended on his leadership; rebuilding became their rallying cry: "We had a common purpose that we were not going to let 9/11 destroy this franchise that we'd worked so hard to build." The team started looking for growth—diversifying globally and focusing on mid-size companies for the first time. They created a success track record that lasted almost a decade, growing that business tenfold.

Ed led from the front, traveling the world to visit employees and explaining the need to reengineer. He mused, "Even if you don't have all the answers, which I didn't, I learned the power of showing up and talking to people so they understand what's happening—even though some were about to lose their jobs. I learned about talking to people directly and honestly, not being afraid to show emotion." Ed realized that out of this challenging situation arose an opportunity to set a high bar for rebuilding. Inspired by Ken Chenault (who became CEO and chairman in 2001), Ed recalls his leader's first address to the employees gathered in makeshift New Jersey headquarters: "Ken stood up on a ledge by a window in the lobby. We're all looking at him and in the background we see smoke coming out of our building and the rubbles of the Trade Center. Ken says, 'Headquarters is not a building. It's us. It's wherever we are. We're committed to make this company stronger.' That was the best display of giving hope when there wasn't a lot. I thought, *There's a lot of work to do. Let's get on with it.*"

The worst of times turned into one of the most rewarding, and Ed was fortunate to be able to contribute. I hope no one reading this ever has to go through trauma to reframe, but in reflecting on Ed's (and Ken's) words, I understand the enormous power—and use—for it.

Reframing to learn

One of Ed's strengths is his humanity. He admitted that it's easy to get into a rut. "I used to think, *I'm just like everyone else. I have good moods and sometimes I have bad moods.* But that's going to impact a lot of people. You have to own your mood. I slip from that and have to be reminded." So Ed makes it a point to surround himself with people willing to call him out: "Giving me honest feedback is not easy to do. And it's not always easy to receive it. I love having people around me who are not afraid to tell me, 'Snap out of it' or 'You're in a crummy mood today' or even a hand signal every now and then. I'm far more effective when I bring a positive outlook and energy. It can be infectious." But how did Ed behave when growth stalled? He reframed:

> By 2010, it was clear the world was changing, because you had hundreds of millions of people walking around with the Internet in their pocket. This could be very disruptive; but there could be great opportunity, too. Well, I was in a four-hour business review with our group serving small businesses. And at the end of a very long day, someone said, "Let's create a day called Small Business Saturday to help in the holiday season." Sitting there, tired out, I realized that this was perhaps the best idea I'd heard that year if not in my career. So I said, "We have thirty days. How much trou-

ble can we get into?" We created a movement within the country.
It was an immediate and huge success for our small business customers.

Ed's team also started a movement within the company. Launching a digital task force, Ed realized that his role had to change from a
financial return on investment mindset to creating an environment of
innovation and taking risks, giving people what they need and getting
out of their way. It was a time of high positive energy, not fear: "I was
exhilarated by shaking off the cobwebs of the financial crisis. We went
from worrying about liquidity to a mindset of *We can move fast, we can
do groundbreaking things*. It changed the way we got things done."

Learning to step back

I wondered if there were ever situations Ed could not reframe. He reframed my question:

> Eventually I come around. You vent a little bit. After a few days
> you have a different approach and are ready to take it on. The trick
> is to step back and call out: Am I personally adopting the right
> mindset or am I stuck in the past? You accept feedback—listen
> and learn—even though it's not easy. You've not seen it all. If you
> think you have, you start to become obsolete.

To Ed, failure is about learning; learning makes growth possible. His
counsel rings in my ears: "It's only a failure if you give up." Fighting
words from a man with endless capacity to reframe!

PART FOUR

CONNECTING

12

BECOMING LINKED

In which we show you the three elements of Connecting; how they help transform relationships and build community; and what you'll find in this section

I t seems that everyone is on the connecting bandwagon these days, with social media changing the meaning of *relationship, friend, linked,* and even *connected.* Sometimes, I wonder if I'm just part of that wave, dressing 1980s' wolfish ideas about networking in sheep's clothing. Should Connecting be equal to powerhouses such as Meaning and Framing? When someone casually suggested that Connecting should be secondary—and my pulse began racing—I realized that Connecting is as important. Throughout my career, I was praised as a great relationship builder. But in reality, I wasn't the connector people thought I was. That's what makes this chapter the hardest for me to write. And the most meaningful.

A Rolodex isn't a network

Cleaning out my office, I found a box of business cards, the most recent at least ten years old. With childish excitement, I went down memory lane, remembering people who I had enjoyed meeting and then forgotten. Many of them were in my contacts, but not in my life. Most had left those companies; many had undoubtedly retired; a few companies had dissolved. So, after twenty minutes of paging through cards, I forced myself to throw them out. Moving on.

I had been diligent in asking people for their cards. Like the baseball cards I once traded (to get the bubble gum), I loved to collect them. But these relationships grew cold quickly. To be fair, a few stuck and continue to mean a great deal to me. For the most part, though, my network is a very leaky bucket. I ignored the holes, telling myself that I'd hold on to my newest relationships. *Get over it! It's a fact of life,* my internal voice chides. You might agree. Maybe you're thinking, *Creating new relationships isn't worth the effort.* It's work to keep our networks healthy. But you'd be mistaken to discount your network's connection to your performance. We depend on others for our success—often people we've never even met; but, clearly, all the people we know can help in some way.

The truth is, Centered Leadership would be nothing without a network. Today, I make new connections constantly. Many I must leave behind, but now I do that consciously, making room for people who share my values and who give and take with positive energy. In other words, my network and purpose have come together in a community that fosters meaning and energy. That's what I want for you.

How did this happen? I thought Connecting would be the simplest of Centered Leadership's dimensions to master, and it may be for you. For me, it turned out to be the highest mountain, and I'm still climbing it. Let me catch you up in the story.

In a crowd, alone

Throughout my thirty-plus years at McKinsey, I was never alone. I joined with a *class* of recruits. I attended training with a global *cohort*. I was part of an *office*. I joined the media and consumer *practices*. I belonged to personnel *committees*, client service *teams*. I advanced in a partner *class*. And then partners everywhere sent notes to welcome me into the global *partnership*. I was pleased that everyone knew me by my first name, like a rock star. Yet it was still torture to go to a global conference or even an office meeting. Despite the people all around me, I always felt isolated. I thought, *What's wrong with me?*

OK. I'm an introvert. For years, I used this excuse as I missed an event, slipped out before dessert, avoided after-hours networking. I told myself that, as a woman, it was uncomfortable to network in a room full of men. I told myself that being a mother, I needed the sleep. I told myself that I had too much work. You get the picture. Until recently, I failed to connect this behavior with the fact that, while everyone in the firm seemed to know my name, I felt invisible.

Fortunately, I connected the dots. I love to teach connecting because you get to use fifty colored markers to draw network maps! Maps are an investigative tool to learn what drove us to build *these* relationships in *this* network rather than other relationships in a different network. In drawing my maps, I began to see that, while densely populated, they didn't include many reciprocal, trust-based relationships—and in fact many important relationships generated negative energy. Walking around the room, I marveled at other maps—positive energy, fat trust lines, double arrows—and realized, *Mine looks nothing like that.* Something deeper was going on.

Mindsets hidden in plain sight

The clues were there from the start. With great reluctance, I joined some participants to work on positive framing. What came back was a shock.

Strangers to each other and to me, my group saw me similarly. They called out my creativity; I've valued creativity ever since I collected colored pencil points at five. But they also saw that I assumed negative intent in everyone I met. They knew that fear was my lens; not wanting to be hurt, my standby. This group suggested that I adopt a new mental frame: *Meeting new people brings opportunity and . . . if I'm hurt, my creativity helps me rebound.*

For those three days, I wept in front of fifteen strangers because I knew I had wrapped myself in yards and yards of cotton batting to insulate myself for years. I understood that if I was invisible, it had been my choice. When I tried to reach through the batting to connect, my arms were not long enough. I remained alone. It would be a relief to live without the insulation. I was afraid to let it go.

It took four more years to understand what the people who loved me too much to hold back meant: I withdraw from connection. (Even David jokingly says that our family hangs on to me so I won't slip away.) Consciously, I have begun to unravel the batting I have worn for over fifty years. I feel naked but free with these mindset shifts:

- I believed that work colleagues wanted to beat me at any cost; I now believe that they're focused on their success *and* happy to help me.
- I believed that being vulnerable would make me a target; I now believe that my vulnerability is a strength *and* creates trust faster.
- I believed that people would stomp on my great ideas just because; I now believe that I am strong enough to protect my ideas *and* hear theirs.
- I believed that people wanted to harm; I now choose to believe that everyone wants to love *and* while not everyone behaves well, believing in this potential makes me more effective and happier.

It was my choice to shift. It didn't happen all at once; to be honest, I am still learning to tell the difference between dangerous situations and those that only appear so. A few experiences got me to this point, and, when I falter, I reflect on them. I'll share just one.

Letting myself be seen

A few years ago, we held a Centered Leadership mastery program in a snowy English town called Hurley. I knew few of the participants and, as usual, had double-booked my time. Neither faculty nor full participant, I felt excluded. Let's go there now.

As the workshop progresses, I find many of the sessions difficult. The next day, a facilitator pushes us to take ownership of our lives, and that's when my rage explodes. I work myself up into a fury. We then move to an exercise in which we use art to recognize our inner voices. In a black mood, I grab paper with ferocity, pushing others aside; I march across the cavernous room to be alone. Deliberately, I rip the colored paper into flames and glue them onto a black background. For an hour, I rip paper loudly. Someone creeps up behind me and hugs me—and I find myself pulling back, uncomfortable with the unexpected kindness. How could he see me? I am visibly invisible. My anger and isolation erupt, literally, into a collage; and, when I step back, I sense a great release. My power is on the paper.

Then I realize, I, too, can be powerful but still be loved.

Always that "but."

Reframe.

I can be powerful *and* loved.

Several years along my Centered Leadership journey, I have reached the point where I can accept myself without judgment.

This is big.

The rest of the program was glorious. I took a walk in the snow along the river with Sarah Wilson—who photographed me leaping in front of a sign that read DANGER at the river's edge. How fitting! She recited poetry as we walked in our Wellies and I imagined her as Ratty from *Wind in the Willows*. Childhood fantasy and friendship relieved me that moody afternoon. Henri de Romrée, Hervé de Barbeyrac, and I took a walk and met a llama—an actual llama. Another moment of wonder and connection. On the last evening, we celebrated. Each participant brought something to share—a story, poem, dance, song. I had arrived empty-handed. Intuition sparked: I made a chain of this group, placing them in height order, each holding hands with the one before and after. At the front of the line, I spiraled the chain in on itself, creating a nautilus. In the center, I was not afraid for the first time in my life to be tightly held in a place without easy exit. Inside this human shelter, I felt only kindness and positive energy.

My transformation from an island to someone with a thousand points of loving connection officially began.

What you'll find in these pages

In this section, we guide you in your own journey to community and connection, starting with trust—and how to strengthen it by focusing on the specific elements of trust we want to deepen. You'll explore what mindsets drive your connectivity, which will prompt reflections on how you build relationships. From there we imagine our desired networks and communities—in service of the vision we most want to create in work and life. By recognizing your networks and communities, you'll experience the positive energy of belonging. The lens through which you view the world is completely up to you.

We then explore one kind of relationship in particular, sponsorship, which deserves a shout-out. I've noticed that some leaders boast about getting to the top on their own and others profess that everyone helped them. In reality, most of us owe a debt of gratitude to sponsors. And the learning never ends. Even CEOs need sponsors.

Playwrights, poets, lounge lizards, and rock musicians have long proclaimed that love conquers all; all you need is love. There must be a reason we humans continue to reinvent those messages. Think about it. Leaders who tap into the greatest human strength of all—to love and be loved—are far and away more effective than those who don't. Everyone can be in that glow. Just turn to the person next to you and see for yourself.

13

FORGING TRUST

In which you'll learn the four elements of trust and where you stand on each, all with the goal to choose actions that inspire greater trust in yourself and in others

At work, we're surrounded by dozens if not hundreds of people. Yet until we build trust-based relationships, we can still feel very much alone. As you think back across the years, who have those trusted connections been for you? How many of them are still active? Who are you developing and supporting? And who are your peers—how are you forging greater connections with them?

Johanne asks us to think back to one person who helped us. Perhaps he or she helped with an opportunity. Possibly that person picked us up when we were down or coached us in a new role. Maybe this person changed our life. Think back and think broadly—beyond the occasional teacher or mentor.

Who helped me?

Who was this person and what do you think they saw in you?

_____

_____

_____

_____

(continued)

(continued)

How did they help you? (What did they do /not do and what was the impact on you?)

_____

_____

_____

_____

How did you cultivate that relationship (at the start, ongoing)? What did you do, ask for, or give?

_____

_____

_____

_____

When I was an associate at McKinsey, I was in awe of the senior partners and never believed I would ever be worthy of their support (just like I thought sixth-graders were such big kids when I was in kindergarten). But when I used this exercise to reflect on my early years at McKinsey, I counted six senior partners who helped me grow (and grow up). Sure, I worked hard to deliver; sure, I stood by those partners, warts and all; and sure, I shared my ideas to help them succeed. In turn, they pushed me, kicking and screaming, through many doors to opportunity. They taught me how to structure problems, how to achieve impact, and how to handle myself in difficult situations—all critical skills. They accepted me for who I was; they behaved with transparency; and they were good for their word. Each one fought for me and stopped me from grabbing defeat from the jaws of success. Back then, I didn't realize that these partners were sponsors. That is, not until they queued up to a pay phone in Germany one Saturday afternoon. One by one, they congratulated me on becoming a senior partner. Sponsors—what a fabulous concept!

You have them around you, too. Like me, you may not realize it. But before you can begin to believe that powerful people are on your side, rooting for you, we'll work on the first and most important ingredient in any key relationship: trust.

Four elements of trust

People grant you trust because of what you say or do, not what you feel or think or even what you intend. Johanne reminds me, "We judge others on their behaviors but we judge ourselves on our intentions," which can lead to a trust breakdown. Trust in others (and their trust in us) depends on four elements: reliability, congruence, acceptance, and openness.

Think about someone you don't trust at all. That jerk! He breaks promises, doesn't deliver, and cannot be relied on in a pinch; even if he means well, it doesn't count. He has let you down. That's a failure of *reliability*—an element of trust. Many organizations implicitly place it above all other virtues. Of course, we all want—and intend—to be reliable, and we give our word. Too often. Here's where I fall down. My husband goes nuts when I'm late. I *want* to be on time, but invariably a last-minute conversation, e-mail, or trip to the ladies' gets in the way. I can't stand being unreliable in David's eyes—and yet I'm late! I love team problem-solving sessions; and, when invited, I always say yes. But reality stung when a beloved team handed me the end-of-project cartoon with a bubble over my caricature's head that read, "I'll be there just as soon as I finish meeting with the Pope and Queen of England." Is that really me? Well, not the part about the Pope and Queen.

Reliability has nothing to do with intentions. Johanne argues that the best test of a person's reliability is to what extent they overcommit. It's all too easy to miss the step of translating that commitment into a promise. If that is you—and it's absolutely me—clarify expectations and formalize your promise (or request), with clear conditions for satisfaction, before agreeing to commit.

The next element of trust is *congruence*—whether what you say is on track with what you believe and do. This is living in line with your values—or "walking your talk." Do you find yourself gossiping about people you don't trust: "He is two-faced," or "She's manipulative," or "He is political," or "You never know where you stand with her"? I get mad at myself when I act without congruence, but I do. Johanne reasons that conflicting values may be the cause. For example, I value hard work and high performance, but I also care about my team's well-being. There have been times when I've promised to send my team home but directed everyone to work through the weekend in service of the client. (And I think of myself as a *nice* person!) If you find yourself in this boat, ask: What do I value more in this moment? Are what I say and do aligned? Decide and tell people. Keep it to yourself, and they'll see you as incongruent.

Acceptance (withholding judgment) is third. We all want to be accepted. Who loves getting misunderstood, criticized, blamed, or worse? So, following the Golden Rule, we never criticize or diminish others by a word or gesture, right? Hmm. An eye roll, glance at a watch, inappropriate joke, even the smallest wink sends a judgment that we find the recipient inadequate. How often do we send these signals without realizing it? I have done everything on this list, unintentionally.

Human beings judge. Our brains jump to judgment to save time and focus. Acceptance means being able to suspend judgment because I know that others are "just like me"—doing the best they can. It doesn't mean excusing bad behavior. We can accept others and still not tolerate inappropriate behavior.

Openness is the final element. We want to be open, but stuff gets in the way. For example, we want to be transparent but withhold confidential information. I think of myself as honest and straightforward but am painfully aware of when I hide bad news to protect someone. We're more believable when we're open about our thoughts and feelings. Even when we deliver difficult news, people appreciate receiving it. Knowing the facts reduces anxiety. It doesn't mean that you must tell the intimate details—or any details—of your personal life. Think of openness as sharing what lies underneath your "iceberg" when making a tough call or stating your convictions—what you think and feel. Reveal your intention, and others will understand why you made that decision.

Stepping back, this trust equation gets more interesting—and challenging—as we each weight the elements differently. Let's say you care most about congruence but your colleagues care more about reliability. Though you believe Superman couldn't meet those deadlines, they expect you to, because you promised that you would. In turn, you evaluate them on alignment of their words, actions, and values, but they don't see it as black-and-white. Do you see the disconnect? It's a good idea to understand what others value if you want to inspire their trust. At a minimum, that will lead to greater understanding. And in combination, reliability, congruence, acceptance, and openness foster meaningful relationships. Strengthen one and inspire greater trust.

What's your baseline? Johanne uses this exercise to build self-awareness of what we implicitly value and believe. Where do you see the greatest differences between your behavior at work and home (proxy for everything outside of work)? What surprises you? What would you like to learn more about?

By the way, this exercise is not about achieving high scores everywhere; each score has a consequence. When two elements are in conflict, in effect we choose one over the other. That said, most of us struggle with acceptance—and self-acceptance. In our zeal for perfection, self-judgment stands in the way of building greater trust. Which elements would you like to deepen? What are the consequences of that for you?

My trust self-assessment

Rate yourself on a scale of 1 (lowest) to 7 (highest) in terms of how consistently others would see you practice these behaviors.

Reliability ratings: Do what you say you will do; keep promises; translate your commitments into promises and do not make ones you cannot keep; meet deadlines; be on time; follow up, follow through

☐ Work   ☐ Home   ☐ To myself

Congruence ratings: Talk straight without playing games; be sincere; make the rules clear; walk the talk in line with your values; don't sugar coat; be clear and follow what you value

☐ Work   ☐ Home   ☐ To myself

Acceptance ratings: Suspend judgment and stay curious, do not criticize or blame; do not put down with technical jargon; delineate the person from performance or behaviors

☐ Work   ☐ Home   ☐ To myself

Openness ratings: Clarify expectations; be honest about limitations; be transparent about your thoughts, feelings, needs; declare your intentions before making a tough call; be willing to be seen and receive

☐ Work   ☐ Home   ☐ To myself

Our final trust exercise is designed to help turn your insight into action. Think about an individual at work with whom you would like to build better trust. What are the costs of lack of trust for you—perhaps drained energy or greater stress? What actions are you ready to choose to enhance trust? Hint: You may want to explore your judgment of that person and your underlying beliefs.

My actions to increase trust

Reliability

_____

_____

_____

Congruence

_____

_____

_____

Acceptance

_____

_____

_____

Openness

_____

_____

_____

What have you learned about yourself? What mindset shifts will allow you to integrate these new actions into your behavior?

_____

_____

_____

Here's my example. I had little trust in a senior partner—let's call him John. John was ambitious. The last thing I wanted was a relationship, yet John's support was critical to my upcoming evaluation. So I vowed to work on my acceptance and openness and scheduled a meeting to welcome feedback. That was a hard pill to swallow. John saw no magic in Centered Leadership. With that on the table, I opened up and asked for help. I proved my reliability by bringing opportunities to use Centered Leadership with John's client; he supported me in the evaluation meeting. Our relationship started to improve.

Try your own action experiment. Identify one important relationship and ask what you can do to inspire greater trust. If that person has not been genuine, you can always move on. But you may discover that the person's trust will grow when you take their suggestions to heart.

Starting by trusting yourself, you often build greater trust in others, as June shows us next.

STORY 6

June Trusts Herself and Her Team

In which June Yee Felix, now managing director and global head of health care for Citi Enterprise Payments, builds trust on her teams

June grew up in Pittsburgh, a first-generation Chinese-American. In her family, trust always meant acceptance. She related, "It wasn't so much whether you got the 100. The question was always, 'Did you do your best?' If it was 85, that was fine if you did the best with whatever gifts you were given. That is stamped in my psyche." From an early age, her role in the family was to negotiate conflict between her younger brother (who spoke no Chinese) and her mother (who spoke principally Chinese). In the process, she learned to stand in their shoes by suspending judgment. Because of this strength, her older brother believed that she could do anything. By the age of twelve, June wanted to be a CEO. In 2000, she got her chance:

> Here was an opportunity to be the CEO of a technology turnaround in a sexy space. The board was filled with senior executives from leading firms. I felt I could bring expertise. It seemed doable. The board had spent $60 million with no revenue yet but it had exciting technology with potential to become the new industry standard. I'd have to raise $20 million quickly. We had to negotiate a deal with banks that did not like the company anymore. It was a turnaround; what I did not know was how fragile the management team was.

Without trust, everything fell apart shortly after: "My entire management team quit (except for technical talent) after their stay package was up. I had to rebuild *and* negotiate a deal with the banks to pay us for the patents *and* raise $20 million."

June focused on careful planning because she promised to deliver, and June's promises were sacred: "I learned to always think about *all* the options. My CFO and I had a plan A, B, C, D, and E to raise $20 million! We got the money, built a new management team, and then experienced 9/11. I had to close the company—fire all the people and give the IP back to our investors."

That experience was both exciting and humbling. June had always believed that if you are smart, work really hard, and have great people on your team, you will deliver. This perfect storm disproved the adage. But in reframing her biggest failure, June discovered the gifts of trust. "I'm quite proud, because a lot of people who went through this with me were grateful for the experience and thought I was a good leader. It was the biggest compliment. People felt that I treated them with integrity and respect, that we made tough decisions, and that we did our best." Congruence, acceptance, openness, and reliability in a nutshell.

Creating a trusting environment

An ability to inspire trust fueled several peak experiences for June. For example, she recalls her time in Hong Kong, leading several businesses for JP Morgan Chase. "The opportunity to build a team, grow a business, and really delight customers in creating innovative new services was fantastic. I worked endlessly, had a child, traveled the region, and came back to New York ten times a year, but it wasn't work. It was fun."

Reliability mattered in helping big corporations manage their cash flows and payments business across Asia. June said, "We were working with CFOs on solving that problem in a period of massive expansion. We were creating new solutions that people hadn't seen before and selling it in new ways. We achieved the number-one position in eighteen months against competitors ten times our size. Winning in the market, creating a high-performance team, and serving clients in a unique way was exhilarating!"

Achieving success took trust. June had enough faith in her abilities to gain confidence. "I went from chemical engineering into brand management and I went from brand management into management consulting, because I knew I could go back. If you feel you can go back, you can go forward." Accepting herself, being open, and sustaining congruence with her core values made June a role model. She inspired unprecedented levels of trust by setting an example:

> It's important to walk a day in other people's shoes. When I was an engineer, I had opportunities to be on the manufacturing line, in process engineering, sales, brand management, research, too. So when I called on people to do something, I had some inkling about what it would mean for them. If you understand someone's challenges, you're more credible. If you understand how they're measured and relate what you do to how they're measured, you have a connection.
>
> Then do what you say. Try to be as consistent as possible and, if you say you're going to do something to support them, do that. Try to provide as much transparency as possible—clarify where we're going, why we're going there, where they fit, why what they're doing is important; and give them support, air cover, and the tools to be successful.

When trust breaks down

The opposite of trust triggers June: when others judge without reason. She shared:

> When my competence is questioned, my heart rate starts going faster. My voice gets higher. I feel angry. Ninety percent of the time, I can control it. Well, I blew up in a meeting with my peers and my boss, who started telling me what to do. I thought, *I'm insulted,* and said, "We're talking about things that I know how to do!" I took a deep breath and, luckily, shut up; the rest of the team jumped in. They piled on to save me!

Even more than loyalty, trust helped June battle breast cancer. She recalls: "I'm standing on line at Delta Shuttle security, and my cell phone rings. I pick it up. I get the news, at which point, my brain freezes. I'm hearing but I'm not processing. I call the doctor back to learn, 'It's early stage, but you need to find a surgeon.' And I'm thinking, *Surgeon? I don't even know what I have!* For those of us that like to be in control, this is the worst. You don't know what to do. So I reached out." June's trust led her to family and friends for support. It helped her take an aggressive stance on a robust approach to treatment. Looking back, a healthy June said, "When you are diagnosed, you have this moment where you say, 'Am I happy with my life? Do I need to go to Nepal? Do I need to seek guidance or recalibrate?' I was happy with my family, my friends, what I was doing and life. "

Clearly, trust paid off for June.

14

BUILDING YOUR DESIRED NETWORK

In which you develop a map of your network, explore the mindsets that drove your choices, and create your desired network in service of your vision

Years ago, a CEO client shared this frustration. "It's like the inmates have taken over the asylum. No one listens to me!" he proclaimed. As I reflect, I see many people who take our Centered Leadership vision forward. So why, like this frustrated CEO, do I also see people as standing in my way? The fact is, the more senior you are, the more important others are to your success.

Whether the people around you are inspirations or insane, allies or obstacles, they matter. Like it or not, networks play a big role in most personal and professional outcomes. Who is in yours? Take some time to list the people you work with and identify those who matter, in light of what you most want to create through your leadership. You may know hundreds of people, but name the ones who count. Whether you have a positive, negative, or nonexistent relationship, put that person on the list.

My list of people

Category	Names / initials
Crucial to accessing resources: info, connection to key stakeholders	
Crucial to my development: coaching, feedback, evaluation	
Crucial for opportunities: creating opportunities or obstacles	
Crucial to my success: primary influencer, higher in hierarchy	
Crucial to my reach: external connections in industry, with stakeholders	
Crucial to my happiness: people whose support matters	

The categories are simply there to help you brainstorm. If someone fits in multiple places, just place them in one. When you have twenty-plus names, you're ready to draw.

Find a large sheet of white paper (bigger than 8 x 10—try drawing paper) along with a set of colored markers. First, we'll walk you through all the instructions and, when you're done mapping, we'll help you explore it.

Place your people

The first step is strategic. Place the words "my vision" in a small oval in the center of your page. Then, using the entire paper, choose where to put each name based on how they relate to your vision and to each other. Avoid naming groups (e.g., the marketing department); take time to place each individual.

Draw a triangle around each name, using different colors to segment people visually. For example, you might use one color for people in your function or department; another color for other people in your company; a third color for business contacts outside the company; and a fourth for your family and friends. That's just one scheme. Choose whatever works for you.

Characterize each relationship

Trust is the first of three characteristics for you to denote. You have three choices in drawing a line between each person and your vision:

- For existing relationships, *thickness of the line* shows the degree of trust you grant. A thicker line represents deeper trust.
- For new, undeveloped, or nonexisting relationships, a *dotted line* shows potential.
- For broken or damaged relationships, a big *X on the line* shouts it out.

Now mark the *reciprocity* in each relationship. Add *a little arrow* pointing toward the other person at the end of the trust line to show that you give or initiate help to that person. Add the little arrow toward you at the end of the trust line if you receive or get help from that person. An arrow on both ends depicts reciprocity.

Next characterize the *energy* in each relationship. Pick contrasting colors that you have not yet used to mark if that relationship boosts your energy or drains it. I usually put a *zigzag line* next to the trust line—in green to show energy-boosting relationships and in red to show energy-draining relationships, so I can easily remember which is which.

Identify your sponsors and potential sponsors

Finally, put a big dot in the triangles for people who are your sponsors so that you can see them easily. Put a lighter-colored dot in the triangles for people who may be potential sponsors. We'll delve more into sponsorship in chapter 12, but for now, consider the senior leaders who stick their necks out to help you develop and advance. If you don't have a sponsor, no worries. In this exercise, you'll explore relationships you've built and spot relationships you'd like to form or strengthen.

What is driving your network?

Voilà! You've drawn your network map—a useful tool for exploring your underlying patterns, mindsets, and outcomes, and to help you plan strategically. If you're doing this exercise with others, we encourage you to share and discuss your maps (without judgment). Look for similarities and differences using Johanne's exercise below to guide you. And if you're on your own, ask someone to discuss your network map with you.

Getting curious about my network

Patterns: What do you see? Any surprises? What do you notice about the characteristics of the support relationships you most value? Least value? And what do you do (and not do) to build support relationships? What feels natural? What makes you uncomfortable?

_____

_____

_____

_____

_____

_____

Mindsets: What are you learning in terms of including how you build your network? What are you thinking and feeling when it comes to seeking development support and sponsorship? What do you need more of? What stands in your way of making that happen?

_____

_____

_____

_____

_____

_____

Outcomes: How are these mindsets serving you? Not serving you? How would your approach be different if anything were possible?

_____

_____

_____

_____

_____

_____

My first map showed a broad network (all over the page) with mostly skinny lines, more negative than positive energy, but lots of reciprocity and giving. My sponsor relationships were long defunct. Digging in, I realized:

- I believed relationships were after the real work.
- New relationships were draining (there's that negative intent assumption).

- My network was global, diverse, helter-skelter, and ad hoc.
- My map was not aligned with my vision for Centered Leadership.
- The people I most needed to collaborate with were not on my map.

Get curious about your network as you explore what drove you to build it.

With fresh colors and fresh intention, now you get a chance to revise your map. Place new names of people you *want* to connect with (you might choose a different color to help you spot those people), and cross out people who are not helping you carry out your vision. If you like, be bold and take a fresh sheet of paper to draw your desired network from scratch, using Jo's questions to guide your reflection:

My desired network map

What new people belong in my network? Which existing relationships should I rekindle or focus on?

_____

_____

_____

_____

Who should I remove (because they are not supportive or actively helping me carry out my vision)?

_____

_____

_____

_____

How can I make better use of trust to strengthen relationships?

_____

_____

_____

_____

_____

_____

Which valued relationships can I transition from energy draining to energy boosting? How?

_____

_____

_____

_____

_____

Who are the sponsors and potential sponsors I'd like to cultivate? And who will I sponsor in turn?

_____

_____

_____

_____

_____

I added in several people able to extend Centered Leadership in and outside the firm. I also added several people who would be energy boosting and let go of others no longer germane to my emerging vision.

The beauty is that you can redraw your map periodically and find new insights—for example, when you change jobs. Be thoughtful about the people you place on your desired network map and who you leave out. Consider whose trust you want to strengthen and how you can be generous in your giving. Look for opportunities to convert inactive relationships to ones that provide positive energy. Look for new sponsors and who you want to sponsor.

Planning next steps is the best part—and if you have the ear of others, talk over your plans together.

My network plan

Who is my focus to strengthen my desired network in light of my vision?

Name _____

What requests will I make _____

_____

What promises will I make _____

_____

Deadline _____

Name _____

What requests will I make _____

_____

What promises will I make _____

_____

Deadline _____

Name _____

What requests will I make _____

_____

What promises will I make _____

_____

Deadline _____

Be sure to carve out time on your calendar for relationship building: an hour a week minimum. As I learned, connecting isn't something to put off until your "real" work is done. Making those connections stronger is real work to carry out your vision! So put down your colored markers, make a plan, and connect. A master community builder is up next to inspire us.

STORY 7

Monique Builds a Community

In which Monique Leroux, chair of the board, president and CEO of Desjardins Group, defines a network and a community, and how she built both in service of her business

Elected to her second four-year term heading up Desjardins Group, Monique Leroux had already spent most of a lifetime building networks—and community. When Johanne connected us, I was delighted to meet the master connector.

Defining terms

Monique goes by the adage that business comes down to people. She related, "What was very important in what I was able to achieve was always the connection—learning, working, and doing things with people. Sometimes you don't see the connection to community, but it's there." So we asked Monique to define network versus community:

> A *network* is a list of people you know and people who know you. That's the basis to start a community. A *community* is when you bring life to a network. It is much more about support and interactions. You can have a great network and do nothing with it. But if you have a real community around you, it's because you're able to activate the relationship between all the people in your network.

Monique learned about relationships with Ernst & Young in Canada. Her first professional network turned out to be the basis for a lifelong community. She said, "You cannot predict what will happen with the community you build. One connection will bring you to somebody else and to another level of responsibilities."

Using community to lead

Network and community activities are essential to Monique's leadership. She sees her role as finding a way to ignite and connect people, mobilize them, help them feel confident to act. Monique takes this to heart in her organization's transformation. For sure, the transformation process is about strategy and execution of initiatives, with action plans and timetables and all the "hard" meetings and reports. But value is achieved through connectivity: "We want to be better in implementing our strategic initiatives. But at the end of the day, it is about connecting people to take the lead to achieve that. It's creating the positive energy within the organization and the various 'communities' of Desjardins for the benefit of our members and clients." She leads 45,000 employees, so the best way to engage the organization and its external community (with over five million members in the group) is by inspiring every one of the vice presidents, general managers, and management committee members in addition to 5,000 elected officers involved in local *caisses*. Monique remains true to Desjardins' original 1900 philosophy: contribute to the well-being of individuals and communities.

> My role is to make sure that I can pass this flame to other Desjardins leaders so that they will do it with the people around them. Engaging their hearts and spreading the dream is a big part of my role. Some people might say it's communication. Really, it is much more; it's connecting with the community around you. I prefer to think about community rather than the typical communication line within the hierarchy. There is a partnership notion here.

Desjardins' tailored leadership development program is an unprecedented investment for the board and management team. The training focuses on executive leadership—bringing one's whole self to leading the transformation. Monique recalled that it took some encouragement to get her top senior executive team to undergo the training. "Some were not convinced that we had to do it ourselves! The exercise was quite important for me personally, but also for members of the team." Monique believed in it so much that she attended many of the subsequent sessions to personally connect and observe the participants' commitment firsthand:

> Half my time is related to hard tasks in formal meetings to tackle issues of governance, performance, management, strategy, and in meetings with members and clients. The other 50 percent is for informal meetings to share the vision, connect, and get input—being there with people to answer any questions in a very personal way. Sometimes you have to admit that you do things well, and sometimes you have to recognize that we should have done it differently. These informal meetings have a direct connection with the success of our projects and strategic initiatives. They appear to be unrelated, but they are not.

Monique role models the internal/external community relationships Desjardins must strengthen:

> If I go to visit elected officers, employees, or managers, let's say in Quebec City, we will start talking about issues internally, but we will structure the activity with members and clients. One of our challenges is to better serve them; I hope that employees and elected officers will replicate this approach.

Desjardins' transformation depends on leveraging a network effect. Monique reflected, "I can do a certain number of meetings and connections, but the real success will come if there is engagement across the organization." In addition, Monique started a community outside the walls of Desjardins, even outside the borders of Canada—inviting the CEOs of cooperative organizations around the world to come together as part of the Quebec International Summit of Cooperatives (*le Sommet international des coopératives*). Monique is excited about this next horizon for the community:

> Some people said, "It's very interesting, but why are you doing that? What are the benefits for Desjardins? What is the business purpose?" The Summit is a "cooperative connecting platform." The leverage that we got within Desjardins is partly an outcome. It helped us facilitate two recent transactions with cooperatives and build new relationships. Something will happen over time if you have a vision and if you are committed to provide "life to the community."

Learning to connect

If Monique is a natural, she started with a keen curiosity about people and organizations. She mused, "I began at Ernst & Young. Some people think auditing is really boring work. But when you are an auditor, you can observe. And when you do, you can learn a lot." Twenty-five-year-old Monique observed a senior partner with the skill to handle any situation and come away with stronger relationships. She also observed a successful entrepreneur building a tremendous global network, enabling creation of an impressive business. Naturally, we wanted to know what the young Monique took away.

For her, it boils down to their profound interest in human beings: "Some people will listen to you but really, they have no interest talking to you. People who are good at building relationships are with you when you are with them. You can feel it in the way they talk to you, in the way they do the conversation." Her mentor—a very successful partner—taught her this lesson. She remembers, "When we were together in his office, he was fully dedicated to my problem or my questions. I'm sure that if he was like that with me, he was like that with clients, partners, and colleagues. That's part of building a community, but that's also part of being a very strong leader." Today, Monique tries to do the same, concentrating with discipline to avoid the distraction of other priorities.

Keeping the flame going

What does it take to tend the flame of community? Monique was not sure—and confided that she grapples with this issue: It takes significant dedication. What she does is set priorities—looking at the calendar weekly to make sure she is balancing her attention. She told us, "I'm not sure that my answer is as profound as you would like, but I'm trying to make sure that my time is allocated in line with our strategic objectives and with the right people. I make sure to consider the soft side—continue to build the relationships, the communities, and the connections to people required to achieve my objectives."

Stepping back, Monique sees connecting—and, in particular, community—as a crucial part of the solution to today's challenges:

> We are living in very difficult times bringing a lot of changes to people and to society. It's a major transformation in the world. In the nineteenth century, there was an Industrial Revolution; maybe there is a connectivity revolution now. My philosophy is that when you are in reasonable health, the rest is opportunity almost all the time. When you start to look at things that way, it helps you get positive energy. And when you start to communicate that, you get the same from others. Being connected to people is very, very important to keep us in balance.

Whether we are introverts or extroverts, we need community. Thanks to Monique, we know what that means.

15

CULTIVATING SPONSORS

In which you'll take steps to strengthen your sponsor relationships and cultivate new ones to accelerate your development and impact

We were taught to find mentors to support our development and then we learned we really needed sponsors. Both are good; but what's the difference? Many people use the term *mentor* to mean sponsor; many sponsors are mentors. There actually is a difference, though, and it's important. Confused yet? We'll shine a light on it.

Great mentors are generally well along in their careers. You find them everywhere in the organization—at the top but also throughout the hierarchy. They truly understand the place and have a perspective worth knowing. For me, the best mentor of all time is Yoda from *Star Wars*; he is elderly, diminutive, green, and has huge ears—but boy is he smart. Yoda challenges Luke to develop. His remarkable wisdom strikes a deep chord in all of us. It's easy to find someone who can recite Yoda's advice (with his accent): "No! Try not. Do, or do not. There is no try."

Who wouldn't benefit from this advice in a new situation? Mentors may understand your situation, but even if they don't, you value them. That's because insights from *their* work and *their* life experience bring you value. In contrast, sponsors are all about *you*. They are "all in" when it comes to your career and life. They're willing to take a risk on you because they've seen you perform and believe you have what it takes; you've already helped them. Maybe the best way to truly explain the difference between mentorship and sponsorship is to share a story. It's a bit of a detour, but hang in to find your sponsor's essential role.

Portrait of a sponsor

A few years ago, we were in Israel. Jetta was about to turn fourteen, which happens to be the minimum age to skydive in Israel. Naturally, she wanted to go, and David was keen. "Joanna," David says, "join us!" I stare in disbelief, swallow my expletives, and reply, "No thanks. I'll be on the ground praying as I *watch* my baby fall out of the sky."

Skydiving, I learn, involves much fanfare. First Jetta chooses a brightly colored astronaut jumpsuit. People (including me) photograph her getting attired. Then she lines up with the others and, in single file, they march to the plane. I notice that this plane is different. It has a large black hole in its side, which is the doorway. She enters, sits on the floor, doors close, and the plane takes off.

Put yourself in her place. Here is what happens when the plane reaches planned altitude. Your turn comes. You stand up and walk to the doorway. Then your arms involuntarily grab hold of the sides in terror. You think, *Am I crazy? Who wants to jump out of a plane at twelve thousand feet?* You are paralyzed. Holding on for dear life. Naturally, when this happens to you, someone needs to help. Know what he does?

Push you out of the plane?

Right!

And that person is . . . a sponsor!

You bet!

He offers an exciting opportunity for you to leave your comfort zone behind and he pushes you through the doorway to that opportunity (disregarding your fears). He is on the ground ready to pick you up and dust you off, sharing in your learning adventure. He tells everyone about your achievement, with evidence to show.

By the way, I watch Jetta descend. She is thrilled by the jump and wants to go again. As it turns out, her "sponsor" was clipped to her and made sure she left the plane as planned!

A lot of people adore skydiving, but what limits many of us at work can feel as frightening as jumping out of an airplane. A great sponsor goes beyond creating opportunity—he or she helps us seize it.

Tough love: It's up to you

So how do you find a sponsor? Walking up to somebody you admire and asking, "Will you be my sponsor?" is not the way. Sponsors *choose you*—but you cultivate the relationship. They choose you because you performed, helped them succeed. If you were to proclaim, "Great work doesn't always get noticed—so isn't this a crap shoot?" you would be spot on. Let's assume great work and figure out how to get noticed. I've asked sponsors what gets their attention; here are six ideas:

- **Excitement creator:** Use the occasion of a success—not to boast, but to share results. I used this technique with a senior partner. Each time he missed a meeting (a regular occurrence), I left him a detailed voice mail relating the high points. He was appreciative and shared those voice mails to press for my election, successfully.
- **Counsel seeker:** Ask someone if you can buy them a cup of coffee in return for advice on an issue. The person makes the time because he is pleased to be asked. Over time, this relationship may build as you find ways to work together. John Donahoe of eBay uses this technique time and again.
- **Great questioner:** Ask the senior person about a specific issue you're working on, via e-mail, an impromptu meeting, a quick phone call—whatever she prefers. Sheryl Sandberg uses this idea to form a great connection, efficiently.
- **Unsolicited helper:** Make a practice of sending helpful articles or ideas. I was preparing a proposal and one day, a new consultant left me a relevant book. When I read the book, I felt grateful and assigned him to my team. Thanks, Michael Silber!
- **Steadfast helper:** Sometimes we get the chance to work directly with a senior person. Though it can be a double-edged sword, take it. As long as you perform (and you will), this is a great opportunity to get to know that person.

- **Upward coach:** This approach requires more skill but has more upside. Point out what works well first, suspend judgment, and be kind. Leaders rarely get honest feedback and know even less about what's happening on the front line.

Cultivating effective discussions

Potential sponsors exist, and we can gain tremendous value from discussions with them. However, not all sponsors are the same. From her research on archetypes, Carole Kammen helped us understand their differing natures, and worked with us to develop this list:

- **The Visionary:** Dreams boldly and helps you see into the future; sparks creativity and innovation—but not interested in the details.
- **The Sage:** Offers wisdom, teaching, and experience; links the work with deeper purpose and helps you get the distance to see it—but cool and distant, too.
- **The Devil's Advocate:** Challenges and shifts your perspective; pushes your boundaries of thought; provides you with a reality check—but always challenging.
- **The Relentless Coach:** Pushes you to develop new skills; provides tough love, won't give up on you—but exhausts you without accepting your limit.
- **The Hero:** Takes on significant personal risk to open doors, clear obstacles, and fight for you; saves you in a tough situation—but demands personal closeness.
- **The Godfather:** Goes to the mat for you, uses his considerable power on your behalf, and is loyal—but demands extreme loyalty forever.
- **The Caregiver:** Nurtures, provides reassurance, and protects you in "the system"; has a sympathetic ear—but won't push you when you need it.
- **The Connector/Navigator:** Links you with people, ideas, and opportunities; helps you navigate—but expects you to close the loop on your own.

You'll see that each archetype is distinctive, with strengths but also limitations. Every individual has a primary archetype, but may not be aware of it. Though we can shape-shift, we revert to our primary behaviors under stress or pressure. For years I thought I was a care-giver when in reality I was a relentless coach, feared by many! With awareness, I began explicitly to change shape to provide other kinds of support. By asking for what you need or want, you can influence how your sponsor shows up.

Which archetype best describes the potential sponsor who can help you carry out your vision? Think deeply about him or her, using Johanne's exercise below.

Getting to know my potential sponsor

My sponsor's primary archetype:

_____

Top 3 strengths: What are the best things about that archetype? What kinds of problems or situations are handled best by that archetype?

_____

_____

_____

Top 3 limitations: What constrains this archetype in helping to grow others? Are there personalities or situations it is not well equipped to sponsor?

_____

_____

_____

Building a relationship: What is the best way to forge a relationship with that archetype? What would you do (not do) and say (not say) to establish trust?

_____

_____

_____

We encourage you to do this exercise with colleagues and friends, so that you can exchange views and brainstorm how to build trust with the sponsor you're cultivating. If you're on your own, ask for ideas from people who know your potential sponsor.

We suggest investing in preparation for your upcoming sponsor meeting. It will help you stay grounded in the discussion (avoiding potential hijacks) and strengthen your presence; your sponsor will receive you with greater respect. These discussions tend to be infrequently held and brief, so preparing also ensures you use the time well.

Sponsor meeting preparation

1.   *I am feeling . . .*

_____

_____

For example, "I am feeling excited, but also nervous, because I have been waiting a long time for this meeting."

2.   *I want to have this discussion because . . .*

_____

_____

For example, "I want to have this discussion because X has ability to direct resources to help me but he does not really understand what we're working on and so I need to bring him up to date."

3.   *What I most want for—and from—myself in this discussion is . . .*

_____

_____

For example, "What I most want for myself is to open the door to X's support. What I most want from myself is to withhold judgment and see him with compassion to understand his view on my initiative."

Johanne encourages you to use a Check-In to foster trust. Prepare two or three questions to open up the discussion. You go first and then ask your sponsor to respond to the same questions. Here is an option:

- *Today I am feeling . . .*
- *My goal for this discussion is to . . .*
- *What I most need from you today is . . .*

The Check-In will help you learn if your sponsor is distracted or hurried, what she wants from this discussion, and what she needs or expects from you. Follow up on the conversation with a thank-you e-mail summarizing next steps. Whenever you can, offer support to reduce the burdens of follow-ups.

And don't forget to let your sponsor know how you're doing. The best gift you can give your sponsor is your success.

STORY 8

John's Sponsors Make the Difference

In which John Donahoe, president and CEO of eBay, Inc., shares his approach to cultivating the mentors and sponsors who helped him grow into a leader

Anyone who meets John Donahoe is impressed with his natural warmth and kindness; a (very) tall man, he is in no way intimidating! As we perched on high director's chairs for our interview, in front of a stunning Golden Gate Bridge view, I was riveted by John's openness and honesty; he is the perfect teacher on cultivating sponsors.

A pattern of trust building

John sought out support early on: "I've been blessed by having a variety of sponsors and mentors throughout my career. They don't just magically appear, though. You have to seek them out and then cultivate them in an authentic way." His first mentor after college was Tom Tierney, his boss at Bain. John recalls, "I thought he walked on water. I thought he was god reincarnated." Tom's first lesson for John was to develop several relationships:

> He told me, "John, you have to change your paradigm. Your definition of mentor was this swami-like Buddha figure who could endow you with the wisdom of life, liberty, and happiness. At times, it was intimidating." No one person had all the wisdom I was searching for. You need to learn a little from a lot of different people.

Tom invested early in John's development. John recalled, "He took an interest and spent time with me as a young up-and-comer. There was encouragement but he never glossed over the development message to just say, 'You're wonderful.'"

John's leadership potential gave Tom the confidence to become his sponsor. Indeed, Tom recruited John back to Bain after business school. Down the road, when Tom was elected head of the firm, he appointed John (then a first-year partner) to head the San Francisco office. John recalled, "I followed in Tom's footsteps. When Tom completed his term as managing director of the firm, I was elected next." The two men remain close to this day; Tom serves as eBay's lead independent director and continues to coach John.

The scary part

At Bain, John had led from within, answering only to the partners. But eBay's public company environment required a more top-down leadership. John reflected, "As a leader, you set the tone. You have to make difficult decisions, which by their very nature can distance you from your team. Within my first few months at eBay, I made the difficult, but necessary, decision to reduce ten percent of our workforce. That was hard. You have to learn to harden your heart a little bit." Harder still was leading eBay's turnaround, which was being followed closely by the media:

> In 2008, I remember hearing that an eBay seller had threatened one of our employees by posting a negative video about the company on YouTube. So I went to YouTube, searched for "eBay" and the first four pages of eBay results were all hate videos about me. It was absolutely sobering. The first video compared me to Hitler, and in an edited scene from the movie, *Schindler's List*, superimposed my name on a German guard's forehead and "eBay Sellers" on a Jewish prisoner the guard was shooting. The CEO "textbook" says you should have thick skin. But that really hurt.

John's word for that period? "Brutal." He reminisced: "I remember telling my oldest son that I thought I might have made a mistake joining eBay. He replied, 'Do you still believe in the things you believed about eBay when you joined?' 'Yes,' I said, 'I believe in a core purpose.' And he said, 'I thought you were in charge. Why don't you do something about it?' His words were like a necessary slap across the face. He held up a mirror for me. Here I was casting myself as the victim and letting circumstances beyond my control shape my internal personal narrative. I shifted to be the resolute leader I needed to be."

Like most of us, John has an internal critic who constantly presses him to do better, wearing him down. John confided, "Like most people, I want to be liked. If I have an interaction which I feel doesn't go well, my internal voice starts up. I've since learned to identify and dismiss it before it becomes debilitating. I tell myself: *There's that negative voice. That's all it is.* It's important to recognize your own patterns so you don't fall into a place where you're less effective." I was knocked for a loop. John appears so confident. "I can pull off the confident facade. I'm trained to have it," he told me. "We're all alike in some ways. It can be liberating to remember that the person across from you feels as insecure as you feel at times." Clearly, trusted connection—with mentors, sponsors—builds confidence.

Even CEOs need support

It can be intimidating to ask a leader for support, especially when you're a leader yourself. I was excited to learn what John did when he became eBay's CEO:

> I had heard John Chambers speak, but I'd never met him one-on-one. After I became CEO, we got together, and he said to me, "John, it's great to meet you. Here's the deal. I'll give you an hour of my time each quarter to discuss your agenda—whatever you want. The executives at HP did the same thing for me on the condition that I return the favor to a new CEO down the road.

That same condition holds for you. Being CEO is a lonely job. It only gets lonelier the longer you're in it and the more successful you get."

He continued, "So share what's on your mind. Bring me your worst problems—your worst nightmares. I promise they will never leave this room. You can feel safe, and I'll listen. Odds are, I'll throw out ten ideas. Some may be good or even great, but I won't know which ones. It's your job to figure that out! You've now got fifty-seven minutes."

In that first conversation, John Donahoe confided that he was scared about the pending layoff; he worried about damaging the culture and that people would hate him. John Chambers empathized and counseled, helping the younger John gain conviction.

How John wins mentors and sponsors

John still reaches out to other CEOs today. He advises, "Start with your peers. Go to the people you think you can learn from, who you see doing something well. If you focus on each person's strength and appreciate that, you'll learn faster and give back through your appreciation." He advises starting with a simple offer. John mused, "Some of the most powerful sentences you can say to anyone are, 'Can I get a little advice? Can I pick your brain? Would you be willing to have a cup of coffee with me a couple times a year and share your thoughts?' I've got a dozen CEOs who I've said that to and who I learn an enormous amount from. I haven't had anyone say no yet. Then at the meeting, I respect their time. I don't show up with baloney, but real issues on my mind."

I was excited to apply this insight, but felt clumsy. John counseled me how to do it: "Say, 'Here's what I'm trying to accomplish. Here's where I'm really struggling.' Showing vulnerability is often a great way to start a conversation. It's not a matter of showing off how wonderful you are but a way of asking the other person for experience or insight in dealing with your issue." John explained that his approach shows you have a real problem and that you're open. A good conversation can open the door to another down the road. John underscored, "But pay it forward."

Why sponsors do what they do

I asked John why he takes time out of his busy day to support others. He returned with his own question, "When one of your most talented people comes to you and asks for some help, how do you feel? Even if you're really busy, it's human nature to want to say 'yes.' I don't care how busy I am, helping is a fulfilling and rewarding thing. It keeps you centered!"

I could not agree more.

PART FIVE

ENGAGING

16

BECOMING A FORCE

In which we step into our presence, and then step outside of our comfort zone, taking risks and actions; and what you'll find in this section

I thought of myself as having presence until a client gave me pause. As you know, pausing can be a good thing. At dinner, the human resources head of a global company spilled, "The feedback I got from a senior male executive about you was very odd." My heart sank. She went on. "He said that when he walked into the room, you were standing off to the side and not looking like much—a small, older woman—unassuming." Just what I had feared—*people don't see me as powerful*. My thoughts wandered somewhere when I caught these words, ". . . but the minute you opened the session, you turned into a force. He didn't know what hit him!"

So aligning intention, attention, and emotion does make a difference! Whenever I forget to align, I recall my own incredible "before and after" picture. And I keep in mind that my "after" photo only happened in 2012, once I said "no" and "yes."

Before/after? No/yes? If none of this makes much sense to you, let me catch you up quickly so that it will.

Reaching alignment

We've been talking about intention since the early pages of *Centered Leadership*. What do you want to bring forth more fully in your leadership? What do you hope for in this difficult conversation? These are all examples of setting intention—consciously.

With Johanne's encouragement back in 2009, at the start of every day I woke up with the question: *What do I really want for—and from—myself today?* before turning to the needs of others. The outcome of that practice was mind-boggling. My impending workshop turned into an exciting opportunity. I began to connect more deeply. I began to look and feel stronger. Even as the day ran away from me, I came back to my intention. Like a glass of freshly squeezed orange juice, setting intention boosted my energy. It was my first sustaining practice, helping me focus my attention, which comes next.

Then I tried these questions: *Where am I choosing to place my attention? Does it match my intention?* Attention is not about time so much as where you choose to focus. How many times have I been with my family but sneaking peeks at my BlackBerry? It clearly is an addiction! The same happens in tedious meetings, when I travel miles away in my thoughts. And, yes, I've sneaked a chance to do e-mail while on a conference call, even checking a shopping site and the news. Sometimes I go through the motions. That's spending time but not attention.

When intention and attention are aligned, you're present in the moment. You feel calm, curious, connected, compassionate. You feel alert and nimble. People see you being there for them. And when you bring emotion into the picture, now you're cooking with gas. What explicit feeling are you choosing to convey? Excitement? Calm? Confidence? Warmth? The best of intention and the greatest presence in the moment will convey even more to others when you add in the right emotion. This can take a while. It always takes practice.

Back to the story.

The "before/yes" picture

The year 2009 marked a milestone. I aspired to shift my focus from traditional client work in industries I knew well to a new program/new work: building Centered Leadership into a global program for clients. I loved this idea so much that I called the chair of our partner evaluation committee for his support. He asked how long it would take to prove this innovative platform. Naively, I said eighteen months. He agreed, and we had a deal.

With more experience, I would have known that eighteen months pass by before you know it. My time was up, and Centered Leadership was hardly out of the gate; I was back in conversation but from a very different position. That was when I began to see myself as the Little Red Hen from the children's story—you know, the plucky hen that plants her seeds, grows her wheat, harvests it, grinds it into flour, etc. There I was, trying to grow wheat and surrounded by hungry animals demanding bread. I was afraid to share what little I had. "You don't share all that well," David reflected. Right-e-o. Ouch.

At evaluation time, things weren't working out so well. Several colleagues counseled me to return to my old program. Lucky me, David is a guy who loves adventure. His view, I distinctly remember, was that given my tenure, it wasn't really a risk at all. "Go ahead," David advised. "If you don't try now, when will you?" He then pointed out that I would probably fail, grinned, and exclaimed, "Just do it!"

I kept on planting wheat and also working as hard as I could to bring in traditional client work. If this sounds like two jobs, it was. In effect, I never said no; I said yes and yes to everything—and that was exhausting! I rushed here and there like a chicken without its head. My new Centered Leadership team did not get much support. We grew too slowly for a startup. I was risk averse and people wondered what I stood for. Naturally, my performance suffered even though I was working harder than ever.

The year 2012 was my turning point. Confused and afraid of getting fired, I was overextended to the breaking point. Wise old David told me to cut it out, but I had stopped listening to him—or to anyone, for that matter. I had convinced myself that chaotic transitions were normal, even five years of them. In this state of turmoil, I participated in a Centered Leadership program for rising senior executives, and the voices inside me rose up to have their say.

This is the part where we go off-road in a jeep without brakes, so feel free to skip ahead if that makes you nervous.

Johanne invited performing artist and coach Anne Gottlieb to help us communicate intention with emotion through an evening of poems and stories. So far, so good. Anne gave me a poem to read about a slave, and I actually *felt* as though I were that woman—an angry, determined, fierce, proud fighter who persevered despite her losing odds. I sat down in shock.

The next morning, I met with Anne and she asked to speak to the voices in me. My internal critic immediately piped up and went on a rant, confiding, "Thanks for asking—I'm exhausted from watching out for Joanna 24/7! She screws up at any moment of any day! It's my job to try and stop her. Is she trying to drive me mad? I'm working so hard. She makes [expletive] mistakes all the time! She's got such potential, too! What am I to do?" Anne asked that voice (actually, me sitting in a different chair) if she needed a vacation. "Vacation? I haven't had a vacation in years!" the critic exclaimed. "Sure, I'd like a vacation! But who's gonna watch Joanna if *I* don't?" Anne promised to do that and then asked me to change seats.

In a new chair, my internal child spoke up. "I want to play but Joanna locks me up and tells me to hush! She is so mean. I want my mother, but she just died. I'm all alone now. . . . " Then she wept tears held inside for months; she felt unloved and unlovable. So Anne did what her instinct told her to do—she hugged that child for a long time and assured that child safety. Sitting in a third seat, I came back to myself, strangely calm. The voices were quiet, and I felt whole. I stepped off the path to burnout and I saw myself and my future with clarity.

My voices have been reasonable since. I named my internal critic Edna (after Edna from *The Incredibles*, because she is small, smart, and sharp). I even bought her some jewelry in gratitude; maybe that's why she quieted down! I named my child self Jody (my childhood name); I no longer hide her away. I've learned to be my own mother, too.

Uncomfortable, yes, but that leg of my journey was a breakthrough. I took ownership and felt a lightness, ready for my future. Just as I reintegrated my multiple voices, I reintegrated my spirit with my emotions, intellect, and body. For a split second, I could hold opposing versions of myself and learn to love them all.

The "after/no" picture

Those moments of integration popped up more regularly as I facilitated or participated in workshops. At one Check-In with Jo and facilitator Alex Kuilman, I felt myself floating above the group. Looking up, I saw Alex staring at me. Later, he said that I seemed to be glowing. "You're allowing yourself to lead through love instead of fear," he told me. "I see you making that shift!" That made me shine even brighter.

So, nine years into my journey, hope emerged triumphant. I started thinking about what a life without extreme struggle would look like, whether negative emotions were a prerequisite to creativity, and whether sitting under the Bodhi tree to watch life pass would be as boring as it sounded. Fittingly, I reached out to another artist and facilitator, Diana Theodores, to share this concern. As a program was about to begin, Diana challenged me to imagine the "empty space" of theater and suggested that I embrace it. So that's what I did.

Let me take you there.

I look into the empty space, see that it is dark, and turn back to our program. Hours pass. On a whim, I return to my empty space to contemplate. Suddenly, up pops the Little Red Hen from the children's story again. I see that she has attached large, colorful feathers to her wings and tail, looking quite silly. Imagine the child's costume headgear of an Indian chief combined with a small Rhode Island Red. I watch the barnyard animals criticize and gossip: *Daring to fly! Who does she think she is? When is she going to get used to the fact that she is a small, silly hen whose job it is to make bread for the rest of us? She's simply ridiculous!* I look up, embarrassed, as if my fellow participants know what's inside my head. My Little Red Hen appears tawdry in her fake getup. Look at how risk-taking turned out for her! I tell myself that flying is for cranes, not hens.

The next day, we're sitting in a circle, about to begin the Meaning visualization exercise. But my brain refuses to take the path to the cottage in the woods. Instead, the Little Red Hen shows up again, still in costume. In my meditative mood, I regard her without judgment. I'm curious as to how she attached the feathers (the miracles of imagination). I watch her fly and note that she is proud and free. I see her differently now. Acting on her dream without allowing other perspectives to slow her down. How clever to use someone else's feathers. How confident! Her colors show the world that she feels fully alive and in love with life. I'm proud to be the Little Red Hen, saying no to my old program without regrets and flying without knowing what lies ahead.

Taking a stand

In *How Remarkable Women Lead*, we wrote about standing up to be counted:

> Engaging is where it all comes together—when you choose to cross an invisible line from being a person to whom things happen to becoming a person who makes things happen. It literally means breaking the bounds that circumscribe your career and your life. Making the commitment to do so is one of the best things you will ever do for yourself.

Everyone—leaders, too—hear internal voices telling them they're not good enough, not clever enough, not brave enough. But other internal voices urge us on. We all can stand to listen to those other voices more, use their encouragement to cross the line.

Crossing from the comfort zone to the learning zone is a bit scary, even for those who love a new challenge. Fear can fuel your passage but beware, go too far too fast and you end up in the terror zone where learning stops. The line differs for each of us. Take my family. David loves to kayak in awful weather, battling the elements. But when the winds kick up, I turn green. I clench the paddle in fear as my daughters zip by on two-foot waves. They are explorers in their little boats, as comfortable as dolphins. Much as David encourages me to learn skills such as "wet exit" (fall in and scramble back into your boat) and "eskimo roll" (stay in your boat but flip upside down and then right yourself), I resist. That's the terror zone in a nutshell—where you refuse to do what is clearly in your best interest. Sometimes, our fears are too strong a match for our reason. Other times, our desire is so strong—our vision carries such great meaning for us—that we gain the courage to move past fear and experience life at its fullest.

What you'll find in these pages

Johanne and I invite you to "cross the invisible line" by practicing with new tools, starting with presence. We'll help you enhance your remarkable presence by aligning intention, attention, and emotion. We'll show you how to use personal stories that engage and inspire. After that, we'll guide you in making your own yes and no decisions with an approach to determine which promises you want to keep. Challenges will be in your way, but shifting from problem solving to solution thinking will help you navigate through. Finally, we'll share a process for soliciting counsel from colleagues in a way that invites learning. Altogether, this section is full of practical tools for leaving your comfort zone, embracing your next opportunity, gaining courage, accepting risk, and taking action. We're headed into the learning zone, where life is challenging *and* exhilarating.

You may even surprise yourself with what you find there.

17

BUILDING PRESENCE AS A STORYTELLER

In which you'll gain the tools to be fully present; craft a compelling story to align, engage, and mobilize others; and bring your story to life

I've always been an avid listener, so collecting the professional and personal stories of 160 men and women leaders globally has been a treat. Perhaps you believe that stories have little place at work. Think again. Stories are integral to work—and to Centered Leadership. Since the beginning of time, they have captivated our imagination and ignited our learning in a shared experience. If we want to lead, stories are one of the most powerful tools to mobilize others to follow. Consider the following scenarios:

- You get great feedback on your performance, but there's always that line about increasing your presence. Whatever do they mean by that?
- You lead your team in a difficult discussion about performance, but your mind wanders. Why isn't the team getting your message?
- You're at a crisis meeting, but you're afraid to speak up. What's the best way to be heard and listened to?
- On conference calls with your global team, a simultaneous meeting is happening online. How do you capture their attention and inspire?

- You're leading the organization's transformation but hate the spotlight. How do you bring everyone with you?

Storytelling holds the key to each one of these leadership challenges. And when you are leading change, stories are an especially engaging way to bring your message to life. They help us elicit understanding and conviction; they create buy-in and commitment.

We remember great stories. Leaders who tell great stories seem more present and alive—electric. Though we may not think of ourselves as natural storytellers, we're all expert at *spotting* great stories and storytelling. Yes, it's an art, but one with learnable skills and tools that belong in our tool kits.

Engaging others in your story

You know those people who tell a story about their vacation in the jungle when they got kidnapped by guerrilla warriors and escaped—and you find yourself yawning? But then someone tells you about a trip to the supermarket, and you're on the edge of your seat? Get these three basics right and the latter storyteller will be you:

- Align your *intention* (what you really want to create) with your *attention* (your focus) and your *emotion* (the feelings and sensations that connect you with others).
- Engage the senses to bring your story to life; think of your story as a movie and use strong visual cues to help others step into it.
- Make it personal; keep in mind that the story is not about drawing attention to you, but helping others understand and believe in your message.

Are you ready to experiment? If so, first spend some time choosing an intention you want to convey, perhaps linked to your vision or to a leadership challenge you faced recently or maybe a lesson from the ups and downs that you've experienced. As you pause to plan your story, try this exercise that Jo adapted from the most famous of all storytellers, Dale Carnegie:

Story formula
(percent of the total story time)

1. Frame the story: Direct the attention of your audience to *your intention,* which is the message you want them to take away from your story. (5%)

    _____

    _____

    _____

    _____

2. Convey a relevant incident or example for the audience: Bring it to life by *engaging the senses* and *making it personal.* (80%)

    _____

    _____

    _____

    _____

3. Convey the point, what you want the audience *to learn/do*: Be specific, brief, and link back to your intention. (10%)

    _____

    _____

    _____

    _____

4. State one (just one) benefit or reason; *make it relevant* to your audience, making clear why you are sharing this story. (5%)

    _____

    _____

    _____

    _____

As you do this, keep each point brief. Soon we'll add detail and color. Here is my first-pass example—and I'll build on it as we continue:

1. *Framing:* I want to persuade that honoring an organization's strengths enables people to more easily and fully embrace change.
2. *Example:* I once flamed out by skipping this step with almost disastrous consequences.
3. *The point:* When building commitment to change, start with success.
4. *Benefit:* You'll find that others will follow you with conviction.

Bringing your story to life

With the guts of your story sketched out, add the color that makes it memorable. Try telling your story to someone now—right off the bat. Choose someone you trust to be honest and *kind*. Take a few minutes for a run-through. Your listener will help you refine your story in the next iteration. Then, go back to your story skeleton and hone your message as well as your content in line with the outcome you hope to achieve for your listeners. We've left you room to make some notes here.

Sharpening your story

What intention do you have for your story? What message do you want to convey? What title would you give to your story?

_____

_____

_____

What emotion do you want to convey and spark in your audience?

_____

_____

_____

What is a brief synopsis of the story—what is happening? What is the challenge? Who is involved? What is the impact on you, on others?

_____

_____

_____

What will make your story memorable—what image or metaphor will make it memorable?

_____

_____

_____

What is the primary benefit for your audience? Why are you telling this story now?

_____

_____

_____

In my example, I intend to hardwire that building on strengths is the crucial first step in leading change; my message is that starting with past success opens up the audience to accept significant changes. My title might be: "Appreciation Turbo-charges Change!" To reinforce my message, I want people to stand in my shoes and feel the charged atmosphere. In a nutshell, my story is about the time I presented to the firm's senior leaders with a (too powerful) video that showcased a vision for our firm. The video backfired. By talking about changing *everything*, I succeeded . . . at triggering *everyone*! The image I'll use is a heroic battle (where I am the enemy). I had a professional near-death experience. Luckily, I survived. Appreciate what is working before seeking to change things, and your probability of success will skyrocket.

We're almost—but not quite—done! To what extent are you mindful of the stories you tell as a leader? Do they energize, inspire, build hope and pride? To what extent do these stories move you in the direction of your desired change? There are no right or wrong answers here, just information to use as you build your presence, story-crafting, and storytelling skills. We suggest another iteration: Tell your story out loud a second time to simplify your message, personalize it, give it memorable color, infuse it with emotion, and cement the learning you most want to create. I won't leave you room because this is an oral exercise, but I will leave you with my story, honed a third time.

Johanne offers an important insight to keep in mind as you craft your change story: People don't resist change, they simply protect what matters most to them. In my case, the senior partners rose in unison to protect their beloved firm. Today we chuckle. Back then it was another story.

See what you think!

Third try

I'd like to illustrate how honoring the past paves a sure path for leading change. Today, I make it my business to do this, but it wasn't always so. My career almost met its end back when I was a brand-new director. Let me take you to 1995.

Encouraged by our managing director to be bold, my colleagues and I decide to make a video about the future of our firm. Six months later, there we are, two colleagues and me, pacing outside a fancy hotel meeting room. We're waiting to show the firm's governance committee how to reinvent the firm. The doors open just as we're ready to leave, but instead, we enter and meet twenty of the most powerful partners sitting around a big U-shaped table, their discarded papers thrown into the "pit" in the middle. I can tell this isn't going to end well.

Pleasantries over, we roll our ten-minute video, and surprise! Their smiles turn to increasing displeasure. Halfway into our presentation I am no longer facing colleagues but twenty fierce warriors armed for battle. They shoot down my colleagues, they bayonet our ideas, and then they corner me. I'm still alive. One elder statesman exclaims, "Why did we elect you?" A sponsor comes to my rescue, fielding that question with, "We were young once, too." My life is spared.

Thankfully, it's over and I leave the room dazed. The next day, I "get it." The senior leaders believed that we would destroy everything they had built. Naturally, they went to battle to save the firm. If I had only started by sharing what our new director group loves about the firm—its many strengths—the leaders might have listened openly. Thankfully, this story ends happily. In time, many of our ideas found a home. My colleagues and I worked till old age—and no one was fired. Yes, I was young once, too.

Filling the room

People often judge us on "executive presence"—how we fill the room. Jo and I hate that phrase, but we hear it regularly and people always ask what it means. Recently, one of our facilitators asked a group of executives to define it. They took less than four minutes. Impressive! I'll recap for you.

Start with the *physical elements*: good posture, a confident stride, eye contact. Try striking a power pose for a few minutes as a warm-up exercise before entering the room; walk in like you own the place; use your gaze, posture, and gesture to fill the room; stand up straight but in a relaxed manner. Project confidence even if you don't feel this way ("fake it till you make it"). Next come all the things you can do with your *voice* to increase presence: Project it; lower and slow it down; modulate it; wait a few beats before opening your mouth. Use silence, too, to underscore something important. You can also practice the *intangibles*; connect through eye contact, a meaningful look, a nod, a gesture.

Think about a leader you know who has "presence." What do you observe? Almost everything you see and admire can be learned.

My observations on presence

Name of leader whom you are observing _____

Physical characteristics (e.g., stance, position in room, movement, attention, energy)

_____

_____

_____

Vocal characteristics (e.g., loudness, sound, modulation, speed)

_____

_____

_____

Intangibles (e.g., authenticity, congruence, openness, connectedness)

_____

_____

_____

The impact on you (feelings, sensations, understanding, conviction, and motivation to act)

_____

_____

_____

Claude Stein, facilitator and voice coach to singers *and* leaders, encourages you to *exaggerate* in the "practice room." Why? What is normal to other people may feel extreme to you. For example, you think you're shouting but your audience strains to hear you. Go on, really shout! When you practice, the words don't matter. People listen for your intention and emotion. Claude illustrates by asking us to imagine how we feel and act when we sing a lullaby to put baby to sleep. "Is that what you do to hail a taxi in NYC?" he sweetly coos. And from the back of the room, waving his arm, Claude yells, "Probably not!"

Presence starts with a process others don't see: setting your intention even before entering the room. Taking a moment to gather your thoughts on what you want to achieve will help you engage with others through the physical space in the room. This all adds up to being perceived as convincing, trustworthy, authentic. "That's a lot to manage!" you say. Spot-on. If you do nothing else, clarify your intention and rehearse once. Typically, we observe a 100 percent improvement in second attempts. A few adjustments make all the difference:

Presence checklist

_____ Do you connect with your intention first, so that what you care about most comes through?

_____ When you enter the room, do you stand up straight and walk to the table smiling?

_____ Do you connect through eye contact consciously?

_____ Do you make sure you speak at least once in the meeting's first few minutes?

_____ When you have the floor, do you take a few seconds to center yourself and command attention?

_____ Do you slow your voice down and lower it to calm yourself and everyone else?

_____ Do you give everyone your fullest attention, as if this were the most important thing in the world you could be doing at this moment?

_____ Do you connect with your emotions and manage them to project what you intend?

_____ Do you take your time to land your point (voice coming down instead of ending on a higher note)?

You intend to do this, and with practice, you will. But when things go awry, Johanne reminds, recenter. Take a deep breath starting with your exhale, breathing deep into your belly. Feel your feet on the floor, imagining roots anchoring you so that you are strong, sturdy, and stable. Focus on your intention. Keep in mind that stories get better with practice.

Let's turn now to a CEO who tells stories with mastery. Enjoy.

Fabrizio's Stories About the Magic of People

In which Fabrizio Freda, president and CEO of the Estée Lauder Companies, shares a few stories that teach as they inspire

Fabrizio is a visionary leader who sees what is not yet there—and achieves it. He explained: "Looking at reality without putting any filter is the starting point of any big achievement. We tell ourselves things are already as we want them to be; we settle without giving ourselves the chance to influence reality." Growing up in Napoli, Italy, Fabrizio began to form this philosophy out of his teenage experience:

> When I was sixteen—the age when everything looks like a disaster, when your girlfriend leaves you, and you are the unhappiest man on earth, when not having money to go to the disco is probably the biggest problem you're facing—I discovered real issues, people suffering from poverty, from injustice, physically. I had a big rebellion when I realized this.

After joining a friend taking handicapped people to a sanctuary, Fabrizio coordinated students to launch a service community:

> We would split our time—organizing beautiful weekends, even bringing people in wheelchairs to ski with us or to the disco! The people we helped were enjoying their very difficult lives a

bit more. My friends were growing in their ability to understand their power in life. They gained energy, passion, and balance. This creation of positive energy marked my life.

Perhaps the best way to learn from Fabrizio is through his stories.

First story: The magic of hope

One of Fabrizio's most fascinating stories is about the power of a seemingly impossible goal. His intention is to inspire us to repeat the magic created here. *I love how he paints this scene. I imagine the town, feel the urgency!*

I was managing the global snacks business for Procter & Gamble. In the middle of a very important year, a tornado hits our main factory in the United States. It happens to be the only factory in the United States. Somebody calls me; my first question is, "What happened to the people?" The caller says, "Everyone is safe but we are out of business for months. The factory is completely under water. Nothing works. The entire town has been hit. There is no electricity, nothing. Our competitors will be happy to fill our shelves with their products tomorrow. We are at risk." So what do you do with that?

Good morning, here's a new adventure! The way we react to this crisis is amazing. We create a small team of decision makers. We go to the factory in the middle of the destruction. We take care of the people. When the people are safe, we start taking care of the business. We get the best engineers on location from around the world. We create a room where everyone can look at all the machines we must rebuild. And then we take the corporate plane to our biggest customer. We explain the situation and hear, "We have an issue. In a few weeks, either you are back or I'm afraid you're out forever."

Forever? Now I'm hooked to find out how he is going to solve this.

We return to the team, to the room with the engineers, the marketers, everyone sleeping there, and say, "In one week, we are back producing." And they say, "That's impossible. The factory cannot even produce the new machine we need in one week!" I reply, "That's the task. Let's work with this in mind." That's the start of the mission: setting this impossible goal, putting it on the wall, and getting this incredible talent thinking in this better way.

We start creating ideas for how would this be possible, ideas we would not have gotten without an impossible goal. In the end, this team succeeds. We start running the factory exactly ten days after the tornado, before the city has electricity. We are back on the shelf two weeks later. The factory people work day and night with amazing passion. It was an incredible experience for the entire organization. When we achieved this mission, the business had the best twelve months it ever had. Nothing had changed in the market. Because of the way the crisis brought people together, the organization was the most united, the most collaborative, the most decisive, the most precise on priorities. We were never more conscious of the important things and the less important things. For a year after, we were still speaking about these ten days, having fun about what happened and what we learned.

Fabrizio now reinforces his message that when talented people share a bold intention, almost anything is possible. This story of hope shows what happens when the team comes together in its most resourceful state.

Second story: Building great organizations

As Fabrizio tells stories effortlessly, he told another one—this time about building on strengths. *Note his message and benefit for the listener right up front.*

I look to build a team wherever I go, because the whole team is always greater than the sum of its parts. In particular, you have to find the strengths of each individual and of the organization—and then you can create magic.

I joined Estée Lauder Companies in 2008 and the first thing I did was listen.

I've learned that, to share a dream, you speak to people. That's why I went to all the cities where we have a business unit. This takes six months; it's not a one-minute exercise! I fall in love with the people, with what they represent, their achievement. I don't think you can create passion in others unless you respect them. By listening, I try to understand what moves them before understanding what moves me. I really get the sense of the strengths of the organization from a business standpoint. I get the sense of the emotional strengths of the organization. Then I can start to face reality and form a vision that could be inspiring for them and interesting for the business. At that point, I begin to have the heart of the organization with us.

Team building is his strength. The next part shows how to do it.

We are all shaped by some unique strengths; we are blessed to have some things that we do particularly well. It's better to draw in people who are brilliant in a specific area and then bring this talent together to form a team. If you are the coach in the Soccer World Championship, and you have somebody who is very good at defense, you wouldn't tell this person, "I would like to try you at the attack, because maybe you can improve ten percent there." You position him to do the best defense he can do. You will place somebody else on offense. The same is in business. You need supertalented people who know they need to do what they do fantastically well. And when your leadership team takes the same attitude, you create a culture where each one can give his or her best.

The terrific soccer analogy drives home his point.

> There were moments in my career where senior people decided
> to build my talent. Everyone has had the experience of a boss
> saying, "You're good at this, but let me tell you about this ten per-
> cent that you have to improve." The boss spends the next hour
> speaking about that, and it never helps me develop one inch. The
> experience that transforms me is when my boss looks me in the
> eyes and says, "You are amazing in that. I want to see you doing
> more of that. How can I help you?" Even better is when he calls to
> say, "I'm going to support you becoming even greater. Let me give
> you another challenge, another opportunity to do what you know
> how to do best, even better." One day a very senior leader—three
> or four levels above me—sends me a note after a presentation. I
> had been in a meeting with twenty people, and I had made a cou-
> ple of controversial points. And this little note says, "I am watch-
> ing you. I was impressed. I'm sure you will impress me again." I
> am twenty-nine at the time. Nothing gives me more energy than
> knowing that somebody so senior would watch me.

Great example of personalizing the story to make it compelling.

Final story: The magic of always learning

One day, Fabrizio told his team an unexpected story about strategic
thinking.

> In a crisis, you realize that having the right questions is much
> more important than having the right answers. My story comes
> from a book for children written by a Norwegian author. It is a
> story of two children, the first from Earth and the second from
> Mars. They meet at night in a garden and start a conversation.
> When the guy from Earth asks a question, the Mars guy takes
> a big bow. And when the guy from Earth answers questions in a
> very sophisticated way for a child, the guy from Mars does not

even smile. So, after a while, the guy from Earth cannot resist and asks, "Why do you reward every question with a bow and then when I give you all these intelligent answers, you don't even smile?" The guy from Mars says, "In my world, we reward questions. They begin every story of change. Answers are the end." This children's story inspired the team to really get the importance of questions.

You gotta love the context—a children's book—to teach such a sophisticated idea! Sitting with questions is a great practice in itself, and one that I'm working with as I write this.

18

FACING FEARS
THROUGH HOPE

*In which you'll build confidence to act by learning your yes
and no; and engaging your voices and others' to increase your
courage and confidence*

If work were smooth sailing all the time, leadership would be a
piece of cake! But I know all too well—I set intentions to make big
changes and, six months later, I haven't acted on them. We overcommit and then we fall behind, and time does what it does well: It
flies by. We keep telling ourselves that we are going to change after the
next deadline, and then the next one after that. One day, we have to
face up to the fact that we have yet actually to do anything. That's certainly what happened to me between the highs of that first book and
our leadership development program in 2009 and my real progress in
becoming a centered leader.

It wasn't until 2012 that I found the courage to throw myself
fully in. What was getting in the way? Doubt rained down on me.
I thought that hedging my bets while collecting more data to prove
Centered Leadership would erase my doubt, but it didn't. *What if
you're wrong?* my doubter voice kept asking. It took me a few more
years to learn that there is always doubt. Hope outweighs it. So I
turned inward to find more hope.

Learning to say no

How often do you find yourself overcommitted? Johanne explains: "When we say yes to everything—in effect, we say no to our own intention. We make competing commitments, overcommit, and cannot follow through on what matters to us most." Quick reminder: When we overcommit, we let everyone down, most of all ourselves. That's why we must learn to say no to what stands in the way of our intention.

It's hard. There is a good reason why. "No" represents a concrete stance, a statement of what you do not want. Just saying the word causes discomfort; it feels like an affront to the relationship. Plus, letting things go causes a sense of loss. By contrast, when we say yes we create positive energy and direction. But "yes" takes time, attention, and energy; and we have finite resources. That's where "no" comes in. For me, "yes" got easier when I realized that Centered Leadership trumped other client work. Everyone else had seen that, but I continued to overcommit until I saw it, too. Naming your "yes" before your "no" builds conviction.

So, going back to your personal vision, what do you most want to say yes to—and what do you need to say no to? Johanne's exercise, adapted from William Ury's work, will help you plan.

Setting priorities and boundaries

What do I want to create and stand for as a leader? What really matters to me that I choose to say *yes* to—the needs, interest, and values underlying my vision and this stand?

_____

_____

_____

_____

(continued)

(continued)

What small steps can I start taking to live more fully into my *yes*?

_____

_____

_____

_____

What do I have to say *no* to—specific requests I have to decline or promises I must renegotiate?

_____

_____

_____

_____

How can I renegotiate or help that requester in turn? In other words, what can I say *yes* to?

_____

_____

_____

_____

What will be my greatest challenges in implementing my *yes/no/yes*—in me or with others?

_____

_____

_____

_____

Let's put our plans into action.

Listening to the voices

Even when we know what we want to say *yes* to, then what we will say *no* to, and what *yes* we can bring back to the requester, we have a hard time doing it. Here's what happens. We're resolved to take that next step into the unknown. In no time at all, our doubting and fearful internal voices speak up. We bravely try to ignore them. So what do they do? They get louder until they drown out our intention, and we take the path of least resistance. Before we know it, we've unintentionally said yes—again.

What if, instead of trying to silence these voices, you did the exact opposite? What if you put them on the loudspeaker? That's what Johanne advises us to do. Don't limit this exercise to the usual bunch of critics and doubters; call on the rest—your visionary, sage, coach, and others. They offer hope. Respectfully listen to each voice in turn (after all, they're part of you). Then revisit your intention; clarify what really matters to you. I admit that talking to your own voices seems weird, but put that aside and embrace Johanne's voices exercise below. Please keep in mind that these voices live inside you—but you are not them. The best way to keep them separate is to place a chair for each voice and one for you. As you imagine that voice speaking to you, sit in its chair. Afterward, come back to your own. So, remember your recentering exercise? Sit comfortably, close your eyes, and consciously relax. Breathe, exhaling and inhaling deeply a few times until you resume normal breathing. When ready, move to the chair you have designated or picture an image for that voice. Listen and take notes below.

Talking to your voices

Visionary (*The visionary is the voice that sees magnificent possibility and dreams big with no limitations.*) What does s/he say to you? What do you say to your visionary?

_____

_____

_____

_____

(continued)

(continued)

Doubter or Critic (*The doubter is the voice that attempts to create safety by pointing out limitations, raising concerns, and criticizing.*) What does s/he say to you? What do you say to your doubter?

_____

_____

_____

_____

Sage or Wise Person (*The sage is the voice of wisdom that may show up as a man or woman guide or beloved teacher.*) What does s/he say to you? What do you say to your sage?

_____

_____

_____

_____

Coach (*The coach is the voice that knows how to begin to implement a vision, keep ourselves moving forward, and remove obstacles.*) What does s/he say to you? What do you say to your coach?

_____

_____

_____

_____

Caregiver (*The caregiver is the voice that loves without demands, tells us that "we are enough" when we need to hear it.*) What does s/he say to you? What do you say to your caregiver?

_____

_____

_____

_____

If you hear other voices, put them on the loudspeaker, too. We tend to favor our negative voices. Please resist that temptation!

You've already heard from my critic, Edna. My child self, Jody, is the voice who creates, who delights in mischief, who enjoys a bit of silliness, and who shines onstage. I don't know what she'll do ahead of time—that's part of the deal. Jody says, *Come with me into the realm of no logic and trust in me.* I plead with her, *Assure me you'll always be there. What if I step out and you've abandoned me?* She answers wickedly, *No assurances!* She is right, of course; and, the funny thing is, only when I trust her do I shine, too.

Now that you have the swing of it, what do these voices have to do with saying yes and no? Edna is good friends with my fears. Her job is to audit my performance; and, if she had her say, I'd play it safe. Jody is good friends with my visionary and she offers hope. Listening to her brings me greater balance, and as the next story shows, balancing hopeful *and* fearful voices helps propel us forward and grow.

.

Sheila Learns to Balance

In which Sheila Lirio Marcelo, founder and CEO of Care.com, recounts how she learned to embrace the polarities of leadership and let go of perfection

Sheila grew up in the Philippines, with a plan to become the lawyer in the family; the family's first four children were designated to be the doctor, dentist, accountant, and engineer. As Sheila recounted, "Top politicians or businesspeople went to law school and so my parents always thought that my opportunity was law. In my teenage years, it was etched in stone. But, deep inside, I really wanted to be an actress or a singer."

Sheila's story is about how she learned to say yes to what she really wanted, and importantly, no to those things that stood in her way.

Planner, problem-solver

Sheila was a precocious child, affable, friendly, smiling, driven, and focused. "I had a to-do list at three: I got up, dressed myself, I had goals! My parents always encouraged me to just be who I was—and they never held me back."

Propelled by her achievement goals and "to do" list orientation, Sheila completed a joint law/business degree at Harvard and then chose to become an entrepreneur, like her parents. She stuck to her formula of ambitious goals, with discipline and a push for action—and had great results for years. Sheila remembers the moment when this approach stopped working. She was a founding employee at Upromise, an Internet company devoted to helping members save for college:

I would go into a meeting. Even though I was not the designated person to run it, I always found myself not waiting for the title. I would observe inefficiency and just *take over!* I'd say, "It seems that we're not progressing here. Hey, let's get stuff done!" I wasn't very diplomatic then. I would look at somebody and say, "Last week, you said that we would get to this. What's the status?" I didn't appreciate people's feelings; I didn't wait for permission. And I learned that no one really enjoyed working with me.

You can't get to the goals unless people know you, trust you, and understand what you are aiming to do. But I was black and white, driven by the outcome more than how to get there with people helping.

At Upromise, Sheila started journaling in her second year—an approach that helped her get distance to see herself. In year three, she started meditating. In year four, self-awareness began to set in. It wasn't until year five that Sheila recognized the fear holding her back from her true intent: "letting people know you're human and you're vulnerable." Being vulnerable was uncomfortable. Sheila mused: "I was taught to create a facade of having it all solved. That's what's going to help you grow in your career. That's what people look up to. Bringing down those barriers was not easy." To say yes to leading, Sheila had to give up perfection. She had to say no to what had made her successful so far.

At the core of the shift

As Sheila evolved and matured, she began to see balance in opposing forces:

When I was young, I focused on goals and my to-do list to learn discipline—to get stuff done. As I became a leader, I had to let go of control. I have to be comfortable with things I can't control so that I'm not stressed out.

When you're young, you're taught to be passionate. And when you become a leader, you're not supposed to take things personally when you're given feedback. You're not supposed to be overly passionate—that's confusing, right? That's what I mean by opposing forces.

Sheila herself is a force. Holding back on her passion takes self-regulation. She told me: "So much of what we have to do is this nuance of grays. There's no perfect to-do list. There's no perfect efficiency. There is no perfect letting go. There are times when you need to be goal oriented and clear. There are times when you've got to take it easy—let others find their way to solutions."

By saying yes to letting go (and no to her formula), Sheila became more inspiring and engaging. Her vision—to grow Care.com into a global company that matches caregivers with families needing care—has no bounds. At the time of our interview, Care.com had grown to six hundred employees and had helped hundreds of thousands of customers and caregivers find a match.

19

TAKING RISKS AND ACTIONS

In which you'll experiment with a few tools designed to help you look at your challenge differently, increasing your comfort with personal risk taking and setting out

It fascinates me that most of the leaders I interview spot opportunities around every corner. It's not just that they're optimistic. They take risks, they see possibilities. Either their comfort zones are broader than mine, or their fears more limited—probably both. They're open to adventure, willing to go to the point where their stomachs are on edge. Why? Because the upside is worth it, it's exhilarating, and the learning is valuable. What's the worst that can happen, really?

When fear overwhelms me, I lose my gumption, and my excitement for new opportunities is dampened. Fear usually comes disguised as an innocent question: *What could go wrong? Everything, of course!* My shiny, new idea loses luster. The everyday routine doesn't seem so dull. I convince myself that the opportunity is really a chore or, worse, a risk—until the weeks and months pass by, and I'm kicking myself. You only really verify that something is an opportunity in hindsight, when the facts are in. At the time, it didn't look like much. Nowadays, I realize that challenges are indeed opportunities to expand my comfort zone. I take more risks. Hey, I've even ridden in a clear plastic helicopter in São Paulo—thanks to my colleagues.

So before avoiding your next big challenge (or opportunity), use these tools to find the courage to reach out and grab it.

The questions you ask

We want to act. We're ready, but there's a problem. We explore it, and more problems follow. But what if you could find opportunities instead, simply by changing the questions you ask?

It's all in the question. Are you wondering how it can be that simple? See for yourself. Think about a leadership challenge you're grappling with now—something sufficiently complex for which you'd like some coaching. Now, field Johanne's questions in Experiment 1—with a partner if you can; but, if not, have the dialogue internally.

Experiment 1: first set of questions

- So, what's the problem?
- What happened?
- What are the root causes?
- Who is to blame?
- What have you tried that hasn't worked so far?
- Why did that fail?
- Why haven't you fixed it yet?

When you've worked through these questions, write down how you feel physically and emotionally, and what you're thinking about (don't hold back!):

_____

_____

_____

_____

Good. Now let's try Johanne's Experiment 2. Talk about the same leadership challenge but use these questions to guide your conversation:

Experiment 2: new set of questions

- What would you like to see happen or create?
- How far have you come already—e.g., times when a solution is present, at least in part? What made that possible?
- What resources do you already have?
- What small steps could you take that would make the biggest difference?
- What support do you need?
- What have you learned from this conversation so far?

Write down your physical and emotional feelings, and what you're thinking about now:

_____

_____

_____

_____

How did you experience this set of questions? How did you feel? What happened to your energy? What new thoughts came to mind? How is your confidence now?

When I tried the first set of questions, I practically had an amygdala hijack! Irritable and defensive, I couldn't help but think, *When is this going to stop?* The second set, on the other hand, made me feel open, hopeful, and optimistic. My discussion partner boosted my energy and encouraged new thinking.

That's the magic of appreciative inquiry. Johanne says, "Ask about a problem and you will find a problem. In Experiment 1, people typically experience defensiveness. Perhaps you felt your body tensing. You focus on the past, looking for blame. But ask for solutions and you will find them. People typically experience openness. Maybe you felt your body relaxing, for example. Your attention moves into the future, looking for ideas."

Both sets of questions have their place; it all depends on the challenge. The first set can help you find root causes, especially when the problem is of a technical nature. When you face adaptive challenges, however, try the second set. Johanne articulates the first mindset as: "My organization/team is a problem to be fixed" and "my role as a leader is to solve problems." Jo sees the second mindset as: "My organization/team has resources and creativity to discover" and "my role is to engage them in the process of discovery."

So when you're not getting the response from others that you'd hoped for, check your questions. Almost all of us revert to deficit-based questions; it's second nature. Before going there, try on a solution-focus for size. You can lead more productive discussions by asking questions that inspire hope, spark creativity, and engage others energetically.

Looking risk in the eyes

Our fears can also be a catalyst for action. They keep us in touch with reality. The role hope plays, on the other hand, is to envision what could be without the limitations imposed by fear. Jo suggests the best mix to be one-third fear, two-thirds hope, though I have found that even half and half is better than no hope at all! The combination helps us to see possibilities *and* produce the adrenaline that propels us into the unknown. This exercise balances them.

Balancing fear with hope

What is your biggest opportunity or challenge right now? (Choose one that gives you butterflies.)

_____

_____

_____

_____

What worry or fear may hold you back?

_____

_____

_____

What benefits can be gained from moving forward—for you, your team, and/ or your organization?

_____

_____

_____

What else can be gained?

_____

_____

And what else can be gained?

_____

_____

And, again, what else?

_____

_____

One more time, what else?

_____

_____

What I love is that five iterations trick us to go beyond self-imposed boundaries. The act of asking with persistence forces us to dig deeper until we see the real upside of the opportunity, which helps us push past fears. A variation is to ask several people to help you identify the upside (*not* downside, which we're sure you know) of this new opportunity. Once you're satisfied that you understand the upside, compare it to the downside of the status quo.

Opportunity versus Standing Still

What is the *upside* of my opportunity?   What is the *downside* of standing still?

_____   _____
_____   _____
_____   _____
_____   _____
_____   _____

When you have fully exhausted these lists, and only then, consider the downside of your opportunity versus the upside of standing still. Shifting the order of your inquiry changes what the opportunity feels like.

The downside risk could be large; and, assuming it is (big opportunities often carry big risks), let's embrace it! Here's an exercise that invites fear to the rehearsal; it's a *premortem*. Gather colleagues or friends and ask, "What is your nightmare scenario—the very worst outcome that could happen here?" Use the left column below.

My nightmare scenarios

Worst that can happen   If that happened, what I could/would do

_____   _____
_____   _____
_____   _____
_____   _____
_____   _____
_____   _____

When you have a rich set of nightmare scenarios, brainstorm how to mitigate risk in each and record these ideas on the right. Hanging on to this exercise will help remind you that, as Daniel Gilbert poses in his book, *Stumbling on Happiness*, our reality is almost always better than our imagined future. Plus, if the storm hits, you'll be glad that you rehearsed in a calmer moment.

Engaging others to help

Chances are, you have given or received plenty of feedback in your career. Feedback can be a slippery slope; judgment can trigger a downward spiral. That said, don't you wish for forward-looking, nonjudgmental input—in other words, feed*forward*? Johanne adapted the concept as a way to help you enlist others to observe your development. She learned that the greatest obstacles to change may come from the people around us; it's easier for them to stick to how they've always seen us. For example, do your parents still see you as a difficult teen? It happens. Try these feed*forward* processes with colleagues or loved ones.

Brief "feedforward" (one-on-one)

- Identify what you want to practice, based on your leadership journey.

_____

_____

_____

 (for example: learning to ask solution-focused questions instead of problem-focused ones)
- Share it broadly with your team and ask them to tell you when they see you use that practice.
- Ask and note what impact your new behaviors are having on them.

(continued)

If your challenge is complex, or you're working in a group, use this structured process.

Structured "feedforward" process

- Spend 2–3 minutes stating your challenge, what you are struggling with, and what you hope to achieve. People need only the skeleton of your issue to be helpful; avoid the details.
- For the next 10–15 minutes, listen as the group speaks freely, giving ideas based on experience, on their observations, or through analogies. Be a "fly on the wall" and take notes, resisting temptation to answer.

_____

_____

_____

_____

_____

_____

- When the time is up, thank each person for his or her input and reflect on the notes you've taken; give your group one takeaway that is meaningful to you and one action you will carry out.
- Close by asking the group to tell you when they observe you acting or behaving in the new way.

Workshop participants report that this process brings new light to the challenge; even when the discussion validates their plan, they see a twist that will make it better. What surprises everyone is the tremendous value of people who don't know you well.

Engaging others builds hope. Hope builds courage and confidence. With courage and confidence, you can use fear to propel you to do great things. Meet Biniam next, an amazing leader whose hope helped him face grave risks in traumatic circumstances.

Biniam Masters His Fate

In which Biniam Gebre, born in Eritrea, follows hope in a zigzag path to survive childhood, provide for his family, and reach for his dream

Biniam Gebre remembers very little from his childhood. For good reason. When he was born, Biniam's dad—a member of the Eritrean rebel force in the war for independence—was arrested and taken away to be killed. Hoping to find a way out to Yemen, Biniam's mom (a spy for the rebels) left him when he was three. When I asked about his strengths as a child, Biniam chose survival in the midst of chaos. He said, "I don't give up. Without thinking, I have this unstoppable need to keep fighting. I want to master my fate." Even when he secured his freedom in the U.S., Biniam believed that, eventually, a good life would result from hard work and suffering.

What I found in Biniam was strength to face adversity of the worst kind. He finds glimmers of hope in disaster, each offering a little more opportunity. His long journey has been filled with trauma, danger, poverty, and also acts of kindness—ultimately leading to a place where his dreams can flourish with hard work, but suffering no more.

Born into risk

At age two, Biniam almost died when he was kicked in the head by a donkey. Not long after, his mother left to find a better life but, instead, found herself in a violent battle, nursing a severely wounded man back to health. When that man was approved to enter the U.S. as a refugee, she went as his wife—with a dream to reunite her family. Once in the U.S., she worked for years to save enough money to send for her son. Biniam related, "She paid smugglers to take me from Eritrea to Sudan. I was there for about a year with her friends who then traveled to the U.S. with me. We landed in New York. They went to California, and I went on alone to Atlanta, where I met my mom. I was eight and didn't know her." Happy ending, right?

Not yet.

Biniam, his mother and stepfather (the man she nursed back to life), and baby half-brother settled in Atlanta. As the war in Eritrea came to an end, Biniam's mother received news that her first husband (Biniam's father) was actually alive. She decided to find him. Biniam recounted, "In Eritrea, girls have arranged marriages by twelve years old. Of all her brothers and sisters, my mother was allowed to marry her true love. Inspired by the hope of reuniting, she left my stepdad, and we moved to California. A year later, she went to Eritrea, found my dad in a large rebel camp, and returned with plans for him to join us."

Once again, Biniam's mother worked hard to save money for the ticket. But her true love never joined them. Biniam shared, "We learned that he had another family. He had no intention of coming, which broke my mom's heart. At the time, I didn't care. Getting plucked from family to family, it didn't really matter to me. But on reflection, I'm angry about it."

Biniam lived with his mother and brother in a San Bernardino Housing Authority unit in Redlands, California. At thirteen, he got into trouble and was placed in a summer job program for at-risk youth—what turned out to be a lucky break.

> My punishment was to work in a high school library until I graduated. It was just me and the librarian for three months each summer. One task was to place every book in its right place in the stacks. I read a lot of books. I was planning on trying to be an electrician or pharmacist or maybe a physicist.

But history repeated itself. In trouble again, Biniam was sent to Saturday school, and one day, to a college fair—another fortuitous break:

> I noticed a booth where a lady presented how to get into elite schools, and I went over to meet her. The next weekend, we spent time together to talk through colleges. She insisted that I apply to liberal arts schools. I didn't have enough money to apply to more than two. My Williams application was pretty crappy—in pen with lots of whiteout. I even forgot that I applied. But on a Wednesday, a small letter came—the kind you assume contains a rejection, and surprise—I got in.
>
> The next day the admissions officer called and invited me to visit the school. The most beautiful woman I ever met was also visiting that weekend. We fell in love and are still together. That place was paradise.

At this point, Biniam had decided to become a physician—serving others and creating a better life. Living his words, he brought his young brother east and looked after him. But in his junior year, Biniam realized that it would take a long time to make enough money to care for others. A good friend suggested he apply for a job at McKinsey instead, which made his soon-to-be wife angry. Biniam explained, "We spent the prior year as activists. We accused the administration of colluding with consulting firms and investment banks to manipulate students to do this work! Our project was about 'the man is trying to take us down.' For me to turn around and say 'I'm going to work for the man' was selling my soul to the devil!" But consulting would provide more opportunity to give back, Biniam figured. He signed up.

Ten years later, Biniam made partner and switched to a public sector program: "We're doing work to fix the $30 billion gap in funding needed to improve public housing infrastructure. I remember cockroach-infested housing and parks where we used plastic bags as seats for the swings. I'm living my dream of solving these problems."

Happy ending time? Patience. It's not yet time.

The turning point

Biniam's story almost ended poorly, but Centered Leadership turned the tide for him:

> Physically, I've been lower: I've been in comas; I've nearly died. But emotionally, I was at my lowest point. My wife and I were not talking. I was not getting along with anyone at work. I was barely seeing my kids. I had to do something. Then this amazing young lady enrolled me in Centered Leadership training and I agreed to go. That was the turning point in my ability to navigate the stuff I was going through. I don't think I've ever cried in front of anyone; this was the first time I let go. The sessions got me emotionally riled up. I went into the woods and punched a tree. I was angry, sad, upset.
>
> The facilitator and her sister gave me support and connected me with a trauma therapist in D.C. For a few months, it was slow going. And then I started opening up. I didn't fear being ashamed; fear about being judged melted away. In three months, I was awake. My wife tells me that I've become a completely different person. I'm wide open and engaged.

Biniam Gebre was on top of the world: with a loving wife and family, great job, and awakening from trauma after thirty-six years.

New perceptions

Centered Leadership helped Biniam to get in touch with what drives him:

> I have to live a life with much greater meaning where I'm contributing to society. Tons of kids like me weren't as lucky. I came to this country through the refugee program. I lived on food as-

sistance. I grew up in government housing. The same programs that helped me survive are suffering; I feel an obligation to help make them work better.

My source of meaning is this: to work in ways that will touch more people than I would have been able to if I had become a doctor. I've been given this opportunity to have impact at scale so I shouldn't be shy about it. I should just do it.

Biniam has come full circle. Finding his path, he decided to take the biggest career risk yet: leave McKinsey and become the general deputy assistant secretary at the Department of Housing and Urban Development—Federal Housing Administration. With this new role, Biniam began a life of complete engagement, perhaps for the first time ever.

And that's a really happy ending.

PART SIX

ENERGIZING

20

BECOMING ENERGIZED

In which we make renewal and recovery your responsibility to sustain your path as a leader; and what you'll find in this section

For about two years, I hounded David to acquire a contraption for our home. This miracle machine would alter the course of his life, I argued. "It wards off depression, delivers *elixir vitae*, introduces discipline, and reverses shapelessness." Two years of procrastination later, several strong men delivered it. And on our twentieth anniversary, David proudly presented this gift to me. There it reigned in its supreme ugliness, taking up my half of our bedroom.

An elliptical machine.

I can hear you chuckle. You're thinking, *So how's that working out for you, Joanna? Great clothes rack?* Maybe you've been down this road. Maybe, like me, you've joined gyms and attended—regularly at first, then periodically, then sporadically—until one day, you don't remember your locker number. Maybe you've acquired treadmills, stationary bikes, spinning bikes, or miracle cures bought off late-night television infomercials. Well, three years later, I can honestly say—on behalf of the family . . . this big, gray, ugly machine is beloved! Just look at my journal: 900 workout sessions recorded. After my many failed attempts, why is it working this time around? What's different?

Drumroll, please.

It's not about fitness or weight loss.

I work out to feel good.

It's that simple.

Shifting mindsets

Seeing the workout as a way to lift my spirits turned out to be the difference between an abandoned gym locker and thirty-plus minutes a day of elevated heart rate. Positive psychologist Tal Ben-Shahar reported that exercising three times a week outperformed psychiatric drugs on the market for depression, sadness, or anxiety, and I was hooked.

So why do we view taking time out to recharge as less important than other priorities? Why is working long hours a badge of honor, even at the expense of physical and emotional health? When the head of our firm once wanted to compliment me in front of our partners at the global meeting, he called me "the Tasmanian Devil." And it wasn't the first time—many teams called me that due to my unbounded energy and tolerance for (making) chaos. They didn't know I turned into a zombie at home. They didn't hear David complain, "You should rest at work so you have enough energy for us. We're the only ones who will still love you when you're too old to be useful!"

Sadly, our research shows that Energizing is the dimension people most often neglect—even the handfuls of masters who routinely practice Centered Leadership. Ignoring energy management is a foolish short-term strategy. Burnout destroys intention and purpose, no matter how noble. Burnout fuels negative emotions—such as fear, anxiety, and stress—that spread through an exhausted organization like a contagion. Burnout eats talent for lunch.

You already know the importance of regular exercise, eating healthy, sleeping enough—of course, because you read books, scan magazines, take classes, go to gyms and even take fitness vacations! So why do we find it so hard to live by? The answer, once again, lies in our habits of mind. Three years into my elliptical experiment, I had shifted my mindsets, without knowing it:

- *From* "I'd better exercise to get fit before it's too late" *to* "As I exercise regularly, I create the experience of vitality and joy."
- *From* "I need to lose twenty pounds at least" *to* "As I take care of myself, I feel worthy and deserving."

- *From* "I need to be more organized and productive during the day and rush home to my family" *to* "As I work out in the morning, I gain access to my creative thinking."

In other words, today I work out most days because it helps me create a richer experience of life. On the days I exercise, I feel more generous and loving for hours. The more I exercise, the easier it is to sustain the practice; like any renewal process, the cycle is self-reinforcing:

- I feel more *physical* energy because I'm gaining muscle strength and endurance.
- I feel more *mental* energy because I get ideas out of the blue as I focus on breathing.
- I feel more *emotional* energy because my body releases mood lifting chemicals.
- I feel more *spiritual* energy because I'm doing something that matters to me.

So how can we persuade you to take time out from your frenzied, always-on schedule to renew and restore your energy?

Managing your energy to be more in balance

Our research confirmed my worst fears—for those who want to advance in demanding fields, work-life balance is a myth. Something had to give, and I was Exhibit A.

I admit I was the lady who failed to show up at Lamaze class because of work, and my blessed husband had to go it alone with just a pillow for a mate. I admit that I was on the phone with my team and client twenty minutes after giving birth. And I admit I went to a client meeting a few days later (had I attended Lamaze class, I might have learned that sitting in long meetings was not a great idea). But it gets worse.

When Gaby was a baby, I flew to the West Coast weekly to lead my dream project in the movie business. I thought it was going well until Gaby learned to say a few words. Imagine me, arriving home from California in time for eleven-month-old Gaby's bedtime. David excitedly tells her that mama will put her to bed as he holds her in his arms. A child prophet, she raises her right hand and points at me, saying (I kid you not), "No dat one!" Did I learn anything? Not yet.

Six years later, toddler Jetta is lying outside the bathroom door when I arrive home from a weeklong business trip. I'm really disappointed that she doesn't stir from her post. I hide it well as I bend down to kiss her. "What are you doing?" I ask nonchalantly. "Waiting for Daddy," she says, "He's in there but he says he's coming out soon!"

This story ends well; hang in there. Most of us want to reach old age having lived a full life, including loving relationships, enjoying activities, and meaningful contributions outside of work. "So," you naturally ask, "how do we get everything we want without work-life balance (and don't pull the wool over our eyes with 'work-life integration')?"

By managing our energy.

It's your choice. Managing our energy works. That's a bold statement, especially coming from me. No, I'm not a hypocrite. It took me a few years to get it. Energy is the fuel for everything we do. Only by managing it carefully, and renewing it regularly, can we sustain high performance—at work and at home.

If managing energy is so important, what gets in our way? Bosses who issue urgent requests on Friday afternoons? Teams with endless meetings all day long? Inherently high-stress jobs, whether in the Emergency Room, on a trading desk, in a call center, or wherever? Or, perhaps, we're in our own way. At least that's what I learned about myself. Do you recognize yourself in these examples?

- Every morning I woke up and remained anxious as we walked our kids to school. I counted this as family time; but, because I wasn't fully present, David refused to count it—and we argued.
- Feeling guilty for getting to work at 9:00 a.m., I worked nonstop and ate lunch hastily. Too often, the food literally stuck in my throat—I'll spare you the details.

- I traveled. A lot. Sometimes, I really didn't need to make the trip but was afraid that work would dry up if I stayed home. I knew I was in trouble when I melted down at the airport from missing a plane. My assistant, Helen, is a saint.
- I was late coming home to family dinners more often than not. When I got there, David fumed and the kids were cranky and I cleansed my guilt by industriously washing up.
- I routinely tossed and turned in uneasy sleep, reliving the day's stresses and worrying about what could go wrong the next day. I woke up tired—ready to leave my job, my family, and my life.

Anxiety, stress, guilt, shame, fear, fatigue, anger—what a way to live! Of course, it wasn't always bad. I loved the fruits of work: the highs of coming up with a creative solution, delighting clients by beating expectations, having great discussions, seeing a colleague's face light up, winning new work; and the list goes on. Some days flew by.

But, looking back, I was *not* working at peak performance as much as I wanted. I was working in some other mode—one that made it harder, more draining, and less fun. The worst was feeling this way in a strange city. Coming "home" to a hotel is only a treat when you don't do it a hundred times a year.

Today, managing my energy brings me into greater balance. In moments of high positive emotions and intensity—Excitement! Fun! Passion! Love!—the workday equivalent of a great run—I'm in peak performance mode. Now that I know it's not possible to operate in peak mode all the time, I have also come to enjoy the calm and peace of low-energy moments and emotions. By allowing myself to recognize and experience both states, I found a way to recover and renew.

Sustaining renewal practices

It took me a few more years to stop thinking that wearing myself out would make me worthier. I had to let go of a belief I had cherished since childhood, when I read about Madame Curie collapsing in the street from overwork (and illness). Helping mankind by working to death? I hardwired that one. It was a great way to avoid living.

Taking off the occasional afternoon was a guilty pleasure, and so I denied myself until I had "earned it." But recovery is integral to energy renewal, and not something to feel guilty about! Indeed, staring out the window for ten minutes may help you recover; holding a one-minute dance party for yourself may do the trick. Days without recovery are going to drain you, and as I learned, waiting weeks or months to fully renew means you never will. Regular recovery is the key to sustaining high performance.

I accept that work (life) is not a cakewalk. There are stressful and anxious times and times when grief and sorrow take over as well. The bottom line is that I'm ready to take care of myself, because I want to have the energy to take care of others and carry out my vision. That's where sustaining practices come in—to integrate recovery into daily work and life. Like brushing your teeth, a renewal practice becomes hardwired if you keep at it. Here are some of mine:

- *Remembering to say thank you to my assistant and team*—they help me every day. This is a form of gratitude, one of the few universal recovery techniques.
- *Walking in the park with David*—the Centered Leadership Project idea was born during an early morning walk; walking conversations can be your most productive times—and renewing.
- *Remembering to say "I love you" to family members* when we hang up the phone or take our leave. Touching base with loved ones offers quick recovery.

What you'll find in these pages

If you want to end the day, week, month, and year with that feeling of living life fully, let go of pursuing elusive work-life balance and instead work toward the positive goal of managing your energy. In this section, we help you reframe your mindset from focusing on managing time to focusing on managing your balance of energy sources and uses. By gaining self-awareness of where your energy comes from and what you do with it, and by observing your emotions, you'll find the direct link to your energy state. Our hope is that this self-reflection yields one or two immediate practices for recovering when you are caught in the throes of work.

From there, we step back to reflect on energy states, so you can make explicit choices about where to channel your energy at work and outside of it. In particular, Johanne teaches us a form of meditation as a mindfulness practice. I'm not ready for yoga, but this practice does help me regain my center during a draining or stressful day. You've practiced it already, here Johanne gives a more detailed explanation.

Finally, we invite you to define and commit to a sustaining renewal practice. Just as I made the transition from awareness to choice to repeated practice, you can, too. We offer you an exercise to help you hardwire your chosen renewal practice.

Do we promise you will instantly have more energy, more positive emotions, and a richer experience of life? Remember Johanne's principle: Promises made must be delivered. We promise that we'll put the tools in your tool kit and do all we can to excite you to use them.

Energized leaders ooze the positive emotion and inspiration needed to build momentum and sustain followership for a bold mission. Energized leaders infuse energy when their teams and organizations flag. So please use these tools and practices to become that leader who creates a self-renewing well. And when you do, take note of what positive impact you have on yourself, the team, and the organization.

21

NOTING YOUR ENERGY LEVEL

In which you'll experiment with understanding how emotions link to energy state; recognize your own patterns, and find ideas for recovery during work

I f you're reading this book at the end of a long workday, the words may be dancing on the page as you try to focus dead-tired eyes. If you're reading on a plane after a fruitful business trip, it would be natural to nod off as the engine purrs. But if you're well rested, curious, and engaged, that's a very different state, right? *How much energy do you have to fuel your attention, creativity, engagement, and commitment?* Before you answer, let's take a look at your four sources of energy:

- Physical energy has to do with your body's state of well-being. This is the fuel you have available in your tank. Ask: *How active, fit, nutritionally satisfied, and rested do I feel right now?* Sometimes a quick stretch or a glass of water can change your response.
- Mental energy has to do with how present you feel. Ask: *What is the quality of my focus—to what extent am I intellectually engaged (without my mind wandering to a different issue)?* Sometimes, recentering on your intention can change your response.
- Emotional energy has to do with feeling open and experiencing positive feelings. Ask yourself: *To what extent am I feeling genuinely curious, connected to others, and positive?* Sometimes, asking colleagues what they hope for can change your response.

- Spiritual energy is about making meaning, tapping into what is most important to you. Ask yourself: *Am I spending my leadership time and energy on what I believe really matters?* Sometimes, taking a moment to celebrate success can change your response.

Noting your energy

We offer a simple exercise, adapted from the work of Jim Loehr and Tony Schwartz, to set your energy baseline. Rate how energized you feel right now—or during a typical day at work—on a scale of 1 to 6, where 1 is very low ("I could fall asleep—literally") and 6 is very high ("I could climb a mountain—figuratively!"). Please be honest with yourself. Fill in just the column under "Now."

How energized am I?

Score yourself from 1 (low) to 6 (high) to note your energy level now (or, if you choose, on a typical day).

	Now	After
BODY (physical)	_____	_____
MIND (mental)	_____	_____
HEART (emotional)	_____	_____
SPIRIT (meaning)	_____	_____

Here's an experiment to see if we can raise your energy scores. In the box below, Jo invites you to write down as many things as you can that you are grateful for. Include anything you are genuinely happy and joyful about. Please be as specific as you can be, and frame your statement appreciatively ("I have been healthy all year" versus "my health"). Remember to record as many items as you can. Quantity counts.

The wrinkle is that you may take only *one minute*.

Sixty seconds. OK?

Ready? Got the timer ready?

Set? Your pen has ink?

Go!

Expressing gratitude

One minute up? Good. Please add up the number of things you wrote and put your total here:

Return to the exercise above, "How energized am I?", and rate your energy again, this time in the column under "After." Did any scores change? How do you feel right now?

When we debrief participants, almost everyone notes energy increases in at least one dimension. It takes physical energy to write fast and mental energy to think fast! Connecting touches the heart and spirit. For some, this exercise reminds us that we've been out of touch. If this is you, please reframe this as the perfect time to reach out. You'll boost your energy—not to mention theirs.

How many things did you put on your gratitude list? Most people register somewhere between five and ten. Over fourteen puts you among the most grateful people! If you stopped at three or four, you probably are just having trouble being specific. Start a gratitude journal and you'll find that it gets easier to allow your gratitude to flow.

We use gratitude to make the point that you can recover more quickly than you might expect. In one minute! Full recovery, of course, will take more effort. First, you must recognize your energy state; you can do it by recognizing your emotions. This sounds easy, but in reality many of us find it difficult to put a name to how we feel. We tend to use a limited vocabulary (e.g., feeling good or feeling bad) and assign judgment (e.g., "good" is good!). Instead, regard your feelings with curiosity. They are neither good nor bad. Grief, anger, anxiety, fear, and sadness are a part of everyone's life, including the happiest individuals. Remember, we have emotions but we are not our emotions. You can choose how to experience the situation.

We admire the tool from Loehr and Schwartz to help you categorize your emotion/energy state. It pinpoints positive and negative emotional experiences along with the intensity of energy.

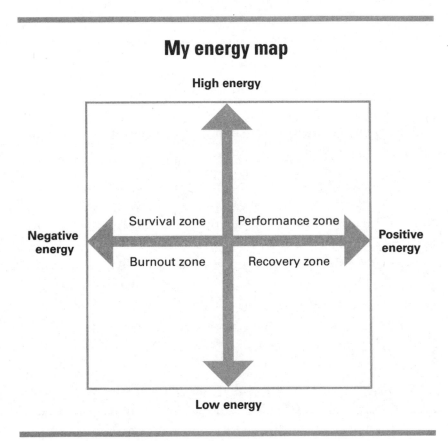

My energy map

High energy

Survival zone   Performance zone

Negative energy   **Positive energy**

Burnout zone   Recovery zone

Low energy

Johanne adds a twist: For each quadrant, remember a time when you were in this state. Use your body to re-create your feeling and energy level from that time. Your body knows your state before your mind does—so, in this exercise, we let our bodies do the talking. With this awareness, you create more choice to move right.

Now, recalling your moments in the *high energy/positive energy* zone, what are you doing? What are you feeling? What does that look like physically? (Participants often leap for joy, give the high sign, or throw their arms in the air for victory.)

_____

_____

_____

Moving left, recall moments when you felt *high but negative energy*. What are you doing? What emotions do you feel there? What is that physical manifestation? (As Madonna might say, strike a pose—probably a tense and angry one.) Give it your all!

_____

_____

_____

_____

Shifting into the bottom-left quadrant, recalling moments of *low and negative energy*, what are you doing? What emotions do you feel? (I loved when one participant slumped in her chair, not even bothering to stand up; she embodied this state perfectly.)

_____

_____

_____

_____

Finally, move right into the bottom-right quadrant, and recall when you felt *low and positive energy*—noting what you are doing physically and what emotions you feel. (Participants often show floating, meditating, rocking—gentle, and at peace.)

_____

_____

_____

_____

Of course, only one of these states is the Performance zone. As much as we'd like to live in it all the time at work (and at home), that's not possible. Athletes know that energy oscillates constantly and so they must build recovery days into their training plan.

In which state do you find yourself most often? Where would you like to be more often? Use your emotional experience to find your typical and desired states:

Emotional range

_____ Performance zone: Enthusiastic, optimistic, challenged, absorbed, alive, passionate, etc.

_____ Survival zone: Impatient, irritable, frustrated, angry, defensive, worried, etc.

_____ Burnout zone: Exhausted, sad, hopeless, depleted, grieving, depressed, etc.

_____ Recovery zone: Relaxed, peaceful, grateful, receptive, calm, rested, etc.

Moving squares

As I stared at the four quadrants, I experienced one of those "aha!" moments of what happens to me. I bet you've felt this way, too. Thinking I was in the Performance zone (that's where I started), but—thanks to prolonged work pressure—I drifted into the Survival zone without realizing. Before I knew it, the Burnout zone became a vacuum that sucked me in. Here's how it works.

I live with a lot of stress: "The business needs me, my family needs me, I need to earn a living," and then I enter the "perfect storm" of energy drainers: unhappy client, unhappy team, angry husband, non-stop work, and a nagging cold. I drag myself out of some awful hotel bed and drink a lot (a *lot*) of lousy espresso coffee as I rush to the client site. I grab breakfast that looks good. I work feverishly till 2:30 p.m., when I'm so hungry I could faint. At that point, I want comfort food. Midafternoon is my low point; and then I want to treat myself. The client's office has the lure of "free snacks" (they sing their siren song, *Joanna, we're here. Come and get us!*). I work late, head back to the hotel, and what I want is a glass of wine. My body aches, my head hurts, and I hardly sleep. When I do, I have anxiety dreams until I'm grateful that day breaks.

To quote Charlie Brown: *"Aaaaaghhh!"* Why don't I slow down, take a break (or at least a breath), and go to the Recovery zone. What stops me?

Mindsets!

I used to think the Recovery zone was for weaklings, naive people who would not get ahead, slackers. Instead, I lived for the adrenaline of high energy—positive or negative (at least it was high!). I enjoyed working hard and I was afraid of the Recovery zone's empty feeling. Not having any familiarity with downtime, what would I do there? But as I recently figured out, the Recovery zone is not a shameful secret. I don't want to be there all the time; that would be dull. But quick, regular trips to the Recovery zone are a requirement for life.

Johanne relates a story that reinforced the power of recovery for her: "I followed my daughter's cross-country ski coach through the team's warm-up preparation on the race course. I was fascinated to hear him say: 'Here is where you take it easy, and here is where you give it your all, your full power, because you know you can recover on the downhill.' He was teaching them to integrate recovery moments into the race to maximize their performance! What surprised me was that this race was under twenty minutes, and still, recovery was part of the winning strategy."

We hope that you practice moving from Performance to Recovery and back, from Survival to Recovery (pause) to Performance, from Burnout to Recovery, as a matter of course. Keep in mind that these four quadrants are neither good nor bad. For example, if your company must lay off valued colleagues, it would be natural to feel sad and low.

And to encourage you, Jamil's story on the magic of recovery.

Please note, recovery is not just for weekends and vacation. It's something you can—and should—practice daily.

Jamil Sees the Signs and Embraces Recovery

In which Jamil Mahuad, former president of Ecuador, recognizes recovery's role in his health and peace on the border with Peru

Jamil Mahuad lived a life filled to the brim with love, ambition, and performance. He had it all. But ordinary life—not in the plan—struck. Forced to embrace recovery, Jamil went on to even higher performance, leading Ecuador in its history-making moment.

Seeded early

What I noticed first about Jamil is his full acceptance of life, going back to his early years. He recalled himself at eighteen: "I loved the concept of being an idealist without illusions. I am full of ideas but, at the same time, try to be grounded on Earth. It's the inner sense of trust that things are going to be OK, that we're fine, that we do not receive more than what we need. That if something happens that appears negative, a part of us needs that experience. Perhaps our rational mind is not ready to accept that."

The seeds of political success were planted early. Jamil had always sought to create belonging. He shared: "Connecting with people on many levels is what makes my heart sing. I love meaningful conversations. We can share ideas. We can share feelings. We can share hopes. Being with people is the most important thing in my life." Jamil's success as a political leader seemed ordained. He operated in the Performance zone regularly, and while he never took success for granted, it came generously to him.

Learning to recover

In 1992, by the time he was forty-three, Jamil had become mayor of Quito. Five years in, during a trip to Spain to share best practices of Latin American mayors, Jamil had a stroke that paralyzed his left side. Hospitalized in Barcelona and then captive in Boston for weeks of recovery, Jamil was able to slowly return to health. But his world had changed. One minute he was at his professional peak, and the next he was handicapped and unsure:

> Trying to make sense of that was nearly impossible. However, I always had this strong belief that everything happens for a reason. I discovered I needed to go through this pain, to this low moment, to reconnect with myself. I was not listening to a lot of spiritual messages I was receiving. I needed this big shake-up to pay attention. Somebody said, "Never ask why, always ask what for?" Believe me, I wouldn't be able to have this interview with you, speaking so openly, if I hadn't gone through that period. It opened my mind. Most importantly, it opened my heart to a lot of feelings I was denying before. I am a better human being now.

His experience reconnected Jamil to emotions he had suppressed early in life:

> Every person, every family, every institution, every country has "allowed" certain emotions to be expressed and other "forbidden" emotions to be suppressed or masked. Socializing educates your behavior. Sadness, for example, was not well received by males in my family. When some of my ancestors were really sad, they averted that emotion by expressing anger. I had the same

difficulty. Still it is not easy for me to connect with pain, with grief.

But by recognizing and bringing this shadow to light, you start incorporating that "new" part into what you are. When one hand is paralyzed, you realize that you need both hands to wash your face. You need both sides of you: Masculine/feminine, light/shadow together do better individual and social things.

In reconnecting with difficult feelings and his bodily functions, Jamil returned to Quito as mayor and put it on the map as one of *Fortune* magazine's top-ten Latin American cities that most improved the livelihoods of its citizens. He frequently checked with his doctors to get their take on his recovery. They gave him a clean bill of health and, because of his new self-awareness, they felt a second stroke was a low probability. So Jamil decided to run for president of Ecuador—and he won. He mused:

> You win elections because you convince the people to vote for you. Do you know the expression, "You should be aware of what you ask for because you can get it?" Well, as every serious study of the Latin American economy shows, the combined effects of historically low oil prices—more than half of Ecuadorian exports—the devastation of El Niño, and the international economic impact, created the worst economic crisis of Ecuador in the twentieth century. I asked to be there, and I got it!

Now that's stress. I would land squarely in the Survival zone. Not Jamil. Instead, he integrated his insights on recovery into his leadership of Ecuador.

Bringing recovery to the country

It was a very difficult moment. Jamil recentered on his intention as a leader and moved ahead. He told me, "I think that peace is in the heart of everybody in the world. But there are no clear medicines for the illness of war. There is time pressure. You have to do things under stress, with no certainty. And if you make a mistake, the risks are so big that many people will suffer. But you have to drive if you're in the driver's seat." Jamil's efforts to forge belonging helped fuel peace:

> Another war was imminent. If you want peace, you need to talk to your enemy. You cannot get it by talking to your friends. At the same time, talking to your enemy can bring many different reactions. Some people could be very mad at you for doing that. "Don't shake his hand. Shut the door in his face!" they shout. It's about dignity, self-respect. Others would say, "'No, you need to talk to him. Negotiate to find an agreement. The higher interest of the country demands it."
>
> We were able to avoid the war and sign a Peace Treaty. Because the Ecuadorians and Peruvians wanted to live in peace, their will rendered this Treaty definitive. Otherwise, it is just a piece of paper.
>
> We humans aren't bad people. We don't like to kill other people. We don't like to do harm. Sometimes people are so afraid, so insecure, and hopeless that they think violence is the only way to protect themselves. But if you can create a container of security and safety and invite people to change inside, they go back to their basic instinct, which is to cooperate. My strong belief is that we are brothers and sisters in this world and if we pay attention, we can connect.

On October 26, 1998, Jamil signed a peace treaty with President Fujimori of Peru, ending centuries of border wars. Jamil said, "It was like Israel/Palestine in our region. Many people were saying, 'Keep trying, but I don't believe you'll resolve it.'" When we signed, President Clinton said, "You have solved the oldest source of armed conflict in this hemisphere." Commerce between Ecuador and Peru is seven times bigger now. We're the best commercial partners after the United

States. And we have had coups d'état and radical changes in both countries but nobody has touched the treaty. Nothing matches the feeling of bringing peace."

The power of recovery

This interview knocked me on my head. I went straight to the Recovery zone and Jamil's closing words brought me full circle to Meaning:

> We come to life with a mission. If you do not play Joanna, who's going to play that role for you? If I don't play Jamil, who's going to play me? There are two or three things that only you or I can do and it is important to discover those things. I think my purpose in life is to help to alleviate human suffering.
>
> We are surrounded by energy and we can tap into it. Instead of using our own batteries, let's plug into the big grid. For many years, I couldn't see it, but now I do. Let's channel the best energies out there to serve the whole human society.

Renewed Jamil is grateful for the stroke that almost killed him. It helped him to value the physical, emotional, and mental energy he consciously builds and uses. And everyone who meets Jamil sees—no, feels—his spiritual energy.

22

PRACTICING RECOVERY

In which you'll learn mindfulness and other recovery techniques that will serve you to replenish energy and recover when you most need it

Imagine yourself at work on a day from hell. You're juggling phone calls, endless e-mails, tedious meetings, irrational requests, urgent decisions, and tough issues. For fun, let's add on that you've just had a quarrel, you're hungry, and you're exhausted. What happens then? In order to simply function, your body shuts down peripheral activities. You lose your intuition, emotional intelligence, and creativity. You might think that this is not the time to stop and practice recovery techniques. But you'd be mistaken.

Communication and emotion overload only increases our need for mindfulness. We fill every second of our day with bits of information—with a tendency to pile more on, and now we're stuck in a situation where we're spinning plates: If we stop, they all come crashing down. But imagine that someone is holding your place. Come practice mindfulness with us.

But how?

Introducing mindfulness

Mindfulness is a practice that helps you to be present, centered, and aware in the moment. It builds your capacity to place your attention where you intend it to be. This helps you reflect on the action while staying in it. You can practice mindfulness by choosing to focus your attention on one thing. Not as easy as it sounds. Our minds are always "on"; our attention wanders before we know it—into past events or what's coming up.

Attention mastery is our goal: choosing to put your attention on one point for a few minutes. In that time, you'll notice when your attention wanders and you'll practice choosing to let go of that distraction to bring you back to your intention—in effect, choosing your response. Mindfulness practice recognizes that body sensations or noises, feelings, and thoughts are always with us. With focus, we can create a welcome stillness that helps us return refreshed, alert, calm, and "in the now." Drawing on the work of Dr. Jon Kabat-Zinn and many others, we found several benefits you should consider:

- **Return to health:** Mindfulness can help you undo the negative impact of stress—physically and emotionally.
- **Improved presence:** This practice helps you broaden and master your attention in the moment, leading to greater presence, which improves connection.
- **Improved reframing:** Pausing is a mini-mindfulness practice, essential to engaging your thinking brain, widening your choices for creative response.
- **More energy:** You access the hormone of good feelings—oxytocin—and calm yourself, returning to the task renewed.

When I first learned about mindfulness practice, I was more of a wriggly pig than a centered leader. My heart thumped, my body itched to move, and my thoughts were like monkeys jumping across the treetops. The last thing I wanted to do was surrender. Let's go back to Australia, 2009, for a moment.

Our second beta test is going well. Having excused myself for a break, I'm in a sunny courtyard outside, talking on my phone (I know, I know!). My call done, I soak up the sun and lazily look through the glass door to our room. I'm now in a boisterously good mood. Missing the telltale sign of people sitting in a circle, eyes closed, I grab hold of the door handle, but it's stuck.

I push.

Nothing.

I try again.

The door pushes back. It isn't going to budge.

So, with force, I throw my weight at it. This time, the door barrels open. I trip into the room, smiling broadly at the facilitator. She is now saying something in a soft, low voice about ignoring background noises as I tiptoe in and sit down. On a chair that squeaks and groans loudly. In slow motion, I look around and notice that I'm the only moving creature in the room. Indeed, they are all attempting to practice mindfulness. Now embarrassed, I try to sit still in my noisy chair, wondering if anyone can hear my rumbling stomach. Moving on.

Mindfulness does not come naturally to everyone. For many like me, it takes deliberate practice. Master it and practice anytime. Some leaders start their day with it; others use the practice to transition from office to home; and still others use mindfulness in the midst of chaos (as we learned in reframing).

Johanne began her mindfulness practice fifteen years ago. The metaphor Jo uses fits perfectly with how we feel. She says, "Imagine that you are standing at a train station. Trains are coming into the station; trains are going out. These trains are your thoughts; they can come from noises or body sensations or what's on your mind. On a typical day, you see a train and board it. Then you get off, but another one comes by in a different direction and you urgently board that one. You ride it for a while and then another arrives, so you switch." Sometimes I spend my entire day riding trains! At nightfall, I wonder where the day has gone and resolve to focus tomorrow. But it happens again. Well, if a Tasmanian Devil like me can embrace mindfulness, so can you.

Mindfulness practice

- **Relax**—Find a nice, quiet place. Get comfortable in your chair, untangling legs and arms, putting both feet flat on the floor, and allowing your hands to rest gently on your lap. Sit up straight, resting your head on your spine and feeling the chair and the floor holding you.

- **Eyes**—Close your eyes to reduce the stimuli that distract, turning your thoughts inward figuratively and literally.
- **Body**—Exhale deeply, pushing all the air out on exhalation and letting the breath flow back in by itself. As you do, feel your body relax, starting with the facial muscles. Feel the space between your eyebrows open up, your jaw drop, and your tongue recede somewhat in your mouth. Feel your shoulders drop and your neck elongate, your belly soften, and the stress release from your arms and legs.
- **Breath**—Gently bring your attention to your breath, letting it resume its regular rhythm; notice the rise and fall of your chest and the breath going into your body and out again. If trains of thoughts come into the station, notice them, acknowledge them but choose to let them go; stay on the platform, bringing your attention easily and lazily to watching your breath. Your attention will go from your breath to your thoughts and from your thoughts back to your breath again.
- **Heart**—If you like, place one or both hands gently at your heart and imagine the sun or an image of a loved one or a favorite place that stimulates a feeling of warmth, openness, and well-being placed at your heart.
- **Intention**—After ten or fifteen minutes, gently bring your attention back to your surroundings, eyes still closed. Set your intention for the day, the meeting ahead, or for whatever lies in front of you.
- **Stretch**—When you are ready, slowly stretch and, if you rub your hands together—where energy stores up—and gently bring them to your face, you may find it quite refreshing.
- **Eyes**—Gently open your eyes and note how you are feeling now.

Practicing mindfulness for ten to twenty minutes daily helps you access presence, calm, creativity, and focus when you need it—like going to the Recovery zone. Of course, mindfulness practice is not the only way to recover quickly at work. We have more ideas up our sleeve for you to restore your energy balance—in even less time.

(Almost) instant recovery

Chances are, you already know a dozen practices for recovery during your work day, but you don't use them regularly. Think about it: Even a small adjustment (ten minutes) can shift your mood and energy. Try this exercise to find mini-breaks for you.

Below, the four boxes represent physical, mental, emotional, and spiritual energy. On your own or with colleagues, go to the energy source you feel most drawn to and jot down what you like to do at work in *ten minutes or less* to recover or renew. Be as specific as you can. Once you have a few ideas down, move to the next box, and so on. If an idea taps into more than one energy source, even better; don't fret about where to put it. Just move on to the next idea.

Ideas for self-recovery at work in 10 minutes

Physical	Mental

Emotional	Spiritual

I love the following ideas from workshops, and thought you'd like to consider them for your list:

Starter checklist of recovery ideas

_____ Take a quick walk *outside.*

_____ Stop and take a mindful drink of water.

_____ Walk up a flight or two of stairs quickly and think about your intention as you slowly descend.

_____ Have a one-minute dance party (on your own or with others).

_____ Laugh about something, anything.

_____ Chat with a colleague about what they're working on.

_____ Stop and ask yourself what you really value about your work or yourself.

_____ Look at photographs of someone or something you love.

_____ Close your eyes and add to your gratitude list.

_____ Reposition your chair to look out the window and spend ten minutes reflecting on the view.

_____ Imagine an "empty box" in your head and go there for a break.

Another great practice uses mindfulness—"square breathing"—and is simple to do: Breathe in for 4 counts, hold for 4 counts, exhale for 4 counts, and hold for 4 counts. It reminds me of when my dad and I attempted to dance the box step (I was four). In a few minutes, you'll access the benefits of pausing—lowering your pulse, calming your thoughts and emotions, and recentering. That's a great one right before a big meeting and also at a low point.

Any of these quick-recovery concepts work with others to restore energy and renew collective focus. Ask for your team's help in choosing recovery ideas—and, ideally, practice them every ninety minutes during a long meeting. Another team idea comes from a participant who uses it in her weekly meeting's Check-In. Each team member shares one success from the prior week, a top priority coming up, and a favorite quote to inspire others (this one's optional).

Building energy long-term

What renews and sustains your energy balance for the longer term? Of course, you already know that enough sleep (seven to eight hours), lots of water, and eating healthy works like a charm. A zillion nutritionists, personal trainers, and books later, I find this one hard to sustain. But two sustaining practices bring me renewal: a ritual for waking up and another for winding down.

1. **Waking-up ritual.** Do you sleep next to a smartphone? Do you reach for it first thing to check e-mails (maybe it also has an alarm that wakes you)? If you take nothing else from this chapter, please remove that thing from your bedroom! Treat yourself to an alarm clock that plays music (and do not, *do not* use your smartphone). Why am I so emphatic? Two things are wrong with this picture. Looking at e-mails first thing in the morning snaps your brain into beta-wave mode. Before you've even had the chance to greet the day, your brain is accomplishing tasks. By going straight to action you're giving up one of the most creative and intuitive times of day—and you're giving it away to whoever wants it!

Instead, Johanne suggests waking up ten or twenty minutes before others make demands on your attention. Take a few deep breaths and ask yourself:

What do I want for—and of—myself today?

This is a bigger question than it might seem. This is not about your grocery list or today's meetings. What do you want to make happen, and have happen, in this day? How do you want to show up? What quality of being do you want to embody? Take the question into the shower and reflect. When you have your intention, it implicitly guides your attention on what truly matters to you. Then you're ready for the kids, partner, dog, e-mails, and the world. There is no right or wrong here—whatever intent you choose is the one you are meant to have. Just remember to note what you want for yourself, but also *from* yourself. There's an important give-and-take here.

2. **Winding-down ritual.** After a long day's work and then responsibilities or activities after work, your amygdala rouses at night. Programmed over thousands of years to scan your environment for physical danger—things that can eat you or hurt you—it remains wakeful. Since it treats emotional danger and physical danger the same way, it will rouse your anxieties, fears, and stresses to the point where sleep is elusive. Do you ever look forward to lying down in a beautifully made bed, and then when you do, your mind conjures up every problem past, present, and future—until you toss and turn all night without relief? Thank your amygdala for that! To prepare for sleep (and a good tomorrow), here's a ritual that everyone in your family can practice—even children can take part! Keep in mind that as you share and listen, avoid judging that family member—and avoid judging yourself.

Nighttime rituals

1. Choose one of these three options and ask:

_____ What three good things happened to you today—and one not-so-good thing? (Note: not the *best* things, but *good*).

_____ What three new things are you grateful for today?

_____ What is one new thing you appreciate about yourself today?

2. If you are listening to others, do not respond beyond a thank-you.

If you are doing this exercise on your own, we suggest writing down your response in a journal (good things or gratitude or appreciation). This record enhances the ritual and serves a purpose: You're more likely to remember to do it and, after some time, you have wonderful reading material that reinforces your new behavior. It takes work to make rituals second nature.

An intention-setting ritual in the morning and a reflection "book-end" in the evening will do you a world of good. A few minutes in the morning will help you set your day, enabling you to focus with greater clarity of purpose. The few minutes of your nighttime ritual will pay back in more restful sleep if you stick to it. If you're someone who loves being busy and productive—your mind always firing on all cylinders—turning recovery into habit might seem impractical (and impossible). But you don't have time *not* to do it. Having used these practices for a few years, I know that time invested in recovery has a double-digit return.

Case in point: Next up is Rebecca's story—using recovery to manage chaotic days as a matter of course.

STORY 13

Rebecca Uses Recovery to Enjoy Chaos

In which Rebecca Blumenstein, deputy editor in chief at the
Wall Street Journal, *thrives in a global newspaper while
raising a family by practicing recovery*

Rebecca lived in Maine until the fourth grade, when her family moved to the small town of Essexville, Michigan, where she was the new (and only Jewish) kid in her grade. It wasn't until high school that Rebecca truly found her footing: "There was a great English teacher with a notorious reputation. When I learned I had her on my first day of high school, I burst into tears. She was tough! But she taught me how to write and believe in myself."

Rebecca went on to gain leadership experience as part of a national Jewish student community. She recalls, "My world opened up. I was president of my state youth organization, and then I went to the national camp. I vividly remember landing in New York and looking out the window at the city. I decided then that I would be back. Sometimes people say, 'How did you get so ambitious?' There are cornfields behind my high school track; it feels like a very surreal place to be from, and that's pretty much why because I wanted to get out of there!"

The oldest of five girls, Rebecca was responsible and conscientious. Like many eldest siblings (and girls in general), she was also studious:

> I had this duty calling to do well in school. There are pictures of me trying to read the *Wall Street Journal*—with no photos and just dot drawings on the front page. I was interested in the world at a young age. At seventeen, I convinced my dad to let me take

a gap year in Israel with a youth group. My father is a wonderful man but I learned early on that his first answer was no. I worked for two years to get him to relent and let me go. I was eventually victorious. I was determined and wore him down!

Put this entire package together—a smart, determined, independent, and worldly young leader—and it's easy to imagine her happily working in the fast-moving and unpredictable (make that a 24/7 endurance-contest) newspaper world. And that's exactly what happened. Today, Rebecca is on the leadership team of the largest newspaper in America as she raises three wonderful kids—two boys and a girl; and, from her perspective, you can have it all—if you want it.

Practicing renewal

How does Rebecca manage to stay sane (let alone energized) with her hectic schedule and a bunch of growing kids? For starters, she has a wonderful partner in her husband, who shares in everything. And there is her extraordinary focus. Rebecca said, "I can be somewhere at one moment and not distracted. I get a lot of e-mails and have a lot of deadlines and a lot going on. I'm comfortable with that; it doesn't stress me out the way that it does some other people who say, 'Isn't it overwhelming?' If I think about it too much, it is."

Second, Rebecca takes things step by step, moving forward. Before making a decision, Rebecca connects, discusses, and closes—even if the conversation is unpleasant. Over the years, she has found that focusing on the outcome and choosing to face the issue releases stress. If these don't sound like renewal practices to you, ask the recovery master:

I believe that you can have it all. There are not enough people saying to women, "Hang in there." It is hard, but at an early age, I decided to make as much out of each day as I can. I had a friend who was my first boyfriend at camp when I was in fifth grade. We were close over the years. Well, in his freshman year at college, he got stomach cancer and died. I think of him a lot. Sometimes when I'm coming into work in the morning, I think how amazing it is that I have had this life.

Rebecca makes it a practice to treasure most days—at work and at home—by being present: "It drives me crazy with everyone e-mailing at home even when they don't have to. We have to be present with each other. Otherwise you float through life and you're not really there. You don't give as much as you can."

Can we really have it all?

Our discussion brought us right back to what it's like being a very senior female executive with family obligations. I ventured into sensitive territory—how does Rebecca do it? After crediting her husband for being a great partner, Rebecca was passionate, adamant, and clear in her view:

> The world is open to us. I've been a pretty good mom. It's important to not tell women what they can't do, but to tell women what they *can* do. Society has told women that if you work, you're a bad mom. It's the message: "If you're a committed mom, you're *not* trying to do it all." Reasonable women should get up and say, "Bullshit. Women have a lot of choices today." Instead of beating ourselves up, it would be good to tell people that it is possible to have a fulfilled, complete life and be challenged.

Rebecca put this in the context of her transfer to China. She recounted, "When I was pregnant with my third, I was a bureau chief. I went to the editor and told him that I'm from a big family. I said, 'I want you to know, I'm still very serious about being a leader here and about my work.' He put me at ease by saying, 'Rebecca, I have been doing this a long time. If you come back to work after one child, you're going to be fine. If you come back to work after two children, you may as well have fifty. You'll be totally fine.'" Still, when the opening was announced, Rebecca felt settled in the suburbs and didn't mention it at home.

That weekend, following soccer practice and the family outing to a pizza parlor, Rebecca began chatting with another mom. She recounts, "I don't like talking about work, but that mom asked, 'How big is the *Journal*? How many reporters do you have?' I told her and she followed up with, 'Are there editors, too?' I responded, 'Yeah, they're in bureaus around the world. We're looking for someone to run China right now.' My husband piped up: 'China? I'd go to China.' So that's how my career development went!"

Assigned, Rebecca's China transition was hard: "A lot of reporters had left, so when I first got there I had to bring in many people; it was hugely challenging. I worked really hard and long, and the late nights in China were tougher because of the deadlines here." She worried about her older son, too:

> He was going to a British school with a blazer and tie and a button-down shirt. I know this sounds stupid, but I had a lot of anxiety about whether he would don this uniform. For whatever reason, he bit on this experience and didn't look up. Quickly we learned that kids rode bikes to school. Within a week, with his tie and shirt and jacket, he was pedaling off to school. I was almost overcome with emotion.

Rebecca's China team won the Pulitzer for international reporting in 2007. And living in China turned out to be a phenomenal experience for the family—with its share of scary moments but, overall, fully energizing.

Strategies for the long term

With age, Rebecca's attention to physical energy shifted—as she found out: "I had this experience, vacationing with friends who are crazy exercisers. I've always thought of myself as very fit, but I couldn't begin to keep up. They were biking up mountains, and then going for a run and then for a swim. I've always thought of myself as in that camp and I realized, 'I have to pick it up here!'"

Like so many jobs, Rebecca's job is an endurance contest. She said, "We are like elite athletes in a certain way. As a journalist, my fingers and wrists and hands are important. People have had all sorts of physical problems—back stress, for example." So Rebecca discovered yoga. She recounted:

> A woman on my block—a very fit, beautiful woman—was all glowy at the train station one morning. She had just exercised. I said, "I like exercising, but I'm so busy I only have time to run on the weekends." She looked at me and said, "Becky, get over it. There's a yoga class at 5:45 in our town, and if you get up and start doing this, your whole life will improve. If you don't take that hour for yourself, you're not going to have any time all day."

So Rebecca took up yoga: "At first it felt like I was getting up at the bottom of a well, but now I go a few times a week. It is good to have this moment of 'What am I going to do today? What's ahead?' It's funny. When you're not in front of your computer in the morning, you can have your best ideas."

Rebecca learned that yoga is a way to strengthen your body and sustain physical endurance for the late nights and early mornings. Yoga has helped Rebecca be more in the moment—clearly something her job demands and that really matters to her in life.

23

SUSTAINING RENEWAL

In which we share how to embed your commitment to recovery and renewal in regular practice that is sustainable

Despite my slow start, I came to love mindfulness, and in 2010, dutifully downloaded *Mindfulness for Beginners* as Jo urged. Every morning, I asked myself what I wanted for and from myself, and practiced. But as happens to the best of us, in time, I forgot to do it. So why is it that I never forget to brush my teeth twice a day, but cannot stick to the rituals I really want?

Researchers assure us that in three weeks we can embed a habit. When I gave up processed sugar, it took me six *months* to stop craving sweets (and still I relapse). When I got the elliptical, it was about *a year* before my new habit kicked in (and still I relapse). Commitments, promises, and habits are very hard to keep. I would be kidding you if I wrote otherwise. And you know the reason why. Mindsets stand in our way. Here is a list of what's in my way:

- Working hard (nights, weekends) demonstrates my commitment.
- Responding quickly to e-mails shows I'm on the ball.
- I need to work harder to prove I'm actually smart enough.
- If I'm not here to fix the problems, everything is going to fall apart!
- If I'm not here to fix the problems, then who really needs me?
- If I don't work on vacation, so much will pile up that I may as well not have left!
- I don't deserve to take care of myself.

- If I appreciate myself, I will get cocky—and then mess up even more.
- You have to suffer to succeed. (I discovered that Jo harbors a Madame Curie mindset, too—and now I wonder how many others have it.)

It's normal that once again, we put obstacles in the road that stop us in our tracks. But as we did in reframing, identify the experience of life you want to create, the desired mindset that you would have to live this way, and the behaviors that naturally emerge. Try this exercise:

Choosing a creative way

First choose to shift your mindset to one that serves what you most hope to achieve:

As I . . .

_____

_____

(For example: "As I choose to set my intention first thing in the morning . . .")

Second, imagine the physical and emotional experience that you create:

I . . .

_____

_____

(For example: "I experience greater mastery and accomplishment throughout my day.")

In other words, the only thing really in the way of creating a sustaining renewal practice is . . . us.

Creating your sustaining renewal practice

Leaders who want lasting impact must find ways to stay the course. Ask: *"What renewal practices would make the biggest difference to help me reach my ideal energy level for performance?"* Choose just one—until it becomes hardwired—before adding others. Jo offers this exercise to make your practice concrete:

My renewal practice

What will I do?

_____

_____

What mindset shift will help me sustain my chosen practice?

_____

_____

When will I do it?

_____

_____

How will I remember to do it?

_____

_____

What will get in the way?

_____

_____

Who (or what) can support me? How?

_____

_____

What becomes possible for me if I do this?

_____

_____

Be realistic, specific, and honest. Each practice should be replicable *and* observable. For example, to renew daily, Johanne set a practice of scheduling "Jo's Time"—in the middle of the day. She goes for a bike ride or skis. She recalls, "One day I was cycling and a client called. I answered and admitted that I was playing hooky. She said: 'Great! Can you promise that I am the very first person you call when you return, as I need you in your most creative state!' That was a real gift. She helped me shift my paradigm from guilt to giving myself some love to serve my client better." With recovery, creative ideas, renewed energy, and greater productivity become possible.

When you keep in mind why you are doing the practice, you may find that many of your internal voices (especially your coach and caregiver) become your ever-present supporters.

We see their influence in Terry's story up next: His internal coach and caregiver taught him to bounce back from life's lowest lows that always seem to follow life's highest highs.

Terry Bounces Back and Higher

In which Terry Lundgren, chairman, president, and CEO of Macy's, Inc., recounts the times he recovered from setbacks only to find greater opportunity in store

Today, Terry Lundgren presides over the largest U.S. department store chain and is a beloved executive, looking and acting like a leader from Central Casting. But years back, it was touch and go with two watershed moments that nearly derailed his journey. Both times, after a painful setback, Terry recovered to experience an exhilarating rebound. In this way, he continued a fruitful and enduring career as a leader.

Setback #1

Growing up in a family of modest means, Terry had not planned to attend college. His parents hadn't gone beyond high school, nor had his five siblings. Terry applied to college only because his friends did, thinking, *Why not?* Entering the University of Arizona, he had a vague idea of becoming a veterinarian, but quickly switched to business, joined a fraternity, and immersed himself in basketball and college life—for two years.

At the end of sophomore year, Terry's father called. "Dad told me, 'Son, I'm glad you're having a good time but your grades are astonishingly poor. I can't afford to pay for your college; so, if you want to go for the last two years, and I hope you do, then good luck. You're on your own.'" Appealing to a man who worked two jobs to provide for his family was not in the cards. Terry blurted out, "You're ruining my life" and his father replied, "No, son. Your life is in your hands, not mine." And that was that.

It took Terry eighteen months to reconnect with his dad and years to recognize the huge gift he had received—his own future. Meanwhile, he picked himself up and got a restaurant job cracking oysters to pay for college. Terry shared, "I mean, it was the lowest job on earth, and I wasn't even qualified." But he worked his way up to become the manager, a new high point. He said, "That's when it all came together for me. I was working full time, playing sports, and my grades got incredibly good, because I had no time to fool around. The busier I was, the better I got at each one of the things I was doing." And the more his confidence grew. I love that Terry received thirteen job offers when the school allowed students only six campus interviews each! He says, "I'd follow people to the parking lot. I'd follow them to the men's room and slip them a résumé. I was just so ready to do something."

When it came down to choosing which offer to accept, Terry passed up a bigger salary at Xerox Corp. to join the management trainee program at Bullock's. Why? The Los Angeles retailer had shown a genuine interest in him. Perhaps the recruiter sensed Terry's passion for retail and execution: "I try to make progress every day. The only way to do that is to love what you do. And if you love what you do, you never work a day of your life. A required skill of any leader is to be passionate about whatever they do. What a terrible thing not to have passion in your workplace. Ditch digger, be passionate about digging ditches and dig them really well."

Terry's passion for work, in turn, fueled his advancement: "I didn't really have a career plan," he explained. "It was always that I was working really hard, doing the best that I could do in the job I was in. You know the adage 'Bloom where you are planted'? I learned that in my first job. The next thing you know, someone was tapping me on the shoulder saying, 'It's time for you to go to the next level.' " What set Terry on a steep trajectory was the ability to connect with senior executives who sponsored him—in particular, Allen I. Questrom, chairman of Bullock's and a legendary merchandising executive.

Setback #2

In twelve years, Terry became the president of Bullock's. One year later, he was out:

> I lost my job when I was thirty-five. A guy by the name of Campeau comes along and buys Federated Department Stores. In the same breath, he sells Bullock's Wilshire and I. Magnin's to Macy's; and I'm out. They hadn't even met me yet and they replaced me! I didn't know what hit me. I thought, "How is this possible?" I thought I was going to retire from this job thirty years later. We were doing great. You know, it was just like a sack of coal in the face.

When the smoke cleared, both Lundgren and Questrom had lost their jobs. The loss hit Terry hard at first. "I was really down. I didn't know what I was going to do," he recalls. "I had two little daughters and they're just running around the house and I'm looking at them wondering if I can afford the mortgage."

But, as the job search dragged on, Terry rebuilt his physical and emotional strength by reaching into his past and retrieving something he had left behind—his love of sports and fitness. He explains: "I started going to the gym and I started running. I started playing basketball again. I started getting physically fit. That got me through. That . . . and my daughters."

Terry was on the verge of taking an offer from a company that ran duty-free shops at airports, when he got a call from Questrom. Allen told Terry not to take that job, but instead to become his right hand at Neiman Marcus, the preeminent luxury retailer. A year and a half later, Questrom was gone, and Terry advanced. "It was like I had died and gone to heaven," he says. "Who would have thought that? I could never have imagined that I'd be the CEO of Neiman Marcus eighteen months after being fired from Bullock's."

The key to rebounding

Terry is a natural optimist: "Guilty as charged," he said with a wide grin. "There are plenty of pessimists. I have some great stories of people who are the ultimate optimists, the ultimate leaders." Among them is Jimmy Dunne, CEO of Sandler O'Neill & Partners, an investment bank that suffered a major toll on 9/11. Terry leaned forward:

> Jimmy taught me a very important way to phrase it. He said, "Your attitude is your choice. You wake up in the morning and you decide whether—on a one-to-ten scale, ten the highest— whether you want to have a one, five, or ten attitude. It's your choice, every single day. If you can't choose somewhere in the seven or eight range or higher, go find something else to do. No one has time to listen to you whine every day about your issues. Get on the bus, make it a better place to be, a better place to work. Don't wait for somebody else to cheer you up, or to motivate you. It's your choice." I love that statement. Don't wait.

I love that statement, too. Don't wait for others to give you permission, help you renew, or make it happen for you. Recovery and renewal are in your hands—if you are willing to embrace them.

PART SEVEN

THE JOURNEY CONTINUES

24

MOVING TO ACTION

*In which you reflect on the commitments to your leadership
vision that truly matter to you and take your stand publicly,
gearing up for action*

You've immersed yourself in Centered Leadership. Your tool
kit has the tools, concepts, and practices that resonate with
you. You've got stories to reinforce them. You are conscious
and self-reflective—knowing what you know and what you don't know.
You recognize and appreciate your strengths. You are clearer on what
you most want to create, and what truly excites you.

Are you ready to take flight?

Even if you don't feel quite ready—we invite you to make a commitment in that direction. Out loud and in a strong voice for others to hear.

This act of vulnerability is important. It's really important. Because when you commit out loud, you are much more likely to act. You
may want to commit in front of people who matter to you—your team,
supportive peers, caring mentors and sponsors, your boss. It sounds
goofy, but witnesses make commitment real. Mind a tendency to want
the pot of gold in one go. You'll be sure to get there if you take small
steps and revisit your commitments as you progress.

In our Centered Leadership programs, we like to close with a ceremony. Participants share their personal commitments by crossing the
line—literally. We put a masking-tape line on the floor and, one by one,
participants cross it—proclaiming their commitments. Sometimes
we stand in a circle, shoulder to shoulder, making our commitments
public as we are moved to do so. Sharing unleashes powerful emotion;

many of us are unused to acknowledging ourselves privately, let alone in public. And ceremonies carry spiritual meaning in the safety of our program. When a group tightly holds a shared image of the future and commits to the success of its members, it creates a strong force for change. However you decide to make your commitment, be sure to take your stand with at least one witness who acknowledges you and who will be there to observe your development, helping you learn from mistakes. You won't regret the companionship.

But before you jump to commitment, take some time to reflect. After all, you're making a promise to yourself that you intend to fulfill. Use Jo's prompts below.

Taking a stand

To live into my vision of . . .

_____

_____

_____

The strengths I will build on are . . .

_____

_____

_____

The shift in mindset I will integrate is . . .

_____

_____

_____

The smallest step with the biggest impact I commit to take now is (be specific) . . .

_____

_____

_____

On my first try, I felt exposed and awkward stepping over that masking-tape line, so I committed to something practical and incremental: setting a daily intention. On my second try, I committed to facing my fear of bullies; that struck a deeper chord. Last year, I committed to building the Centered Leadership community.

Leaders who show their vulnerability inspire others; they demonstrate authenticity. So if this exercise feels uncomfortable, you may be feeling vulnerable. Stay with it. Here is my latest—pretty darn vulnerable—example:

> To live into my vision of moving every soul to action, starting with me and with you, I build on my creative insight, energy, and sense of wonder. The shift I integrate is befriending my mob of fears as I practice soaring. The smallest next steps I commit to are greeting each new workshop as a chance to change lives and regularly telling my family that I love them.

This is no New Year's resolution, meant to be spoken in a boozy moment one night and forgotten a few days later. And this is no time to play small, to dim your light, or to be modest. Stand up and tell your commitment. Boldly.

When I did this, each year going deeper, I learned that it's scary to be great.

It's scary even to *dare* to be great.

It's damn scary.

We all long to be seen and heard by someone—to make a difference. But in the moment when we are seen and heard, we are vulnerable. We feel naked. Don't waste that moment. Greatness lies within, waiting for you to bring it forth. When you do—weird as this sounds (and it was certainly weird when I experienced it personally)—you may feel tremendous love and kindness for all living things; you may feel the boundaries dissolve between you and everyone else, everything else in the universe. I grope for the words to describe that experience of joy, hope, and lightness of being. Ralph Waldo Emerson, a preeminent man of letters, described it well over a hundred years ago:

In the woods, we return to reason and faith. There I feel that nothing can befall me in life,—no disgrace, no calamity, (leaving me my eyes,) which nature cannot repair. Standing on the bare ground,—my head bathed by the blithe air, and uplifted into infinite space,—all mean egotism vanishes. I become a transparent eye-ball; I am nothing; I see all; the currents of the Universal Being circulate through me; I am part or particle of God.

What more is there to say, really?

STORY 15

Band of Brothers

In which five colleagues enter through their doorway of choice, illuminating what it means to be a Centered Leader

I had the most amazing experience before I began writing this book. Fellow partners in our practice met on their own to discuss it. They had followed different career paths, and harbored different thoughts, but in the months following, they voiced their support in unison. Oddly, each enters Centered Leadership through a different doorway. Johanne and I had no trouble matching them to the resonant Centered Leadership dimension. I think it took us two minutes.

As each man shared his story, all that I had hoped for materialized. Together, we could expand Centered Leadership globally, bringing it to leaders, rising leaders, and future leaders. I got so excited that I decided to write this chapter and introduce you to a band of brothers who embody the five dimensions of Centered Leadership and the vision we are jointly creating.

Doorway 1—Zafer finds meaning

Born in Damascus, Syria, McKinsey partner Zafer Achi had three formative experiences that shaped his growth. When the Ba'ath regime took over in a coup, his highly educated and respected father found himself on the wrong side of the political divide, and so he whisked four-year-old Zafer and family to Lebanon. As Zafer recalls, "The first life experience that I can articulate is that of the frailty of roots. It explains why I am a compulsive collector of homes. If anything goes wrong, I have an alternative place to go."

In Lebanon, young Zafer learned his second life lesson. "I grew up speaking Arabic. When my parents put me in one of the best schools in Beirut—the official French Lycée—I was totally disoriented in class and rejected because I didn't speak French." Zafer continued: "When I was seven, I brought home my term grades. I remember vividly that my rank was 27 out of 32. My father, who was not an angry man, scolded me for not showing up better. That experience taught me that in order to fit in and to please, hard work and struggle are vital." A few years later—at about age ten—Zafer's parents moved him to the best school in the country, which happened to be run by Jesuits. He recalled, "The Jesuits teach you critical thinking. They're probably one of the best systems for it. At the same time, they teach you to embrace faith un-critically, and for me, it just didn't work. They instilled in me a lasting allergy to any form of organized religion."

In an uncertain world, Zafer worked hard to fit in—judged by others who held him to the highest standards. He recounted, "This is the best possible formula to be a successful consultant, but it is devoid of meaning." Why then, you ask, is Meaning the door for Zafer?

Fast-forward to 2001. A successful partner in Jakarta, Zafer was leading a team to create the definitive piece on why conglomerates thrive in developing economies. It almost won the global McKinsey Practice Olympics, but Michael Rennie's upstart team from Austra-lia took "gold" with the topic of winning hearts and minds. For Zafer, it was cruel irony: Sharp, critical thinking lost out to fuzzy mus-ings on emotions and the human spirit! Soon after, he transferred to McKinsey's Canadian office, led by his good friend Bruce Simpson. Bruce thought Zafer would integrate best by organizing the partner retreat whose theme was . . . Michael Rennie's work! Was there no es-cape? Zafer flew to Australia to see it firsthand. He recalls,

> I was blown away by the uniformly heartfelt, positive, whole-
> some feedback on the way the firm worked with clients, our re-

sults, and the regard in which we were held. In my lifetime at McKinsey, nowhere had I seen such gratitude for our work; and that was a mind opener. But the teams included the weirdest meditators, facilitators, spiritualists, and gurus! I couldn't make sense of their unorthodox approach.

That's how I got into meditation. I went to the lead guru (Gita Bellin) and said, "I appreciate that you're doing this, and clients seem to find it helpful, so can you please teach me?" Through meditation I rediscovered the spiritual being in myself. I rediscovered what I had buried for thirty years under the need to be disciplined, to work hard, to please others.

That experience changed Zafer deeply. He reflects: "For as long as I could remember, my way of dealing with turbulence had been to take the surging surf head on, fight for breath, and stay afloat. I learned a better way of facing the raging ocean of life: Dive below the surface, hang on to the rock of what you stand for, your own meaning, and let the surf flush away. Resurface, fill your lungs, and carve your own path." Which Zafer did, dedicating his last decade at McKinsey to pioneering client work in mindsets, behaviors, and capability building to drive transformational change, and shaping an innovative learning agenda for partners that drew on this people-centric philosophy.

And all of this is my good fortune. Zafer's support of Centered Leadership has been steadfast from the start.

Doorway 2—Pierre masters reframing

Since childhood, McKinsey partner Pierre Gurdjian—born and raised in Belgium—was supersensitive. He recalls:

I was a pretty emotional child in that I picked up tonalities and emotions quite easily and amplified them in my head. That helped me learn how to interpret environments. I've developed the instinct to frame and reframe. The only way to deal with those emotions—which, by the way, aren't necessarily bad, some are positive and some are negative—was with a mindset to place them, examine them, give them meaning and therefore, avoid the confusion that would otherwise occur.

To illustrate, when little Pierre believed others were rejecting him, instead of letting his emotions take over, he thought it through methodically and rationally. "It's kind of a routine," Pierre remembers. "It's like an app to deal with emotions!"

Today, Pierre has an even better process for reframing to prepare for difficult client situations. He starts by visualizing his situation, including the energy and emotions surrounding him. "I try to visualize what the people are thinking and why they're acting the way they do. I'm almost putting myself in their heads. And then I have almost a visual representation of what is happening—it's a 3-D animated mind map where you have people, objects, concepts, energy, colors."

Once Pierre knows what he wants to achieve, he uses his visual model to play out scenarios of what he could do to move everything forward:

> In other words, what should I say, who should I talk to, what language should I use, what frame should I apply. Words are very important; I try to use the right words that describe the situation. It takes time to find the word that has the right tonality, the right color, the right nuance to explain what is going on. And then if I intervene using that framing, sometimes it's completely useless! But once in a while, I hit the right button.

This approach serves Pierre particularly well when he worries that the conversation may turn ugly and he will be triggered.

> I have the fear of being found incompetent. I can shut down when I feel that somebody is disapproving—not disagreeing, because I can deal with that—but giving an impression that what I'm saying is completely wrong and disappointing. Then the little voice in

my head says, You're an imposter, you're not qualified to do what you're doing, you don't really know what you're talking about!

I need to be very careful. When I have delicate, complex meetings, I spend time visualizing what could happen. I will have thought, "This guy at that moment might say this in a very offensive way and this is why he is saying it, so just react very cool because you know exactly why he's saying it, you've anticipated it, and you're not going to be shutting down because you know how to deal with this. Don't worry."

Pierre may spend up to three hours preparing—framing how to react to potential conflagrations in the meeting. "I need to do this with my eyes shut. It's as if I would be sleeping or meditating." This exercise is Pierre's equivalent of "spiritual exercises" as coined by philosophers beginning in ancient times.

A spiritual exercise is an ability to concentrate your mind on a particular posture that has deep meaning and that helps you anchor yourself in intense situations. Jesuits use a similar exercise akin to mindfulness practice for twenty minutes twice a day. It helps them learn what they could have done better and yet feel grateful for what they have done.

I discovered something in western tradition that is very old. I'm interested in the wisdom of centering oneself through exercises in personal mastery. We approach Centered Leadership through a different lens, but essentially we're talking about the same thing.

For Pierre, reframing goes well beyond the Iceberg. It's an approach to life. Thinking about his eightieth birthday party, he told me:

There's a notion of having expanded my consciousness to the maximum of my ability. To have become aware of the never-ending richness of the world around us and its meanings—all the shades and colors and levels that are there. And through that, to have been able to help, guide, support other people on the same path. I was born with this thirst for meaning, and with my modest ability—or at least desire—to frame and reframe, I can do something with that.

Who better to walk through the door marked "Framing"?

Doorway 3—Claudio connects with everyone

With a Swiss German father and an Italian mother, McKinsey partner Claudio Feser observed different cultural perspectives on life early on. He told me, "One of the things I learned is that two can look at the same object and see it differently, and each is completely justified and rational." Fittingly, Claudio spent his first nine years in Switzerland, the next ten in Italy, and then returned to Switzerland for university.

Claudio loved being around others and leading; he recalls: "It was always a give-and-take; I do something for you and you do something for me." Aah, reciprocity. Every interview reinforced it. But what Claudio said next turned that upside down.

> My perspective changed dramatically when I was diagnosed with cancer. For the first time, I was completely helpless. For the first time, I was someone who could only take. I was at a loss but tons of people rallied to help me. Even though I expected it, not one person took advantage.
>
> I've always been very good about understanding what was going on—more for me to understand what my strategy should be. With my give-and-take framework gone and people significantly more generous than I thought, I've become more able to accept their generosity—and more able to extend it without expecting anything.

I asked Claudio what he meant by "generosity." His self-identity was being someone who generated big results. In his give-and-take framework, he gave opportunities in return for followership. Generosity never entered the transaction. Claudio said, "I believed that people would not be generous simply because. My bias was that I needed to be the strongest, the one creating the most opportunities, closest to the CEO. And as long as I was the big gorilla, the other gorillas would follow and be positive about me."

Claudio knew that insecurity was behind this, and he presumed it drove everyone. He described his behavior: "You go to meetings where, frankly, you're not adding that much value but you feel that—if you don't go—someone will take your place. Well, I was going to every meeting. I was in every situation that I felt determined my ability to be the rainmaker who controls the situation." When cancer sapped his energy, Claudio was surprised that no one pushed their way into the top spot. "That changed my way to look at it. I've become significantly more relaxed. I'm significantly less calculating than I was before, but I have retained the ability to put myself in someone else's shoes. So, if someone is insecure, I try to give more certainty through a role that gives more security. If someone needs more space, I try to define a role that is more entrepreneurial."

This new mental frame altered Claudio's reciprocity principle, and it had the same effect on me. Postcancer Claudio gives without having to receive. He said, "I have nothing to prove to myself. I have nothing that I need to do in order to feel good or worthy. That's all behind me. It's not about me anymore. I distribute leadership. I give credit to who deserves it. It's about the right decision and being honest and authentic." No wonder Claudio is entrusted with building the global leadership practice.

And what will Claudio enjoy remembering at his eightieth birthday party?

> I know it sounds dumb but if I'm thinking about what am I leaving behind, you can say a great career—but in a way, what you leave behind are people you helped, and most importantly, your kids.

My wife and I sit on the sofa when they're about to go out with friends and we look at them. It's just a fantastic feeling. That's my biggest source of pride and the biggest thing I think about. To be clear, my kids aren't perfect. I wish they would be more diligent at school. Yet we are very proud of how they are—the values they have. They want to help people; they are very social; and they are really gentle, nice guys. That is the most important thing to my wife and me.

Though I only met Claudio in late 2012, I immediately trusted him—because I felt his trust in me from the start. He exuded the desire to help. Maybe he had learned that he had no time to waste, or maybe he simply entered Centered Leadership through the door marked "Connecting."

Doorway 4—Nate engages in war and in life

McKinsey partner Nate Boaz, a decorated Marine with two tours in the Middle East under his belt, was mature, responsible, and driven to meet challenges even as a boy. People have told Nate that he was just born older but with an early taste for adventure. "I was raised by hippies—and my mom was adamant about not having guns. One day, she found me outside, sharpening a stick on the driveway, and asked me what I was doing. I told her I was using it to hunt birds out of a nest down the street. I wanted to do something exciting—but I wasn't a risk taker in terms of breaking rules."

Drive took Nate to the U.S. Naval Academy, one of the hardest schools in the country to get into, with one of the most challenging programs. He recalls: "It felt like my ticket out of the life that I was living. It was going to provide me with opportunities I wouldn't otherwise have. I wanted something in my family that would anchor me and that I would be proud of." Family lore had it that a grandfather had pulled his copilot from a burning plane on Interstate 5 in California and another was in a bombing campaign in Japan. Nate saw war as an opportunity to achieve similar recognition.

War is also the ultimate engagement, Nate learned, and he showed that through a story of breaking the rules. In Iraq, Nate led an intelligence unit screening locals at a road intersection; his team had tried to rescue American prisoners but didn't reach the right spot in time. Nate's gut told him where the prisoners had been moved to, but it was against orders to deploy men in another rescue attempt. He takes us there:

> My intention is to make something—at a deep level—positive out of this horrible situation. Like soldiers say, "In the end, you're not fighting for freedom or for your country." I wasn't fighting for anything but the survival of my guys and the folks that had been captured—to bring them home safely. With laser focus, I'm analyzing and pulling together any information my team has gathered, trying to figure out where they're located.
>
> It's one of those movie moments where you don't have communications with headquarters and you can't find the person you need. I'm screaming expletives over the radio. You don't do that in the Marine Corps, and definitely not in combat situations! I yell, "Where the f—k is Colonel X? *Somebody get him down here right away!*" And as I look up, he's standing right there—a tall, skinny, and very fit Lieutenant Colonel—an imposing figure—looking down at me sitting in my vehicle and screaming.
>
> He says, "What can I do for you, Lieutenant?" in a calm, fatherly way. We don't have permission for the rescue. Our mission is to stay at this road intersection. But he says to me, "What is the worst thing that can happen? We get shot at, and that is what Marines get paid to do." You can see in his eyes and hear in his voice that everything in our values as human beings and as Marines makes it clear that we have to go save these folks. So we're going to do that. That gives me confidence to trust what I know is right. We execute the mission and save the soldiers. My team returns unharmed.

Coming home with post-traumatic stress disorder, Nate was haunted for years. He recalled the moment as "a boatload of fear and just a few drops of hope—a silver lining in a dark and stormy sky." He said, "Even though I had this deep feeling in my gut and I knew in my heart, part of me was thinking that I was sending men to do something that could get them all hurt."

Since then, Nate uses this story to stay grounded. He tells himself, "First, this situation isn't as bad as you've experienced or as it could be. Second, the opportunity to do something purposeful here is greater. How do you make the most of it?"

Yet when I met Nate, he had been avoiding the big—uncomfortable—questions. Used to living outside his comfort zone, Nate entered our Centered Leadership program ready to face them. He admitted, "I felt like I'd been living a lie up until that point." He had begun to see that everything he had said yes to was for external validation—the Naval Academy, the Marines, Harvard Business School, McKinsey, and then advancing to partner. Taking a step back, Nate realized that fear of not being good enough had been guiding him all along:

> I thought I was self-authoring. I now know I was seeking achieve-ment that was recognized as achievement. The biggest aha! for me is that I was at a moment in time where everything core to who I was felt like something was off. Who am I living for? I didn't have the answer yet.
>
> Centered Leadership created the space for me to step back and see a pattern for why I've been acting the way I have been. It was a resounding, *Yes. Nate, once you get to the place where you can be self-validating, you can love and trust yourself. It's going to be so liberating. You're going to be able to start doing things because you know it to be right and not because someone is telling you it's right.* For me, achievement comes from satisfaction. It doesn't mean that there isn't fear. But this is truly what I'm meant to do.

With new self-awareness, Nate said yes to his passion—leadership de-velopment work—and no to the generalist partner track. Compared to the Marines, the risk was small and outweighed by an enormous supply of hope and optimism. And when he imagines celebrating his

eightieth birthday, Nate knows that the accumulation of his small gestures of kindness, compassion, and love will be meaningful. He will
have touched the lives of others; and, when he passes on, he will have
left "an awful hole."

Thus Nate stepped through Engaging's doorway and into his future.

Doorway 5—Ramesh activates renewal

Ramesh Srinivasen was born in Delhi, India, the youngest of three children in a loving family. But his father passed away from cancer when
Ramesh was twelve, and in the same year, his sister married, and his
brother left for school. Now Ramesh had to be the "man of the house"
for his grieving mother. Still an enthusiastic boy, Ramesh was told to
contain his sadness and be strong because his mother needed him. So
perseverance, independence, and self-regulation became his strengths.

During this time, Ramesh drew energy from sports, but more so
from academics—evidenced by his national ranking, 39th—at the
India Institute of Technology. He told me, "Early on, I recognized the
need to sharpen my intellect. I was quite strong in math. Attacking
new things gave me energy and built curiosity. I've always been more
interested in abstract, intellectual problems. In Centered Leadership,
I really enjoy artwork and movement, though; I realize that they are as
important as the intellectual side of things."

Driven by a call to adventure, Ramesh and his wife moved to New
York in 2005 with their two children. A year later, their son was diagnosed with leukemia. Ramesh recalled, "It brought back memories
from when my dad was undergoing treatment and how tough it was."
Then in 2008, their daughter was diagnosed with a malignant brain
tumor. Despite the best treatment in the world, they lost her to the dis-
ease eighteen months later. Ramesh related,

> She was a wonderful girl—smart, curious, and beautiful, the an-
> chor of our lives. Losing her shook the foundations of our mar-
> riage and our family. It's been very tough for us, individually and

collectively, to deal with her loss, especially as it came on top of what our son was going through. There were times when both our kids were undergoing treatment and both physically and mentally needed a lot of energy from us. That is part of what triggered my own need to practice Vipassana.

Ramesh had drawn on spiritual energy early on. His mother taught him the scriptures, and he memorized most—if not all—of the Bhagavad Gita, one of India's spiritual texts. The Buddhist practice of Vipassana was a natural step to help him cope. Ramesh mused:

Of late, I believe less in God but have become more spiritual. Vipassana is the practice of staying silent and building self-awareness and equanimity. That has increasingly given me strength and been a source of energy. You learn a breathing technique and, through that, you practice a form of meditation. What I realize now, through Vipassana and also Centered Leadership, is that I remain calm and equanimous by using my head, a little bit by escaping my reality, and using my heart and gut to understand and embrace what I'm going through. It has made me more self-aware. At times it is more painful, but I've become more of a whole individual. I'm living life more fully as a result of all the experiences that I've gone through.

Ramesh also finds energy by connecting, which he says moves him away from his head to his heart and gut. He told me, "At times, I'm a source of emotional energy for people, and it gives more meaning and purpose to my life. But I am also conscious of how do I put myself in situations that balance where I'm giving and gaining equally with situations where I'm giving more than I'm gaining." Physical energy also became a recovery source for Ramesh, really for the first time. He shared: "I realized that unless I'm strong physically, it's hard to have the energy to do the other stuff that I want. It's the foundation on which I can build my own self. That realization is very,

very strong now." With an ongoing need for renewal, Ramesh has a few recovery practices. He described them:

> My signs that I need to recover are when I am either feeling really tired or alone. I enjoy listening to music, especially Indian classical or folk music. I have specific songs I listen to. I also practice breathing and meditation. Talking to my closest friends, my wife, and my son helps me recover. Then of late, hiking. I was just thinking, my practices fall into energy's four categories! I pretty much do one of these practices daily, depending on what I feel I need that particular day.

Physically, Ramesh feels fitter today and boasts of more "good" cholesterol. Spiritually, he says: "I feel sane, I'm still smiling, and I'm talking to you so I must be all right." Mentally, he's excited about his client work in healthcare and organization, and emotionally, he uses Centered Leadership to reconnect bit by bit:

> I feel blessed that my wife and I are together with our son. Frankly, we learned from him the need to be in the moment and take life one day at a time. It's given us a sense of purpose—focusing more on being optimistic, making people smile, showing what the human spirit can be about, and doing it in a way that still makes people learn and be the best of what they can be. But it's also hard. Our family is still working through it.

How will Ramesh feel at eighty? His response inspired me, and I hope it will inspire you: "If I can look back and say, through all the tough times and the good times, I've been smiling and I've been growing and brought that to my family—our son, my wife, to our daughter who's no longer with us, and to my friends, clients, and the world around me—if I can stay true, that will have been a life well-lived and fulfilling."

For Ramesh, body-mind-heart-and-soul energy brings ongoing recovery, and so he shows us the way through the Energizing door.

Five doorways for five brothers

With great courage, each of my "five brothers" dares to live a life true to himself. It reminds me of a jewel of a story related by our facilitator, Andrea Borman Winter: "A tailor from Dvinsk dreams of treasure under a bridge in Krakow. He travels to that bridge and starts digging. A soldier stops him. The small tailor trembles, but the soldier just wants to share that, strangely enough, he too had a dream of treasure. His dream directed him to look under the floorboards of a tailor's house in Dvinsk. So the tailor hurries home straightaway. Lo and behold, under the floorboards in his very own house he finds treasure." For Andi, Centered Leadership is about looking beneath the floorboards to find your true self—and to build capacity to lead your life from that place.

And isn't that just what this band of brothers is doing?

25

YOUR LEADERSHIP
LEARNING PLAN

*In which you'll develop your Learning Plan and prepare for
your "field work" to practice in real life work challenges*

W hat's a Leadership Learning plan? Nothing more than a
way to organize your self-reflection, commitments, and
how you want to track your progress. We've created a
template that we hope works for you. Think of it as the first step of
your "field work"—practicing in real life what you've learned. But
lest you feel like this is some sort of final exam, we assure you that
your plan is all about the learning. No one (including you) judges it.
So be honest and reasonable about your commitments. Every action
should be specific, observable, measurable, and just outside your
comfort zone. Set a realistic time frame—be it three months, six
months, or a year.

Time to plan

We use the template below with everyone who seeks to become a better leader—whether for their personal growth, as a team leader, or
head of an organization. You'll recognize these questions, as they all
appear earlier in this book. We've noted the relevant Centered Leadership dimension in parentheses to help you find your notes, collect
your ideas, and renew commitments you made earlier.

My leadership learning plan

1. What is my personal vision for my leadership that builds on my strengths? (Meaning)

    _____
    _____
    _____
    _____
    _____

2. What am I going to start doing/intensify to live into my vision? (Meaning)

    _____
    _____
    _____
    _____
    _____

3. What am I going to do less of and actively try to let go of to live into my vision? (Meaning)

    _____
    _____
    _____
    _____
    _____

4. What shifts in my mindsets and behaviors will make the biggest difference as I live into my vision? (Framing)

    _____
    _____
    _____
    _____
    _____

5. What reframing practice am I choosing to do to dismantle my triggers and extend my learning? (Framing)

_____

_____

_____

_____

_____

6. How will I know that I am succeeding with this practice? (Framing)

_____

_____

_____

_____

_____

7. What opportunities (challenges) will I take on at work—how and when—to live into my vision? (Engaging)

_____

_____

_____

_____

_____

8. What upside potential will I keep in focus, and what risks will I work through? (Engaging)

_____

_____

_____

_____

_____

9. What relationships will I build in service of my vision—what will I request and promise? (Connecting)

_____

_____

_____

_____

_____

10. What are the one or two renewal practices I commit to in order to sustain my journey? (Energizing)

_____

_____

_____

_____

_____

11. What challenges stand in my way—and how will I shift to meet them? (Energizing)

_____

_____

_____

_____

_____

12. How will I measure my success across these five dimensions?

_____

_____

_____

_____

_____

13. What becomes possible for me as I choose to live this way?

_____

_____

_____

_____

_____

Share your draft with others to help you clarify your thoughts and actions, bring them on board, and role model openness and commitment. As they observe you, they will begin to shift their view of you and, in turn, their feedback will reinforce your new shifts in habits of mind and behaviors. As it catches on, you'll have access to more energy and, voilà, progress will get easier.

What happens next

You and I have been through a lot together so far—and you've seen me without rose-colored glasses, too. As I reviewed the final manuscript, it struck me that you might think my career was a long series of mishaps, mistakes, and mess-ups! I've clearly had my share. But to encourage you, I'd like to share what happens down the road on this journey. It's one thing for me to write about love, energy, belonging, and impact and another to demonstrate it.

The last five of my thirty-two years at McKinsey have been all about shaping and building and delivering Centered Leadership to companies and countries around the world. It has taken me to places as far apart as Malaysia and Hong Kong; Spain and Norway; Canada and Mexico. And, in the summer of 2013, I traveled to São Paulo to facilitate a three-day Centered Leadership program. It's my last story. Promise!

Rushing to the airport that Friday afternoon through the backstreet slums, I find myself in the protests. Crowds are amassing as we desperately seek alternative routes to the airport. Still two kilometers away, my driver decides that it's getting dangerous. Thousands of protesters on the road flow around our car, headed to the airport in slow motion. We turn onto the grass and reverse our course. We find a nearby hotel and I'm fleeced on the room, which looks like a movie set for *Married to the Mob*. In the musty suite, hungry and tired, I open my computer and burst into tears. I'm on automatic but something catches my eye, words popping up in the bottom corner of Gmail: "Ping. Ping. Are you there?" I hastily write, "Yes. And I'm crying." "Hang on, Mom!" comes back. In one minute, Gaby storms the phone operator to reach me. She guides me through a breathing exercise, police helicopters buzzing by my window. Jetta gets on next and makes me laugh about my "secret agent" life. I'm back to center.

The lightbulb above my head flashes: I can access my Centered Leadership capabilities anywhere and anytime. Centered Leadership lives in me, and when I lose it, I simply need to reach out. Someone will help me find it again.

When people ask me what I plan to do now that I've "retired," I answer, "I'm doing what I can to create more and better leaders." They ask, "How can I join up?"

You know how.

The pot of gold is in your hands and so it's time for us to say good-bye. Sure there's more to talk about, but you're heading out on your own journey. Johanne and I know that you'll learn on this voyage more than we could ever teach you. Soon, your story will be the most important thing on these pages. As it should be.

And, as you build capability, we hope that you'll feel the force, too. Your light will shine brighter with it. Others will draw near, but don't worry. Your light will shine endlessly, no matter how many share it. Then you'll feel the extraordinary joy of helping others.

And so, as you reach that birthday when you become your much older self and remember all that you have imagined in these days and weeks of learning Centered Leadership, you'll reflect on a full life filled with love, led with purpose, clarity, and positive impact.

A life well-lived.

ACKNOWLEDGMENTS— FLY US TO THE MOON!

Expressing gratitude is very much a feature of Centered Leadership, and so when Johanne and I drew our joint network map, our shared vision for this book at its center, remarkable people appeared on the map in a rainbow of colors! They help us by supporting Centered Leadership, contributing to its programs, developing us, and making this book possible.

We start with deep gratitude to the leaders who shared their stories with us. From Canada, Ecuador, Eritrea, Hong Kong, Italy, Kenya, the Philippines, and of course the United States, these men and women helped bring our practices to life: Rebecca Blumenstein, Geoffrey Canada, John Donahoe, June Yee Felix, Fabrizio Freda, Biniam Gebre, Edward Gilligan, Terry Lundgren, Mellody Hobson, Monique Leroux, Jamil Mahuad, Sheila Marcelo, Wangechi Mutu, and Zoe Yujnovich. You have inspired us by having the courage to be seen fully and sharing your thoughts with honesty and vulnerability. Thank you. And thank you as well to all the men and women who gave their time to be interviewed for our video archive and the many more who shared their stories in our programs. We continue to learn from you.

There are many additional supporters to thank next: Our clients helped translate our ideas into reality as they applied Centered Leadership tools and practices to their own leadership challenges. It goes without saying that you cannot be a consultant without clients. In our case, you were co-creators, helping us to shape our vision, see our participants and ourselves more clearly, and achieve positive impact professionally and personally. Thank you for this wonderful gift! You gave us confidence because you put yourselves on the line to experience Centered Leadership, advocate for it in your organizations, and provide us feedback so that we could refine the tool kit. We're not going to shout out your names for the sake of confidentiality, but please accept our deepest gratitude.

We did not stand alone at McKinsey either; within the firm, sponsors of all shapes and sizes supported Centered Leadership from early on. Visionaries, sages, coaches, connectors, and plenty of devil's advocates lent us a helping hand at different stages of our journey! Some came on board early—and we thank Zafer Achi and Felix Brueck, along with Aaron De Smet, Scott Keller, Raoul Oberman, Michael Patsalos-Fox, Seelan Singham, Vikram Malhotra, Colin Price, and Tom Saar for taking a risk with us. We would not have gotten very far without you by our side. A special thank-you to Claudio Feser, whose assignment to lead McKinsey Leadership Development coincided with our decision to write this book. You did not hesitate for a moment, extending trust first and asking questions later.

Centered Leadership itself has many mothers and fathers. They came on board year by year to help us bring this work to clients and colleagues. Our current community is 100 practitioners strong and growing. In particular, Mike Bennett, Nate Boaz, Andy Eichfeld, Pierre Gurdjian, Viktor Hediger, Alison Jenkins, Dana Maor, Kirstan Marnane, Elizabeth Schwartz Hioe, Henri de Romrée, Ramesh Srinivasen, and Jin Wang stand out for speaking up. We grew with your healthy challenge and your friendship. Thank you for being part of this journey.

We are privileged to share our vision for this work with the Mobius Executive Leadership community of gifted coaches and facilitators who were our co-creators from the first pilot program. Many of our senior faculty come from Mobius, and in particular, we send our heartfelt thanks to Amy Elizabeth Fox and Erica Ariel Fox for continuing to introduce us to new insights and best-in-class contributors. At the top of the list are Andrea Borman Winter and Alex Kuilman for their dedication, love, and energy; Anne Gottlieb, Claude Stein, and Diana The-odores for their special gifts; Srinivasan Pillay for helping us translate brain science into leadership implications; and Jennifer Cohen for her coaching. You'll find their wisdom sprinkled throughout our book. A warm thank-you to Carole Kammen, too; you helped us crystallize elements of Centered Leadership and show what becomes possible when we lead with generosity and love.

We have also crossed paths with several academics, either directly or by studying their work. We include Martin Seligman, who intro-duced us to Roy Baumeister and Jonathan Haidt, and Tal Ben-Shahar. We add a special thank-you to Richard Boyatzis, Brene Brown, David Cooperrider, Jon Kabat-Zinn, Robert Kagan, Lisa Lahey, Jim Loehr, Annie McKee, Tony Schwartz, and William Ury. Thank you for the work you do, for your inspiration, and for helping us understand and frame what we saw through the stories of leaders.

Our Centered Leadership tribe is large and growing; you are the rock stars who bring Centered Leadership to life! You've stepped up to par-ticipate in the programs, help in the research, organize new programs, and teach them, and you've spread the word from college campuses to clients to your personal communities. A special thank-you to members of this tribe who regularly convene or teach programs (Eman Bataineh, Natacha Catalino, Susan Charnaux-Grillet, Adriana Mascolli, Kirstan Marnane, Thomas Rajan, Naveen Unni, Caroline Webb, and Sarah Wilson, thank you!), create our videos (Steve Lackey, thank you!), edit our writing (Rik Kirkland, Josselyn Simpson, Allen Webb, thank you!), talk to the world about Centered Leadership (Penny Burtt, Keri Hat-tich, Dorothy Roca, Humphry Rolleston, Laura Schalekamp, Leslie Wood, thank you!), write weekly e-mail posts (Kate Barrett, Stepha-nie Coon, Ruben Hillar, Grace Ho, Josephine Mogelof, Sumit Mundra, Amanda Pouchot, thank you!), and create workbooks that sing (Kris-tina Kockum, thank you!). A special shout-out to Susie Cranston (now) Hamilton, who helped start up Centered Leadership and supports us to this day. As is the nature of a start-up, every single one of you took on personal risk and worked like crazy. Your passion and desire to build

Centered Leadership globally makes it all happen. Know that you are everywhere and making a real difference in this world. Together, you can shift the system through your amazing collective strengths. We look forward with eagerness to note the remarkable things that you do for McKinsey, for clients, and for the world.

That brings us to the remarkable men and women who helped bring this book to life—my former client who first believed in me, Larry Kirshbaum, and his friend and my agent, Jim Levine, who lives a Centered Leadership life. I remember Tina Constable holding that first proposal tightly in her arms in 2008 and voicing her full support for the book; in this book, Tina generously added her confidence and warmth to encourage me to speak up; and Talia Krohn graciously brought kindness, insight, and honesty to help this book live into its purpose. Thank you to the unsung heroine of this book committee—Glynnis O'Connor—who read the manuscript with care and shared the reader's view, admitting to laughter, tears, and confusion!

At the core of our networks sit families. Johanne first: "I feel deeply privileged to be able to do what I love to do and live a life so rich in meaning. Thank you to my children, Mélanie and Freya, who help me be a student of my own work through my motherhood every day. You are my deepest source of meaning, my mirrors, and my teachers in so many ways. Our son, who never opened his eyes, but without whom I would not be doing what I do today. Thank you to my mother, who showed me the art of reframing before I was mature enough to understand it, and to my father, who encouraged me to engage, follow my dreams, and take risks. I will also be eternally grateful to Gita and Michael, who helped me at an important crossroad in my professional career. Close to my heart are Zafer, my wise mentor and friend, and Amy and Erica, my soul-sisters. I owe so much to you. You help me see myself more fully. And finally, Rob. You have been by my side for over twenty-five years now, dreaming with me and keeping me grounded when I needed it most. Thank you. I would not be who I am and do what I do without you."

It is with trepidation that I move on, because I don't want to miss the many generous and supportive voices. Thank you to the remarkable women leaders out there for starters—women who stepped up before the men, standing by me during some pretty dark days. In particular, I am so grateful to those who've helped me take Centered Leadership forward: Nora Aufreiter, Michelle Bleiberg, Sandrine Devillard, Anne Fuchs, Andrea Jung, Doris Meister, Zia Mody, Eileen Naughton, Martha Nelson, Susan Peters, Judy Rice, Dori Rubin, Sheryl Sandberg, Sheree Stomberg, Nilka Thomas, and so many more role models. Thanks to the McKinsey men who sponsored me when reason probably told them not to: Carter Bales, Dominic Barton, Dominic Casserley, Ron Daniel, Ian Davis, Dolf DiBiasio, Chuck Farr, Dick Foster, Roger Kline, James Manyika, Mark McGrath, Lenny Mendonca, and Norman Sanson. You are angels sitting on my shoulders to guide me. And one woman sits there with you—the warrior spirit, Johanne Lavoie!

"Hold on," David said to me the other morning. "Just thank *me*! I'm the one who told you to write a book in the first place in your own voice and with your stories." David, you bring me so much: the capacity for loving and being loved, courage, risk-taking, toughness, and truth—and my gratitude is endless. Most of all, you brought me the greatest joy any human being can have in the forms of Gaby and Jetta. Gaby and Jetta have taught me that I am never alone. What a gift!

And dearest daughters, our hope for you—and for sons and daughters everywhere—is to live a life filled with meaning, love and belonging, and action. The world you are growing up into badly needs leaders. So stand up, hold your heads high, and get in there! Sure, you'll stumble and make mistakes; you learned to walk that way and that's the way you'll learn to lead. But know that you're on a journey that reaches well beyond success to achieving positive impact in the world. It took me fifty years to find that path. Please don't wait a minute longer.

I'm standing by to cheer you on—pom-poms waving wildly.

NOTES

page xiii *How Remarkable Women Lead*: Coauthored with Susie Cranston and Geoffrey Lewis and published by Random House/Crown Business in 2009. Even men have a lot to learn from the twenty-five stories of remarkable women leaders inside, a slew of research on the gender issue, and a deeper look at the science underlying Centered Leadership.

page xvi at the same time: With great thanks to Ronald A. Heifetz and Donald L. Laurie, who introduced the idea of being on the balcony and in the dance at the same time as a core leadership competence. Learn more in their seminal article "The Work of Leadership," *Harvard Business Review*, 2001, or, better yet, read *Leadership on the Line* (Cambridge, MA: Harvard Business Review Press, 2002) by Martin Linsky and Ronald A. Heifetz.

page xvi (whom you'll meet soon): In 2009, I led the launch of the Remarkable Women Program for rising senior female executives with colleagues at McKinsey: Elizabeth Schwartz Hioe, Johanne Lavoie, Kirstan Marnane, and Caroline Webb. In 2012, adding in Nate Boaz and Thomas Rajan, we developed a parallel offering called the Centered Leadership Program, for men and women leading major change at our clients.

page 3 *you're Obi-Wan Kenobi:* Played by Alec Guinness in *Star Wars*, written and directed by George Lucas, and first distributed in 1977 by 20th Century Fox. As described by Obi-Wan Kenobi, the force is an energy field created by all living things that surrounds and penetrates living beings and binds the galaxy together. Sounds dramatic, but what I had felt was indeed a life force running through all the interviewees containing emotion, energy, and connection. And funnily enough, one of my sponsors—the wonderful Carter Bales—had been calling me JoBi-Wan Kenobi for years.

page 4 reams of research in relevant academic fields: With Rebecca Craske,

Susie Cranston, and many wonderful team members, we scanned academic research in leadership, neuroscience, evolutionary psychology, positive psychology, organization behavior, and gender studies. We also interviewed a number of stellar professors across universities to understand their work in more detail. I'm grateful in particular to Roy Baumeister, Jonathan Haidt, and Martin Seligman.

page 4 for the current challenging environment: Thanks and a lot of gratitude goes to colleagues at the time, Josephine Mogolof and Josselyn Simpson. With their leadership in 2010, we surveyed 2,000+ men and women executives in companies ranging from small to large in every region of the world. Within this sample, we identified a segment of 100 executives who scored in the top 20 percent in four or five of the dimensions (for frequency of practice). We found that 79 percent considered themselves to be highly effective leaders, 83 percent were highly satisfied at work and home, and 92 percent felt well equipped to handle today's challenges. In contrast, 1,300 executives did not make the top 20 percent in *any* dimension. Only 5 percent considered themselves to be highly effective leaders, 4 percent were highly satisfied at work and outside of work, and 21 percent felt well equipped to handle today's challenges.

page 7 take ownership of your future: Robert Kegan and Lisa Laskow Lahey, in *Immunity to Change* (2009, Harvard Business Review Press), describe a progression in adult mental development from a socialized mind (e.g., team player, faithful follower) to self-authoring mind (agenda-driving leader, own compass, independent problem solver) to self-transforming mind (meta-leader, holds contradictions, problem finding, interdependent). On the second level, we learn to lead and when/if we get to the third level, we lead to learn.

page 13 said the secret word: *You Bet Your Life* debuted on CBS television in 1950. I watched it with my grandmother in the late 1950s. *Wikipedia* reports—differently from what I recall, but memory can be faulty: "Show tension revolved around whether a contestant would say the 'secret word,' a common word revealed to the audience at the show's outset. If a contestant said the word, a toy duck resembling Groucho . . . descended from the ceiling to bring a $100 bill." I thought it was $50; to my five-year-old mind, that was riches!

page 21 challenges are adaptive or technical: Johanne learned the concept from Ronald Heifetz, who coined the term *adaptive* (versus *technical,* or routine, challenges) to refer to a leadership response in situations that are complex, dynamic, and without easy answers. These force a response outside our repertoire. Mr. Heifetz is the King Hussein Bin Talal Senior Lecturer in Public Leadership at the Harvard Kennedy School, where he founded the Center for Public Leadership. For more, read his book, *Leadership Without Easy Answers* (Boston: Harvard University Press, 1998).

page 22 we learn in four stages: The theory of the four stages of learning was first developed by Noel Burch of Gordon Training International in the 1970s.

page 23 *"Pittifaldi Barsh!"*: Emerson Fittipaldi was the youngest World Champion in the history of Formula One auto racing and twice an Indianapolis 500 winner. A Brazilian named after Ralph Waldo Emerson, "Emmo" experienced serious car and plane crashes and survived. David introduced me to the notion and I inadvertently switched the consonants. We use "Pittifaldi" to mean daring speed with a fearlessness that is extraordinary (and not very rational)!

page 25 machines that go "ping!": This comes from one of my favorite comedies: Monty Python's *The Meaning of Life,* distributed in the United States in 1983 by Universal Pictures.

page 35 human beings are "meaning makers": Benjamin Hale, *The Evolution of Bruno Littlemore* (New York: Twelve Books, 2011): "We, and I mean humans, are meaning makers. We do not discover the meanings of mysterious things, we invent them. . . . To admit that something is meaningless is just like falling backward into darkness" (p. 184). That said, Johanne and I each have dog-eared copies of Viktor Frankl's book *Man's Search for Meaning.* It has been reproduced many times since its first publishing in 1946 (Boston: Beacon Press, 2006). We draw on its inspiration for Meaning, but also every part of Centered Leadership. If you read just one book after this one, *read Frankl.* Better yet, read it twice. (Frankl's account is under 100 pages—83 in my edition to be exact—so it's not a big homework assignment!)

page 35 experiencing joy wholeheartedly: Dr. Brené Brown, whose now famous TED talks about her research taught us all about shame and vulnerability, is also the author of many books, including *Daring Greatly,* a terrific book that summarizes her work (New York: Gotham, 2012). We use her first TED talk in our programs to help participants reach their own most vulnerable selves.

page 36 from voluntary activities you choose: Dr. Jonathan Haidt, *The Happiness Hypothesis* (New York: Basic Books, 2006), p. 91. This is a great summary of all the literature on positive psychology and its earliest research.

page 37 Tal Ben-Shahar, in *Happier*: I have had the pleasure of seeing Tal present his material a few times and am grateful to him for convincing me to exercise. He was talking about his mother at the time, but it rubbed off on me! He is the author of several happiness books: *Happier* (New York: McGraw-Hill, 2007) and *Being Happy: You Don't Have to Be Perfect to Lead a Richer, Happier Life* (New York: McGraw-Hill, 2009).

page 39 we had as children: Christopher Peterson and Martin E. P. Seligman, *Character Strengths and Virtues: A Handbook and Classification* (New York: Oxford University Press, 2004). I'm a big fan of Seligman's strengths assessment, as you'll see.

page 41 "results will happen one day": Shikha Sharma was at ICICI Bank in India at the time I interviewed her, and soon after moved to Axis Bank as its CEO. You can read Shikha's story in *How Remarkable Women Lead.*

page 42 jot down your notes: Drawing on research from appreciative inquiry and also positive psychology, Johanne uses peak experiences—what she calls "moments of positive deviancy"—to encourage deeper learning. We also thank colleagues Scott Keller and Carolyn Dewar for the inspiration behind this exercise.

page 45 way to purpose: I have Gail Collins to thank for the notion that while your first dream may not work out, you might have a second that will. Gail is a well-respected journalist, op-ed columnist for the *New York Times,* and author who graciously agreed to be part of our Leadership Archive.

page 46 of "signature strengths": You can take the same survey by going to www.authentichappiness.org, but you must register (it is free). Before you get sidetracked by all the various assessments, look for and take the VIA Survey of Character Strengths. Avoid the short form Brief Strengths Test. David would never allow it! Why? You can fool yourself with twenty-four questions, but it's a bit harder with 240. Take the twenty minutes needed to do the assessment.

page 48 true about you: I first learned about strengths from Martin Seligman, one of the fathers of positive psychology. Read *Authentic Happiness* by Martin E. P. Seligman (New York: Atria Books, 2004). There are many assessments, including the well-known Gallup StrengthsFinder that many companies use. You may prefer to read Tom Rath's book, *StrengthsFinder 2.0* (New York: Gallup Press, 2007), or the books of Marcus Buckingham (who worked on the assessment when at Gallup before heading out on his own).

page 49 come back to your breath: Centering is a form of mindfulness practice, which we draw on from Dr. Jon Kabat-Zinn, whose book *Mindfulness for Beginners: Reclaiming the Present Moment—and Your Life* (Boulder, Colorado: Sounds True, 2011) is a great place to start if you're interested in learning more. Jo recommends a book with an amusing title that appeals to New Yorkers and busy executives: *Meditation in a New York Minute: Super Calm for the Super Busy,* by Mark Thornton (Boulder, Colorado: Sounds True, 2004). Mark used to be an investment banker at JPMorgan in London, so he should know!

page 51 source of inspiration for Centered Leadership: David Cooperrider is the Fairmount Minerals Professor of Entrepreneurship at the Weatherhead School of Management, Case Western Reserve University. When Johanne asked him to recommend further reading for those who want to learn more, he suggested these two articles: Cooperrider, D. L., and Srivastva, S. (1987), "Appreciative Inquiry in Organizational Life," in W. Pasmore and R. Woodman (eds.), *Research in Organization Change and Development* (Vol. 1; Greenwich, CT: JAI Press): 129–69; Cooperrider,

D. L. (1990), "Positive image, positive action: The affirmative basis of organizing," in S. Srivastva, D. L. Cooperrider, *Appreciative Management and Leadership: The Power of Positive Thought in Organizations* (San Francisco: Jossey-Bass), 91–125.

page 58 experts call *flow*: For more on flow, take a look at Mihály Csikszentmihályi, *Flow: The Psychology of Optimal Experience* (New York: Harper Perennial Modern Classics, 2008), Wangechi's comments capture it in an elegant way.

page 80 "amygdala hijack" in action: Actually, Daniel Goleman coined the term in his book *Emotional Intelligence: Why It Can Matter More Than IQ* (New York: Bantam Books, 2006)—a classic book you should read.

page 85 a robust reframing process: With thanks to Gita Bellin, Amy Elizabeth Fox, Erica Ariel Fox, Carole Kammen, Srini Pillay, and Michael Rennie, who helped Johanne directly and indirectly to develop exercises in this section. Johanne is grateful to Gita, a gifted teacher of transformational coaching and leadership, who taught the practice of meditation and living as the creative cause of your life experience. In addition, Jo is grateful to Carole for helping to refine the process of reframing and create sustaining practices. I'm very grateful for all of these exercises—they've done me a world of good!

page 91 starter list of needs: We assembled our list from dozens of workshops, but we have drawn on Dr. David Rock's model of needs: Status, Certainty, Autonomy, Relatedness, and Fairness (SCARF); for more, go to his website and find this article, "SCARF in 2012: Updating the Social Neuroscience of Collaborating with Others," posted at www.NeuroLeadership.org.

page 99 Bill Bradley: American Hall of Fame basketball player, Rhodes scholar, and with three terms as the U.S. senator from New Jersey, Bill Bradley was set to walk Mellody down the aisle at her upcoming wedding to George Lucas as we wrote this book.

page 104 "How fascinating!" Ben Zander uses this mantra all the time, as featured in the book he coauthored with his wife, Rosamund Zander, *The Art of Possibility: Transforming Professional and Personal Life* (New York: Penguin Books, 2000).

page 109 process from start to finish: In addition to the coaches and academics already mentioned, Johanne studied with Robert Kegan and Lisa Lahey, who developed the four-column tool for their approach to reframing described in *Immunity to Change* (Boston: Harvard Business Review Press, 2009). I love how Bob and Lisa show us that there is a deeper and more important mindset stopping us from carrying out the goals we really think we want to achieve.

page 114 feel more centered: Johanne drew from the teachings of Chris Argyris, founder of Action Science—based on the premise that in order to achieve sustainable behavioral change, you must do more than suggest action—you must address the person's frame or mindset. This intervention is what Chris called "double loop learning"—by shifting our mindsets, we cause a natural shift in our behaviors. For more, read "Teaching Smart People How to Learn," *Harvard Business Review*, 1991, or "Double Loop Learning in Organizations," *Harvard Business Review*, 1977.

page 116 in a more powerful way: In our longer leadership programs, Erica Ariel Fox, lecturer at Harvard Law School and president of Mobius Executive Leadership, has joined Johanne to anchor some of our Centered Leadership programs. She teaches leaders to master high-stakes conversations. To learn more, read her terrific book, *Winning from Within: A Breakthrough Method for Leading, Living, and Lasting Change* (New York: HarperBusiness, 2013).

page 119 a growth mindset: Ed is referring to the research of Carol Dweck reported in her book *Mindset: The New Psychology of Success* (New York: Ballantine Books, 2007). Carol distinguishes between a growth mindset (ability to reframe and learn from everything) versus a fixed mindset (dependent on the recognition and validation of others and therefore resistant to any change that would threaten one's performance).

page 125 and even *connected*: Network analysis is an exploding academic field of research as I write, and if this is the thread you're curious to explore further, read *Connected: The Surprising Power of Our Social Networks and How They Shape Our Lives* by Nicholas A. Christakis and James H. Fowler (New York: Little, Brown, 2009).

page 133 key relationship: trust: When we talk about trust, we mean *relational trust*, of course—different from credibility. Technical challenges demand credibility trust: trust in the person's expertise, qualifications, and know-how. When the challenges are complex, you'll need to influence people, reframe difficult conversations, ask others to take personal risks, and more; that's when you need relational trust.

page 133 acceptance, and openness: We adapted our definition of trust from Integro Learning Institute, whose research and consulting work focuses on building trust in the workplace.

page 133 before agreeing to commit: Johanne learned about the work of Fernando Flores, philosopher, linguist, Chilean senator, and a seminal thinker in the domain of linguistics and leadership, from Jennifer Cohen, also from Mobius, who is a somatic specialist. Flores identified five primary moves human beings make in language every day, which he called "speech acts": declarations, assessments, assertions, requests, and promises. An effective promise is characterized by a speaker and a listener; mutual understanding of the request being made; a specified time frame in which to fulfill the request; and specified conditions of satisfaction. For more, read "Fernando Flores Wants to Make You an Offer" by Lawrence M. Fisher from booz&co.'s strategy+business publication (issue 57, Winter 2009).

page 143 personal and professional outcomes: Daniel Goleman, psychologist, author, and science journalist, first introduced the notion of emotional intelligence, but in later work went on to describe social intelligence and how we're wired to connect. For more, read *Social Intelligence: The New Science of Human Relationships* (New York: Bantam, 2006).

page 156 we really needed sponsors: I first learned the term *sponsor* from Ruth Porat and included her story in *How Remarkable Women Lead.* Sylvia Ann Hewlitt published extensive research on sponsorship and followed that with her book, *Forget a Mentor, Find a Sponsor: The New Way to Fast-Track Your Career* (Boston: Harvard Business Review Press, 2013). Many large corporations have begun to encourage senior men and women to step up to sponsoring more women.

page 156 "There is no try": *Star Wars: Episode IV—A New Hope,* written and directed by George Lucas and first distributed in 1977 by 20th Century Fox. Frank Oz provided the voice for Yoda (and also, with Jim Henson, Miss Piggy, Bert, Cookie Monster, and Grover). If you're too busy to watch the *Star Wars* movie (a classic), check out the cool video clip available on the Internet.

page 157 skydive in Israel: Minimum age in the United States is eighteen years old if you're interested.

page 159 develop this list: Carole Kammen is the founder of Pathways Institute and a gifted facilitator who specializes in exploration of human consciousness, building personal and professional skills. Johanne brought in Carole to help us shape our first pilot programs. Early on, Carole had a profound effect on me and accelerated my learning in ways she will never fully know. She found my voices in 2009—along with the bully living in me! In 2012 she encouraged me to face my power and bring it forth for positive impact. Carole studied mythology and symbols as part of her research, and she taps into dreams with exciting insight.

page 164 movie, *Schindler's List*: Steven Spielberg's 1993 award-winning movie distributed by Universal Pictures, no laughing matter. John is referring to the persecution of Jews by the Nazis—a gripping scene from a gripping movie that won seven Oscars, including Best Picture and Best Director.

page 165 heard John Chambers: John is president and CEO of Cisco Systems. He joined the company in 1991 as senior vice president, Worldwide Sales and Operations, and stepped into the top role in 1995. He is credited with leading the company from $1.2 billion in sales to over $23 billion. John is a visionary, an entrepreneurial leader, and a straight-talker, as this story shows!

page 174 performing artist and coach Anne Gottlieb: With personal thanks to Anne Gottlieb, who works with us to deliver Centered Leadership presence sessions. While not the first to find voices in me, Anne honored them and helped me come to grips with this aspect of myself. That led to incredible peace and self-acceptance as I made my way to ultimately appreciating myself more.

page 174 Edna from *The Incredibles*: *The Incredibles,* written and directed by

Brad Bird and released by Walt Disney Pictures in 2004. Edna is as nasty as they come, but you have to love her because diminutive height takes nothing away from her smarts and power! In general, I'm a fan of animated movies (and also ridiculous, stupidly funny movies) as a way of finding relief from constant problem-solving. If you're willing to try animated movies even without a small child in hand, this is one you should see.

page 175 Bodhi tree: It is said that Siddhartha Gautama, who became known as Gautama Buddha, sat under this large and sacred fig tree and ultimately received enlightenment. At this moment in my journey, I was reading Tara Brach's *Radical Acceptance: Embracing Your Life with the Heart of a Buddha* (New York: Bantam Dell, 2003) and gaining an introduction to Buddhism and variations on mindfulness practice as I struggled with the notion of sitting in stillness.

page 175 facilitator, Diana Theodores: With thanks to Diana Theodores, a Mobius-affiliated coach and facilitator. Johanne met Diana at The Banff Center, Canada's premier center for creative leadership and where Johanne is an advisory board member. Together they lead a week-long Centered Leadership program for women, steeped in the expressive arts. The "empty space" is from Peter Brook's book, *The Empty Space: A Book About the Theatre: Deadly, Holy, Rough, Immediate* (1968; New York: Touchstone, 1995).

page 176 "you will ever do for yourself": *How Remarkable Women Lead,* p. 188.

page 176 the comfort zone: Scratch any organization consultant or executive coach or facilitator and you will find the terms *comfort zone, learning zone,* and *terror zone.* The concept is often attributed to Alasdair A. K. White. These zones are an important foundation for Engaging, too. Imagine yourself at work, doing what you know how to do well. It is comforting to know you're skilled, but also a bit boring—ho hum, really. Step outside that zone and you start to learn. Along with learning comes excitement and some anxiety or fear. Keep moving away from your core and eventually you will cross over into the terror zone, where all learning stops. For more, read White's paper, "From Comfort Zone to Performance Management" (2008).

page 180 storytellers, Dale Carnegie: Dale Carnegie, *The Quick and Easy Way to Effective Speaking* (1962; New York: Pocket Books, 1990).

page 184 before entering the room: Harvard Business School Professor Amy Cuddy studies body language and how that affects perceptions of us. Watch her TED talk on "power posing" (standing with confidence) or learn more from her article, "Power Posing: Brief Nonverbal Displays Affect Neuroendocrine Levels and Risk Tolerance," with Dana Carney and Andy Yap (*Psychological Science Online-First,* 2010). I was skeptical at first, but I realized how annoyed I had been watching scores of executives lean back in meetings with their hands resting behind their heads in that wild "I'm so powerful, I can lean back and think" stance. Of course!

page 186 Claude Stein: Claude is a multi-platinum-award-winning voice and performance coach who has worked with Grammy winners and is a faculty member with Mobius Executive Leadership. Johanne brought in Claude to work on leadership presence through singing. Guess what? For the most part, singing boils down to mindsets and behaviors! Don't think you can sing? I watched Claude take a participant with that affliction and turn her into an amazing rock star in the space of fifteen minutes. It's really all about intention, attention, and emotion.

page 194 Hope outweighs it: We learned about the role of hope from Richard Boyatzis and Annie McKee, who coauthored *Resonant Leadership* (Boston: Harvard Business School Press, 2005). I had the good fortune to meet Annie at the EVE Programme in Evian, France, hosted by Groupe Danone (the global dairy company), where 250 women and 50 men come together from over a dozen companies to develop as leaders. Annie taught us the Ubuntu saying, "I am because you are," which is the essence of human kindness. I had been skeptical that anyone would be genuinely good and kind, up until I met Annie.

page 195 "yes" before your "no" builds conviction: Johanne adapted this exercise from the yes/no/yes concept that William Ury teaches in his book *The Power of a Positive No: Save the Deal Save the Relationship—and Still Say No* (New York: Bantam Books, 2007). What a great book!

page 197 Voices exercise: With thanks to Hal and Sidra Stone, we use Voice Dialogue in our programs and I have found it to be very helpful personally and professionally. You can follow up on voices with the Stones' book *Embracing Our Selves* (1989; California: New World Library, 1998).

page 205 magic of appreciative inquiry: Johanne has drawn from David Cooperrider's appreciative inquiry approach in Engaging along with Framing. If you are leading your organization through transformational change, we wholeheartedly recommend exploring this approach.

page 208 it's a *premortem*: This exercise comes thanks to Doug Stern. I met Doug at my second client; he helped me through a tough political challenge there and over the years, transitioned from client to good friend. Doug's love for challenge took him from movies to magazines to media research to cable to newspapers and then to United Media, where he remained CEO until it was sold. To say Doug loves rough weather sailing is an understatement!

page 209 *Stumbling on Happiness*: Daniel Gilbert, who teaches at Harvard and wrote *Stumbling on Happiness* (New York: Vintage Press, 2007), researches cognitive bias. His research reaches intriguing conclusions, for example—more choice makes us less happy. And in the case of risk aversion, he found that our imaginations run wild with what could go wrong; reality is rarely that extreme.

page 209 colleagues or loved ones: Johanne got the idea for this exercise from Marshall Goldsmith, best-selling author on management, executive coach, and leader in the Marshall Goldsmith Group, who coined "feed*forward*" and offers a proprietary tool for it.

page 220 and I was hooked: Here's what we learned: Exercise increases your heart rate, and your brain recognizes that as stress. A protein called BDNF (Brain-Derived Neurotrophic Factor), which has a protective and reparative element that acts as a reset switch, is released. That's why we often feel at ease and see things clearly after exercising. Endorphins, another chemical that fights stress, are also released; they tend to block the feeling of pain and bring on a feeling of euphoria.

page 220 "the Tasmanian Devil": With thanks to Warner Bros., the Tasmanian Devil cartoon character was first introduced in 1954 in *Looney Tunes* and *Merrie Melodies*—two series I watched with great pleasure a few years later, when we got television and I was granted permission on Saturday mornings to watch without waking up the rest of the family.

page 223 recover and renew: Johanne and I draw a lot of inspiration from Jim Loehr (cofounder, the Human Performance Institute) and Tony Schwartz (president, founder, and CEO, the Energy Project). We recommend their book, *The Power of Full Engagement: Managing Energy, Not Time, Is the Key to High Performance and Personal Renewal* (New York: Free Press, 2005). Both the Human Performance Institute and the Energy Project run programs for executives looking to manage their energy for higher performance.

page 224 may do the trick: I love to dance and have discovered many men and women who find movement an extraordinary recovery physically, emotionally, and even spiritually. If you are intrigued and unafraid of going off-road, look into the work of Gabrielle Roth and her five rhythms (flowing, staccato, chaos, lyrical, and stillness). You can watch a tape, go to a class, or read her book, *Sweat Your Prayers: The Five Rhythms of the Soul* (New York: Jeremy P. Tarcher, 1997). What I personally learned is that at work I move from chaos right back into flowing. Eliminating the appreciative Lyrical phase and restorative Stillness phase was draining me on every dimension.

page 224 or take our leave: Ben and Rosamund Stone Zander tell a heartbreaking story about the unintended consequences of leaving a loved one on an angry note in *Art of the Possibility*. Ever since, I have regularly used the practice of ending every family conversation, no matter how brief, with a declaration of love and affection. *Art of the Possibility: Transforming Professional and Personal Life* (New York: Penguin Books, 2002).

page 226 four sources of energy: As laid out in the seminal article by Jim Loehr and Tony Schwartz in 2001, "The Making of a Corporate Athlete," published in the *Harvard Business Review*; it is well worth reading.

page 227 set your energy baseline: We love the four energy states; most people stop at one and so miss the opportunity to refuel in many other ways. If you get in the habit of noticing your mental, emotional, and spiritual energy, too, a host of recovery tactics open up for you to use at work.

page 230 intensity of energy: Loehr and Schwartz, *The Power of Full Engagement*, pp. 10, 38.

page 230 with this awareness: If you find the field of somatics intriguing, we recommend the book by Richard Strozzi-Heckler, *The Leadership Dojo: Build your Foundation as an Exemplary Leader* (California: Frog Books, 2007). Jennifer Cohen wrote a chapter for Strozzi-Heckler's book *Being Human at Work* (California: North Atlantic Books, 2003).

page 232 your emotional experience: With gratitude to Jim Loehr and Tony Schwartz.

page 233 what would I do there: If the fear of downtime is familiar to you, check out Leslie A. Perlow's book aptly entitled *Sleeping with Your Smartphone: How to Break the 24/7 Habit and Change the Way You Work* (Boston: Harvard Business Review Press, 2012).

page 240 with bits of information: More and more is being written about the energy-draining effects of always-on communications. For more, read: Edward M. Hallowell, "Overloaded Circuits: Why Smart People Underperform" from the *Harvard Business Review,* 2005; Hallowell introduces the notion of Attention Deficit Trait (ADT) and its impact on our leadership, decision making, creativity, and effectiveness. In addition, check out "Recovering From Information Overload" by Derek Dean and Caroline Webb in the *McKinsey Quarterly,* 2011.

page 241 Dr. Jon Kabat-Zinn: Dr. Kabat-Zinn is professor emeritus and also founder of the Stress Reduction Clinic and the Center for Mindfulness, Health Care, and Society at the University of Massachusetts Medical School. He began teaching mindfulness in 1979. If you want to begin it, too, we recommend his book or audiobook *Mindfulness for Beginners: Reclaiming the Present Moment—and Your Life* (Boulder, Colorado: Sounds True, 2011).

page 241 choices for creative response: Johanne says that mindfulness practice is directly linked to reframing. For those who are curious to explore this thread, read *Emotional Alchemy: How the Mind Can Heal the Heart,* by Tara Bennett-Goleman (New York: Random House, 2001).

page 242 fifteen years ago: Johanne first learned the Dynamic Mind Practice from Gita Bellin and then, working with Carole Kammen, Jo added the "heart center" into her practice. This is what we use in our programs, as it teaches empathy and compassion. In this variation, you place one or both hands at the center of your chest (at your heart) and imagine a loved one or special image there—like the shining sun. It may surprise you, but many people report soreness where they have placed their hands during this exercise. Carole explains this as the development of your "heart muscle."

page 242 Mindfulness practice: We are grateful to Jon Kabat-Zinn along with Andrea Borman Winter and Alex Kuilman for their gentle guidance through countless programs. In time, I began to taste the alert but calm feeling that mindfulness offers. I went further than you may want to, but found inviting variations (using the concept of loving kindness) in Tara Brach's book, *Radical Acceptance: Embracing Your Life with the Heart of a Buddha* (New York: Bantam, 2003).

page 247 Thank your amygdala: Johanne also studied with Srinivasan S. Pillay. Thanks to Dr. Pillay for helping me realize that fears are with us all the time, in our unconscious; my gift for sensing danger well before anything happens is not bizarre, as my girls and husband note. This is why I don't go to suspense or shoot-'em-up movies with my family—I scream and warn the audience seconds before anything happens, without fail. All the cues are there! On a side note, it is amazing that David and I stayed together after I warned the entire movie theater during a Clint Eastwood "Dirty Harry" movie, yelling out, "Don't go down that street!" David was not only embarrassed but taken aback that I could anticipate action and react to it well before it actually occurred.

page 247 make rituals second nature: If you want to learn more about habits, check out Charles Duhigg, *The Power of Habit: Why We Do What We Do in Life and Business* (New York: Random House, 2012).

page 254 downloaded *Mindfulness for Beginners***:** Dr. Jon Kabat-Zinn, *Mindfulness for Beginners: Reclaiming the Present Moment—and Your Life,* also comes in audiobook, and Johanne recommends it at every program. I took her counsel and listened to it, fully enjoying both Jon's storytelling and his calming, authentic voice.

page 268 particle of God: I included this quote with great trepidation—worried that you would think I'd gone over the top. I read Emerson with my daughters in their respective eleventh-grade English classes. Then I used it in a Check-In to role model extreme openness and vulnerability. It received the reaction I had hoped for: One participant shared her discomfort with the "naked eyeball" analogy but then stepped over the line with me into learning. Ralph Waldo Emerson's essay on nature from *Nature and Other Essays* (New York: Dover Publications, 2009).

page 273 tradition that is very old: Pierre persuaded me to explore Marcus Aurelius's Meditations (Roman emperor and renowned philosopher who lived from AD 121 to 180). Not a philosophy student myself, I found this exploration fascinating and my first foray into the history of self-reflection. If you are interested, read *Meditations of Marcus Aurelius* (London: Penguin Books, 2006).

page 279 "an awful hole": Nate loves Frank Capra movies and, in particular,

It's a Wonderful Life, first distributed by RKO Radio Pictures in 1946. The full quote for Capra fans, in the words of Clarence the Angel: "Strange, isn't it? Each man's life touches so many other lives. When he isn't around he leaves an awful hole, doesn't he?" We are all connected.

page 287 Centered Leadership program: With the help of colleagues and friends Manuela Artigas, Sheila Lopes, and Adriana Mascolli, we organized an amazing program in Brazil with rising senior leaders from fourteen companies. These women taught me that Centered Leadership not only has "legs," but is a powerful ingredient for building community. I cannot wait to return!

page 287 *Married to the Mob*: Directed by Jonathan Demme in 1988 and distributed by Orion Pictures, another favorite of mine. It offers the great combination of home decor, comedy, and adventure.

McKinsey on Leadership Development

Who We Are

McKinsey convenes creative leadership experts, united by their aspiration to help develop high-performing global leaders across all sectors—private, public, and social. Our faculty and practitioners are comprised of seasoned facilitators, coaches, experienced management consultants, senior leaders, and distinguished academics.

What We Offer

The McKinsey Centered Leadership Program (CLP) is one of our flagship offerings for clients. It is a unique opportunity for senior executives to shape how they personally influence and effectively lead transformational change—to lead self, lead others, and lead systems. All of our programs focus on experiential learning, grounded in your own professional context, offering journeys rather than a series of one-off events. Our field and forum offering includes both multi-client leadership programs and customized leadership programs tailored to the organization's strategic imperatives.

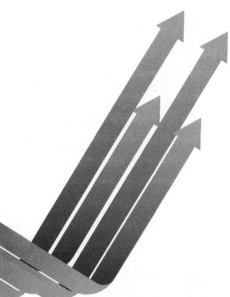

Joanna and Johanne

Joanna Barsh has joined our external faculty this year. After 32 years with McKinsey, Joanna has become a Director Emeritus; she has an ongoing and central role in our Centered Leadership programs.

Johanne Lavoie is a senior executive of McKinsey Leadership and the Dean of our Centered Leadership Programs globally. Our program builds on approaches she pioneered with clients 15 years ago to help them accelerate and sustain performance transformations. Mixing over 2 decades of business and consulting experience, a passion for people and boundless energy, she brings an engaging conversation style as a speaker, a coach, and lead faculty.

How to reach us

You can find us at ww.McKinsey.com/Leadership.

Taking Centered Leadership Beyond the Page . . .

In her keynote speeches, workshops, and programs, Joanna Barsh brings a program filled with practices, tools, and hands-on experience, weaving in the stories of remarkable leaders. Among her lecture topics are:

Moving Mountains Quickly: The Centered Leadership Project

Based on ten years of research and dozens of training programs globally, through an interactive talk or workshop, Joanna equips audiences with a tool kit of practices, based on the five dimensions of Centered Leadership, that helps them lead more effectively, adapt to challenges more easily, and gain more fulfillment in work and life.

How Remarkable Women Lead

In this talk, Barsh inspires women to step up by building on their strengths, connecting deeply, facing their fears, and taking action to recover on a regular basis. It's the new "right stuff" of leadership, helping participants become self-aware and choose the experience of work and life they want, offering practical take-aways and a road map to positive impact.

To inquire about a possible speaking engagement, please contact the Random House Speakers Bureau at 212-572-2013 or rhspeakers @randomhouse.com. A full profile and video footage of Joanna Barsh can be found at www.rhspeakers.com.

Random House Speakers Bureau
THE WORLD'S BEST SPEAKERS UNDER ONE ROOF

INDEX